HELLBOY™

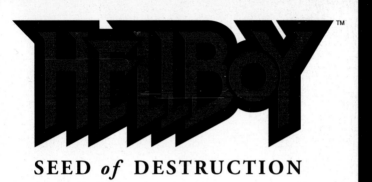

SEED *of* DESTRUCTION

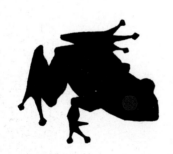

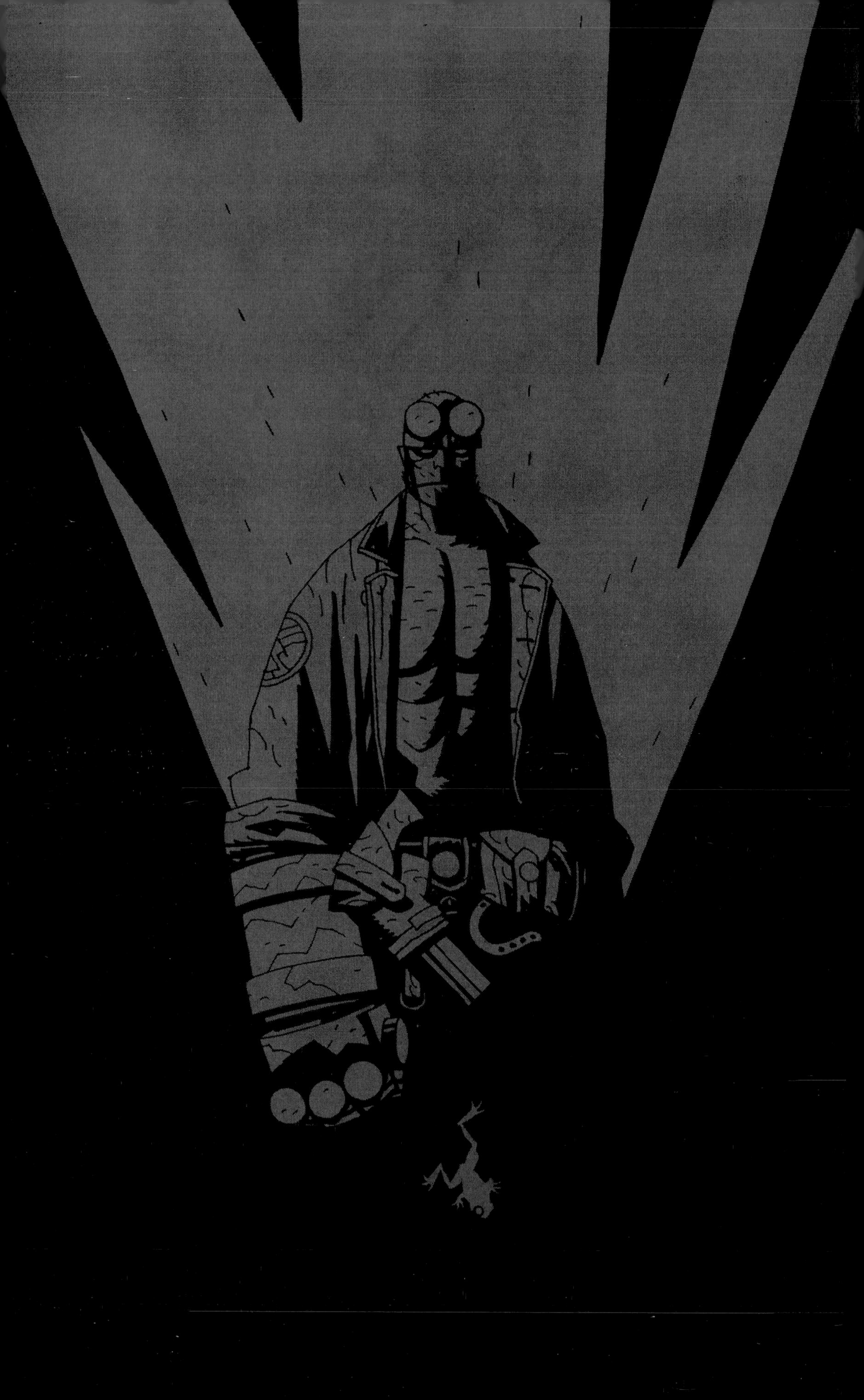

SEED *of* DESTRUCTION

by
MIKE MIGNOLA

Script by
JOHN BYRNE

Miniseries colors by
MARK CHIARELLO

Cover colors by
DAVE STEWART

Short-story colors by
MATTHEW HOLLINGSWORTH

✠

Introduction by
ROBERT BLOCH

Series and collection edited by
BARBARA KESEL *with* SCOTT ALLIE

Hellboy logo designed by
KEVIN NOWLAN

Collection designed by
MIKE MIGNOLA & CARY GRAZZINI

Published by
MIKE RICHARDSON

DARK HORSE COMICS®

NEIL HANKERSON ✠ *executive vice president*

ANDY KARABATSOS ✠ *vice president of finance*

RANDY STRADLEY ✠ *vice president of publishing*

CHRIS WARNER ✠ *senior editor*

MICHAEL MARTENS ✠ *vice president of marketing*

ANITA NELSON ✠ *vice president of sales & licensing*

DAVID SCROGGY ✠ *vice president of product development*

MARK COX ✠ *art director*

DALE LAFOUNTAIN ✠ *vice president of information technology*

KIM HAINES ✠ *director of human resources*

DARLENE VOGEL ✠ *director of purchasing*

KEN LIZZI ✠ *general counsel*

Published by Dark Horse Comics
10956 SE Main Street
Milwaukie, OR 97222

First edition: October 1994
Second edition: June 1997
ISBN: 1-56971-316-2

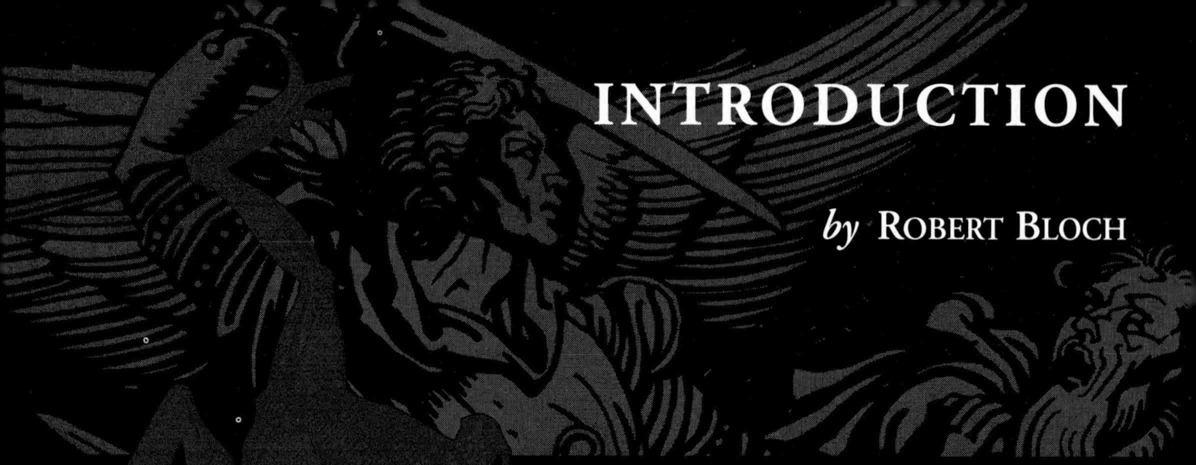

INTRODUCTION

by ROBERT BLOCH

IF SOMEONE HAD TOLD ME FIFTY YEARS AGO THAT I'd ever write the introduction to a collection of comics, I'd have told him he was crazy, and that *I* would have to be crazy in order to do so.

Back then I was writing short stories for the pulp magazines. Neither the publications nor the material I sent them was a major contribution to the status of American literature, but by virtue of it I could at least call myself a writer. Today I probably could have made the same claim — and gotten more critical and media attention — if I'd just gone around spraying out *graffiti.* Nevertheless, even though I lacked such opportunities, I was a published writer. Some of my colleagues, equally proud of their status, were less satisfied with their incomes. Under various pseudonyms they moonlighted, turning out scripts and story lines for the comic books. But this was not something one talked about in polite society, nor spoke of in private. Even in those days there were limits to admitting one's indiscretions; anyone might proclaim himself a born-again Christian, but few would admit to being a burn-again Satanist.

And comic books, to some, were satanic. They were gross, sleazy vehicles of violence, and their creators were the kind of people who gave child-molesting a bad name.

So thought Dr. Frederick Wertham, a psychiatrist who launched an attack on these dime-store demons. The odd thing is that this same Dr. Wertham, a few years thereafter, was quite critically impressed by my first novel, *The Scarf,* and in ensuing correspondence the good doctor and I traded opinions about comic violence, just as though neither of us was aware of the murder and mayhem I perpetrated on the printed page.

But things have changed over the past half-century — things like comics, and myself. And at least some of them — the comics — have improved.

Back then it was easy to trace the roots of the story comics to the pulp magazines, from which many series characters were transported and transplanted to the paneled pages. Artwork showed the influence of newspaper comic strips, cartoons, pulp magazine illustration, and the films of the era. Much of what those early comics offered was derivative, and some of it did, at least in part, justify the criticism of well-meaning do-gooders who feared their children would become read-badders.

And the comics were an influence, no doubt about it. Youngsters who came under that influence grew up to become influential themselves, as writers, artists, filmmakers.

Today, the influenced have become the influential, so that cause and effect have done a flip-flop. Now the comics are the innovators; newspaper art copies *their* style, and other forms of graphic art and illustration frequently adopt their techniques. And the whole "language" of modern film and television seems quite obviously translated from comics in the form of jump-cuts, enormous head shots, rapidly changing POV, and a dozen other innovations which determine emphasis and pacing — and careful editing.

All of this has been generally accepted under the convenient label of "pop art," but there are indications that talented artists, writers, and editors are starting to stretch that label. Not satisfied with endless (and frequently, mindless) repetitions of the mixture as before, they are reaching out to broader concepts, bolder methods of reaching a more adult readership, new ways to tell old tales.

Hellboy is a brilliant example of how to elevate the comic of the future to a higher literary level while achieving a higher pitch of excitement. Its story line combines traditional concepts with modern frames of reference, the whole being swept along by a *virtuoso* treatment of dazzling artistic effects.

As in any experimental venture there are, of course, minor flaws. "Yeah, right" was not a sarcastic phrase used in 1944, nor was anyone or anything characterized as "Looney Tunes."

But these are quibbles — mere flyspecks on the dome of the Sistine Chapel. The total effect of *Hellboy* is that of a true work of art — original and innovative and exciting. Again and again you'll find panels and pages which display a sophisticated and sometimes deliberately satirized awareness of classic modes and content. The product of superb talents, they could be framed and stand forth on their own. Striking use of color enhances their effect and complements the impact of plot and scripting.

This is far from the "pop art" of the Andy Warhol world or the inane imagery of the drug culture. The creative approach found in *Hellboy* is a newly evolving art form of its own, addressed and attuned to today.

Besides, it's a killer read!

For Jack Kirby, H. P. Lovecraft,
my lovely wife Christine, and
the amazing Elmer Newton.

CHAPTER ONE

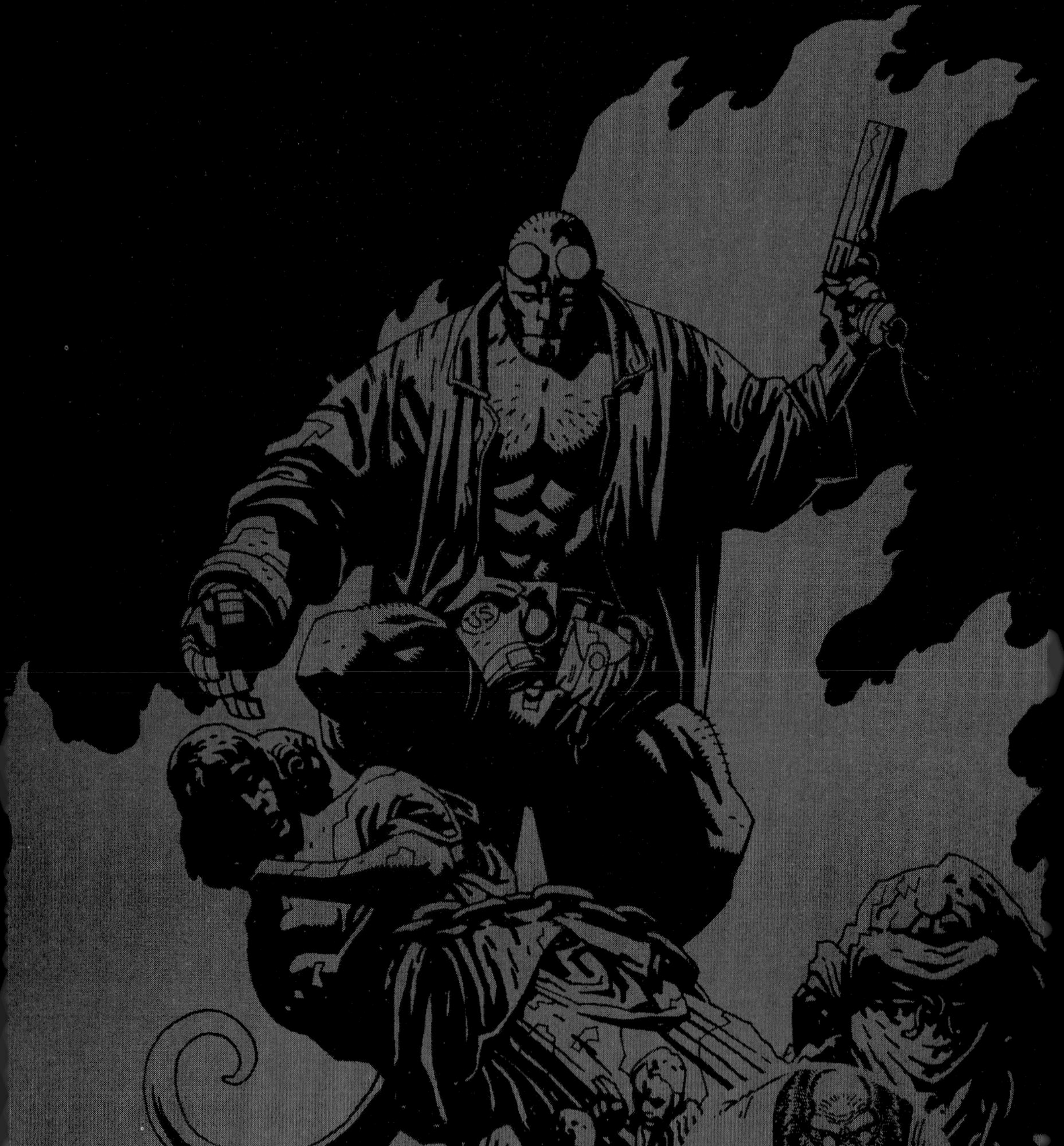
MIGNOLA

Journal of 1st Sgt.
George Whitman, USA
12/23/44
East Bromwich, England.

We've been here for two days now and it isn't getting any better. All of the men are jittery in this place. Maybe if it had a name. Maybe if the people in the village would even talk about it. But they won't.

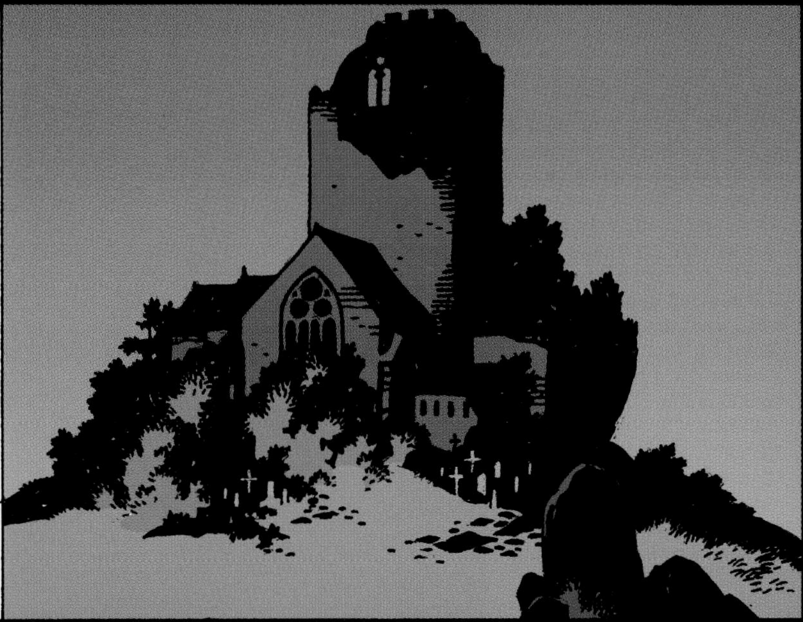

Not even telling them there could be a crack team of Nazi commandos lurking about somewheres gets anything out of them. They just look at you like Nazis are maybe the last thing in the world they need to worry about.

If that were true, we wouldn't be here.

Okay--this is what we think we know: Hitler has sent some kind of team to England. I called them commandos, but there's a trio of people from the British Paranormal Society who say they're more than that. They say the Germans are some kind of spook squad. That the krauts are here to perform some kind of spell or something. Summon monsters. Raise the dead.

Yeah, right.

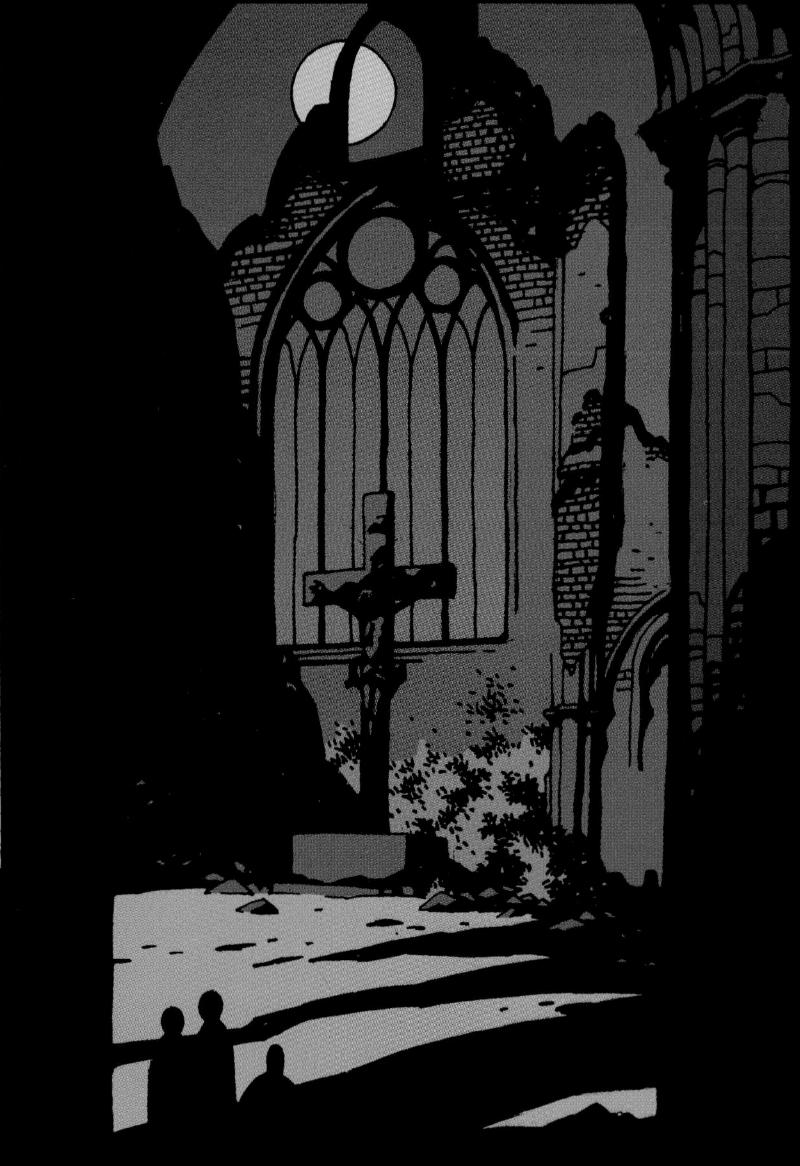

But whatever it is, it's got the top brass worried enough to send a special Ranger unit to look into it. And the Torch of Liberty is here with us. Funny to see him standing there, having a cup of joe with the rest of the guys. I'm more used to seeing him jumping around in newsreels, fighting some cockamamie Nazi menace.

Seems like an O.K. guy, though. And he believes this whole business. He says his own sources confirm the Nazis are in the final stages of something called "Project Ragna Rok".

I don't think our Limey friends were too thrilled to learn it took the Torch's word to make us believe them.

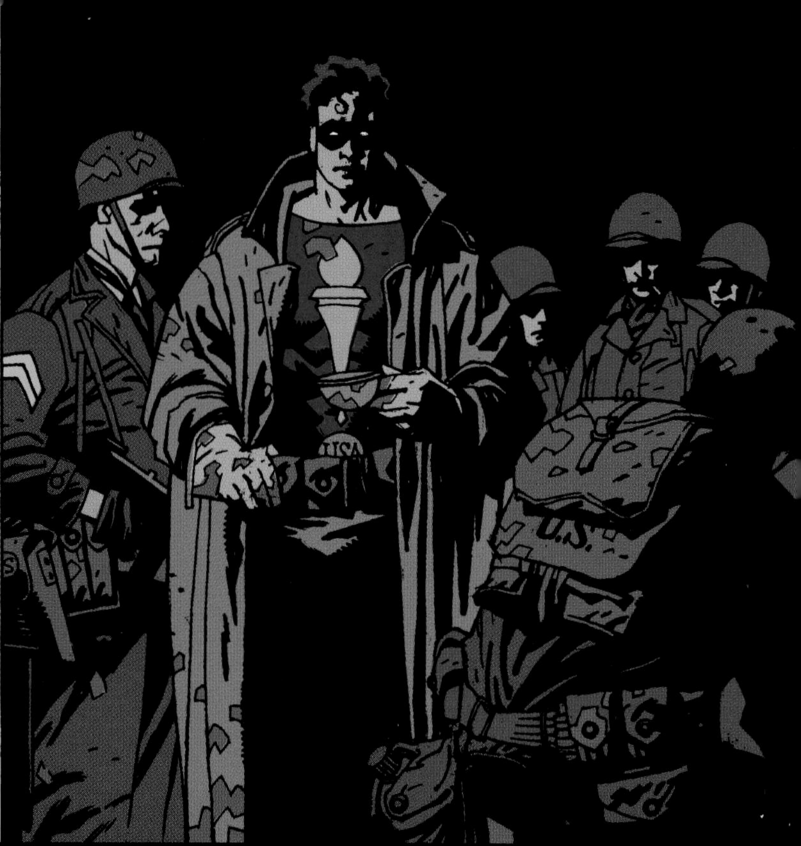

There's three of them:

Professor Malcolm Frost, from Blackfriar's College, stateside.

Trevor Bruttenholm (pronounced "Broom") who's some kind of paranormal Whiz Kid.

And Lady Cynthia Eden-Jones, who's supposed to be England's top medium.

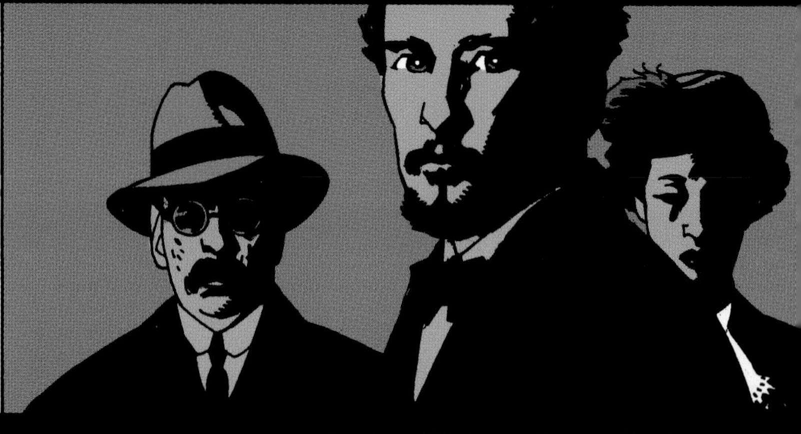

And in charge of this whole Looney Toon party is me, a guy who'd never even heard the word "paranormal" before a week ago.

Anyway, two days camped out in this holiday camp and so far nothing. No spooks. No monsters. No Nazis.

But Lady Cynthia says it's going to happen here. And it's going to happen tonight.

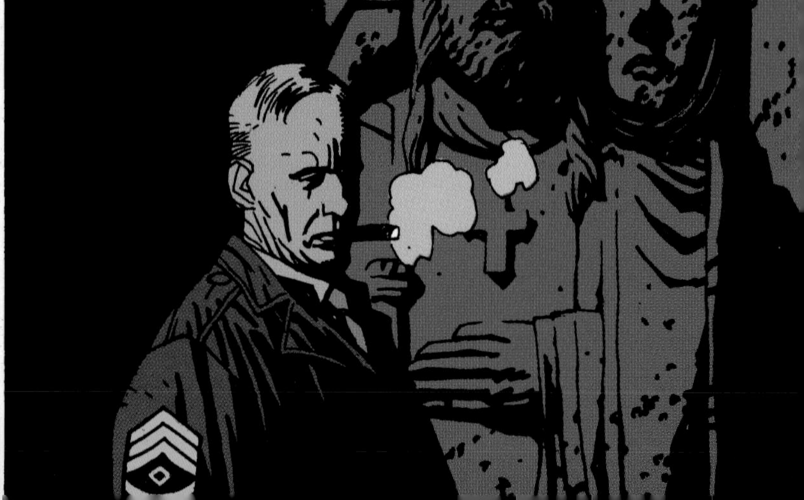

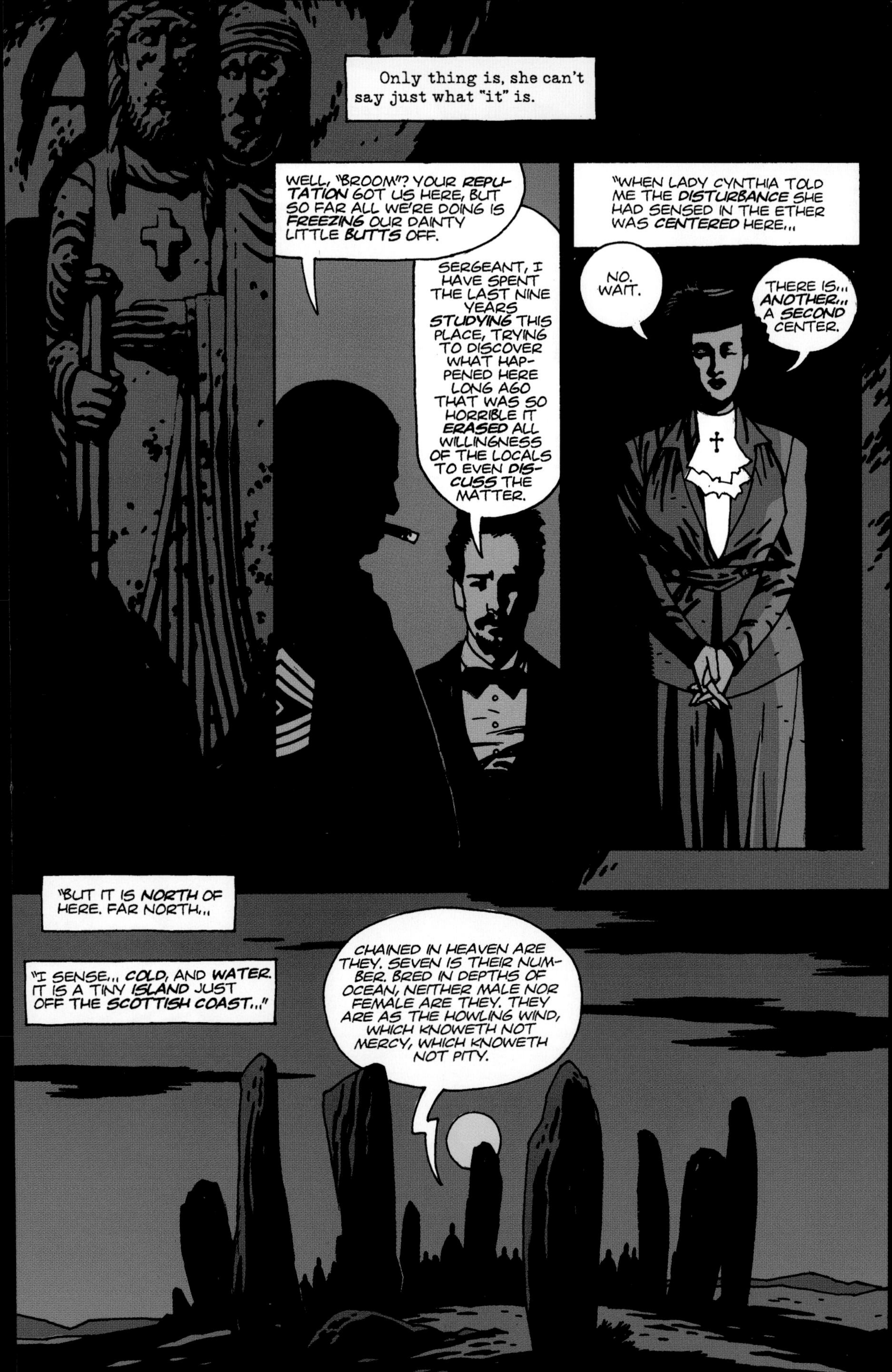

Only thing is, she can't say just what "it" is.
WELL, "BROOM"? YOUR REPUTATION GOT US HERE, BUT SO FAR ALL WE'RE DOING IS FREEZING OUR DAINTY LITTLE BUTTS OFF.
SERGEANT, I HAVE SPENT THE LAST NINE YEARS STUDYING THIS PLACE, TRYING TO DISCOVER WHAT HAPPENED HERE LONG AGO THAT WAS SO HORRIBLE IT ERASED ALL WILLINGNESS OF THE LOCALS TO EVEN DISCUSS THE MATTER.
"WHEN LADY CYNTHIA TOLD ME THE DISTURBANCE SHE HAD SENSED IN THE ETHER WAS CENTERED HERE...
NO. WAIT.
THERE IS... ANOTHER... A SECOND CENTER.
"BUT IT IS NORTH OF HERE. FAR NORTH...
"I SENSE... COLD, AND WATER. IT IS A TINY ISLAND JUST OFF THE SCOTTISH COAST..."
CHAINED IN HEAVEN ARE THEY. SEVEN IS THEIR NUMBER. BRED IN DEPTHS OF OCEAN, NEITHER MALE NOR FEMALE ARE THEY. THEY ARE AS THE HOWLING WIND, WHICH KNOWETH NOT MERCY, WHICH KNOWETH NOT PITY.

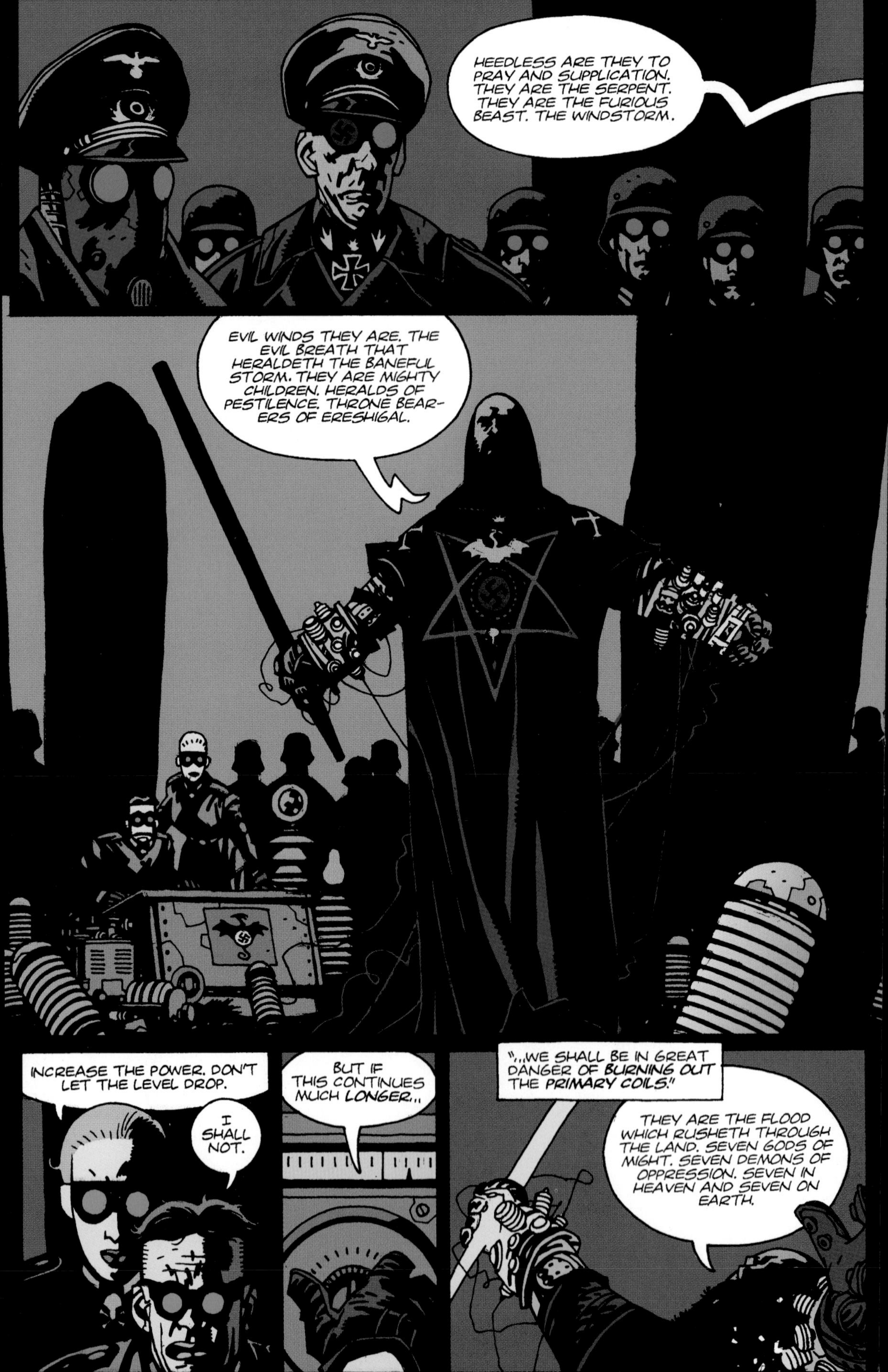

HEEDLESS ARE THEY TO PRAY AND SUPPLICATION. THEY ARE THE SERPENT. THEY ARE THE FURIOUS BEAST. THE WINDSTORM.
EVIL WINDS THEY ARE. THE EVIL BREATH THAT HERALDETH THE BANEFUL STORM. THEY ARE MIGHTY CHILDREN. HERALDS OF PESTILENCE. THRONE BEARERS OF ERESHIGAL.
INCREASE THE POWER. DON'T LET THE LEVEL DROP.
I SHALL NOT.
BUT IF THIS CONTINUES MUCH LONGER...
"...WE SHALL BE IN GREAT DANGER OF BURNING OUT THE PRIMARY COILS."
THEY ARE THE FLOOD WHICH RUSHETH THROUGH THE LAND. SEVEN GODS OF MIGHT. SEVEN DEMONS OF OPPRESSION. SEVEN IN HEAVEN AND SEVEN ON EARTH.

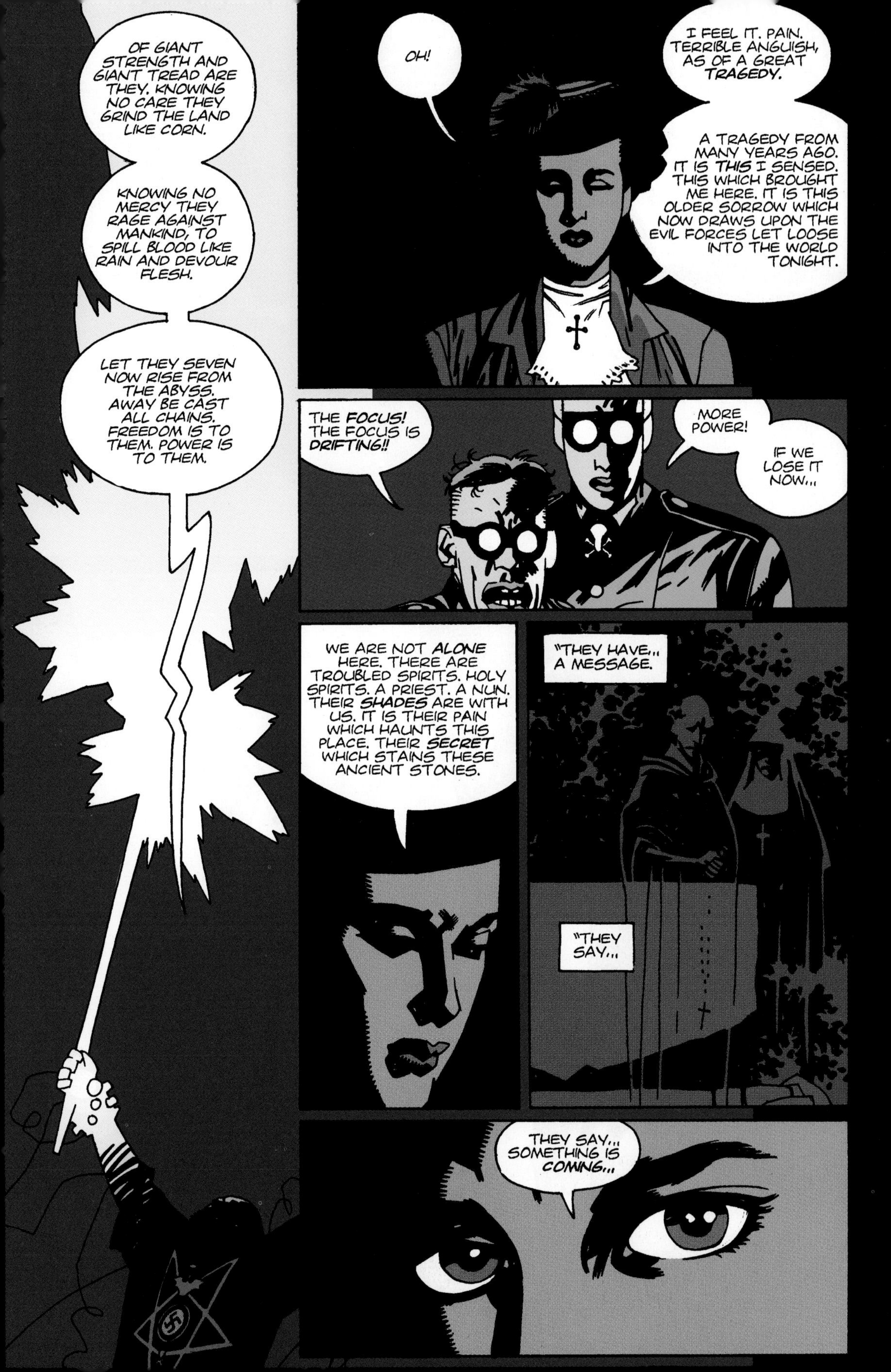
OF GIANT STRENGTH AND GIANT TREAD ARE THEY. KNOWING NO CARE THEY GRIND THE LAND LIKE CORN.
KNOWING NO MERCY THEY RAGE AGAINST MANKIND, TO SPILL BLOOD LIKE RAIN AND DEVOUR FLESH.
LET THEY SEVEN NOW RISE FROM THE ABYSS. AWAY BE CAST ALL CHAINS. FREEDOM IS TO THEM. POWER IS TO THEM.
OH!
I FEEL IT. PAIN. TERRIBLE ANGUISH, AS OF A GREAT TRAGEDY.
A TRAGEDY FROM MANY YEARS AGO. IT IS THIS I SENSED. THIS WHICH BROUGHT ME HERE. IT IS THIS OLDER SORROW WHICH NOW DRAWS UPON THE EVIL FORCES LET LOOSE INTO THE WORLD TONIGHT.
THE FOCUS! THE FOCUS IS DRIFTING!!
MORE POWER!
IF WE LOSE IT NOW...
WE ARE NOT ALONE HERE. THERE ARE TROUBLED SPIRITS. HOLY SPIRITS. A PRIEST. A NUN. THEIR SHADES ARE WITH US. IT IS THEIR PAIN WHICH HAUNTS THIS PLACE. THEIR SECRET WHICH STAINS THESE ANCIENT STONES.
"THEY HAVE... A MESSAGE.
"THEY SAY...
THEY SAY... SOMETHING IS COMING...

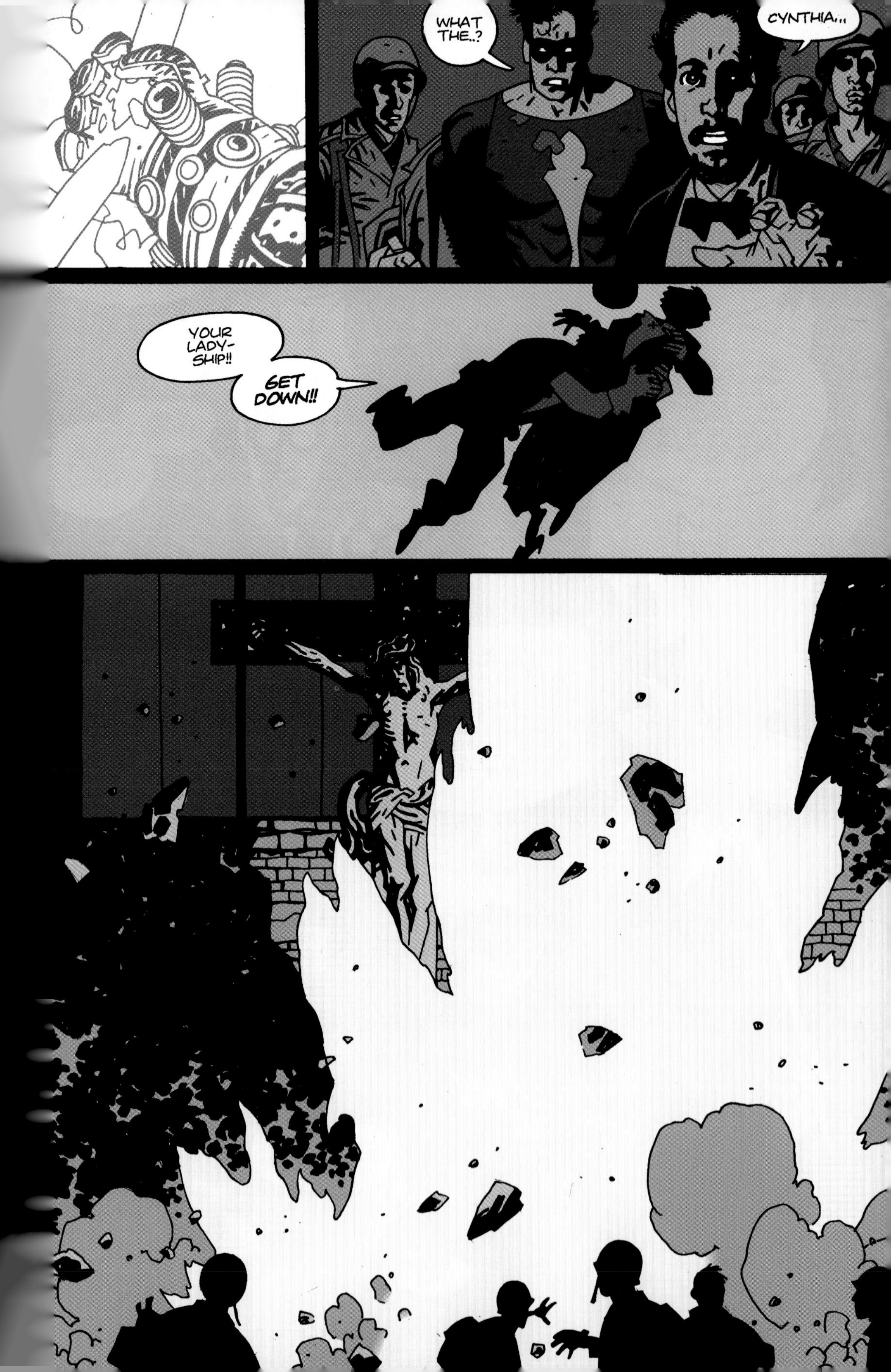
WHAT THE..?
CYNTHIA...
YOUR LADY-SHIP!!
GET DOWN!!

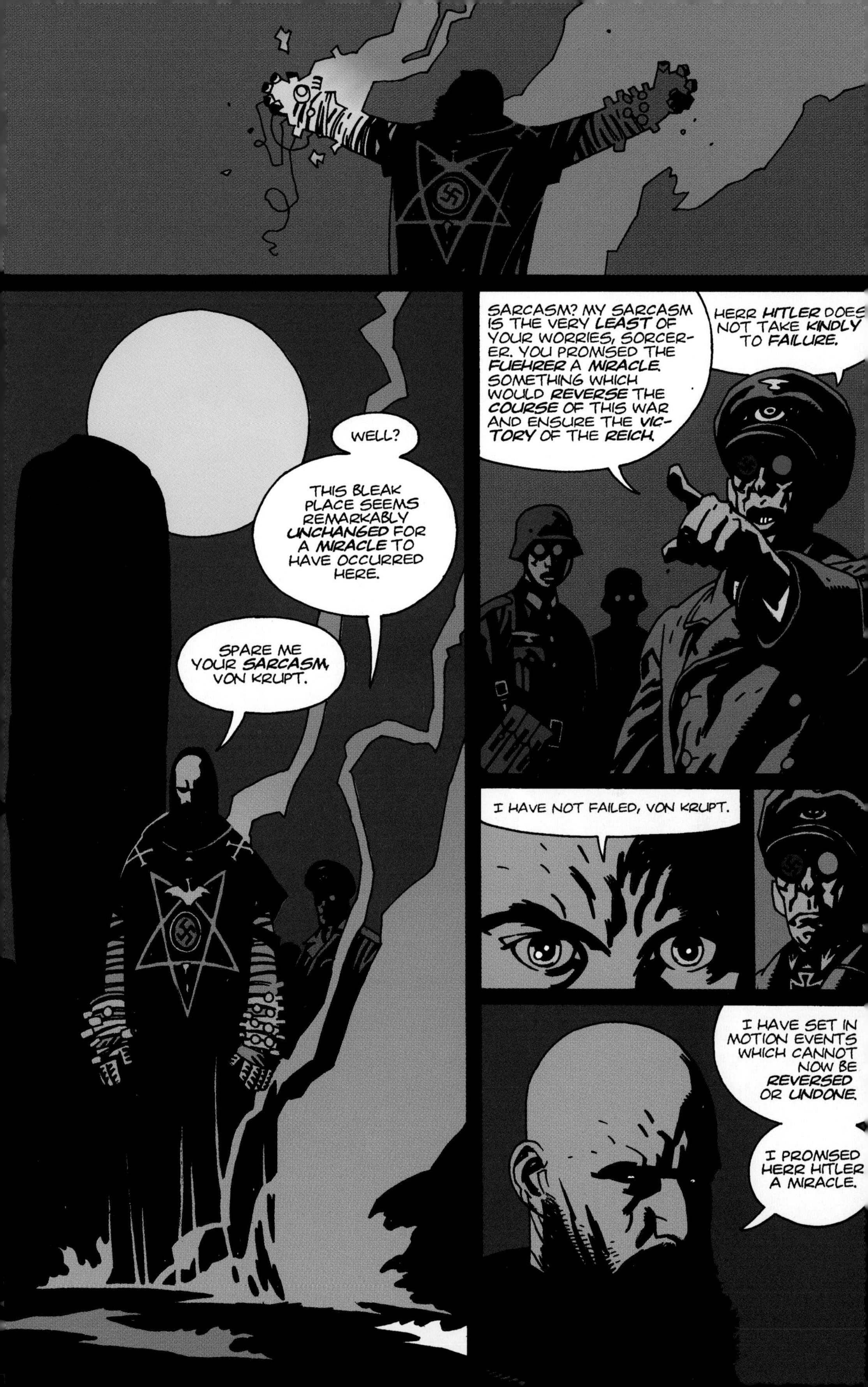
WELL?
THIS BLEAK PLACE SEEMS REMARKABLY UNCHANGED FOR A MIRACLE TO HAVE OCCURRED HERE.
SPARE ME YOUR SARCASM, VON KRUPT.
SARCASM? MY SARCASM IS THE VERY LEAST OF YOUR WORRIES, SORCERER. YOU PROMISED THE FUEHRER A MIRACLE. SOMETHING WHICH WOULD REVERSE THE COURSE OF THIS WAR AND ENSURE THE VICTORY OF THE REICH.
HERR HITLER DOES NOT TAKE KINDLY TO FAILURE.
I HAVE NOT FAILED, VON KRUPT.
I HAVE SET IN MOTION EVENTS WHICH CANNOT NOW BE REVERSED OR UNDONE.
I PROMISED HERR HITLER A MIRACLE.

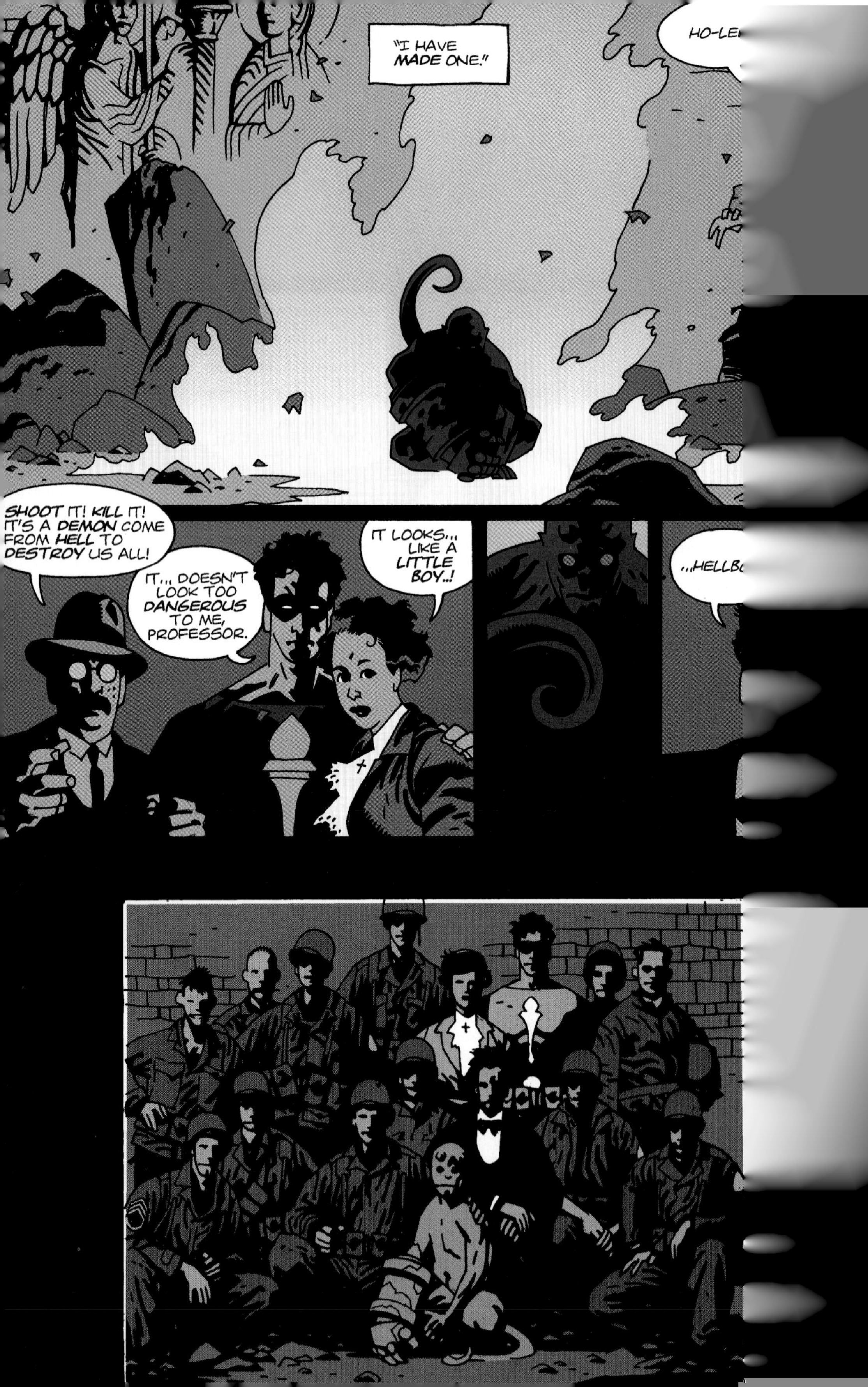
"I HAVE MADE ONE."
HO-LE
SHOOT IT! KILL IT! IT'S A DEMON COME FROM HELL TO DESTROY US ALL!
IT... DOESN'T LOOK TOO DANGEROUS TO ME, PROFESSOR.
IT LOOKS... LIKE A LITTLE BOY...!
...HELLB

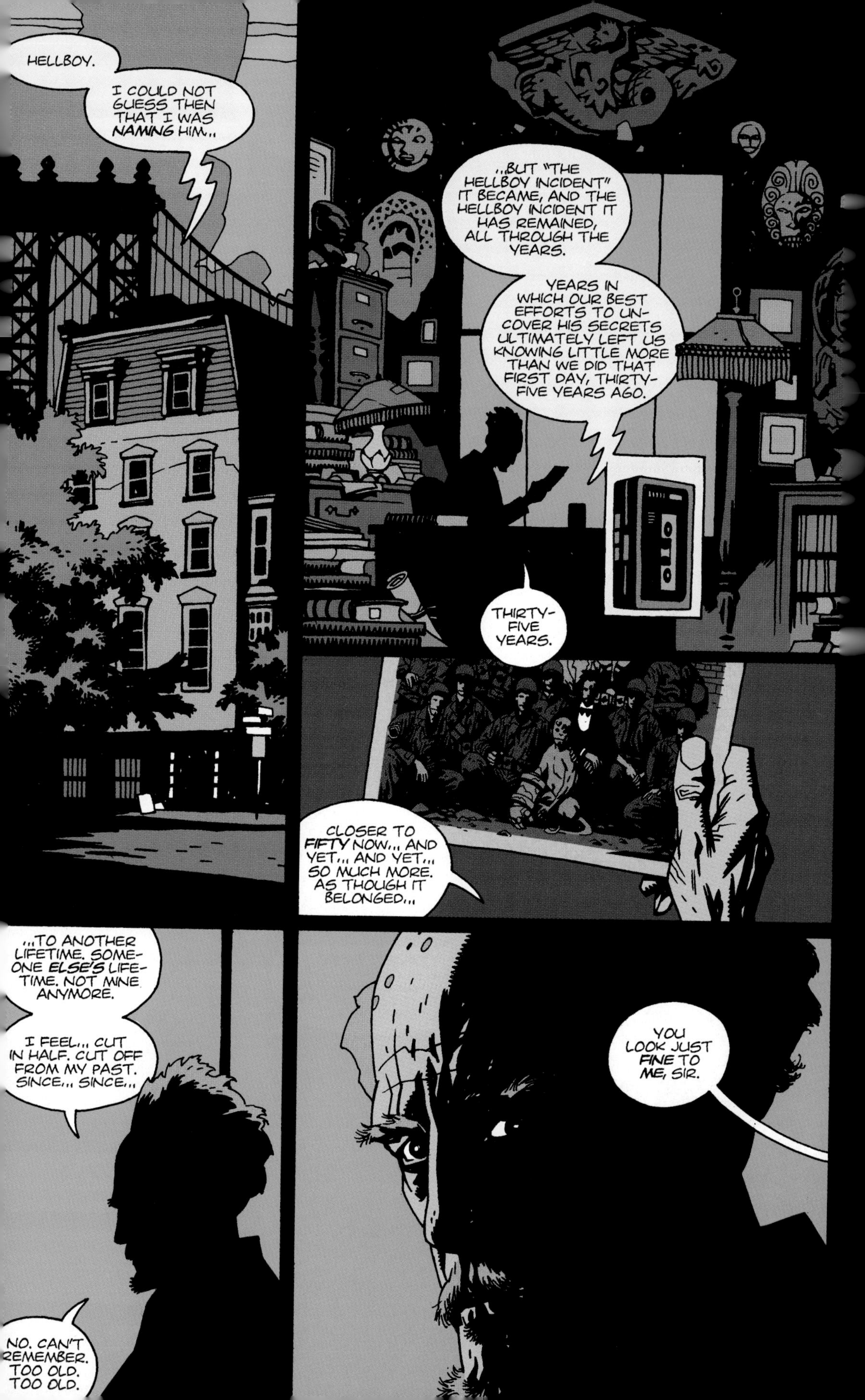
HELLBOY.
I COULD NOT GUESS THEN THAT I WAS NAMING HIM...
...BUT "THE HELLBOY INCIDENT" IT BECAME, AND THE HELLBOY INCIDENT IT HAS REMAINED, ALL THROUGH THE YEARS.
YEARS IN WHICH OUR BEST EFFORTS TO UNCOVER HIS SECRETS ULTIMATELY LEFT US KNOWING LITTLE MORE THAN WE DID THAT FIRST DAY, THIRTY-FIVE YEARS AGO.
THIRTY-FIVE YEARS.
CLOSER TO FIFTY NOW... AND YET... AND YET... SO MUCH MORE. AS THOUGH IT BELONGED...
...TO ANOTHER LIFETIME. SOMEONE ELSE'S LIFETIME. NOT MINE ANYMORE.
I FEEL... CUT IN HALF. CUT OFF FROM MY PAST. SINCE... SINCE...
NO. CAN'T REMEMBER. TOO OLD. TOO OLD.
YOU LOOK JUST FINE TO ME, SIR.

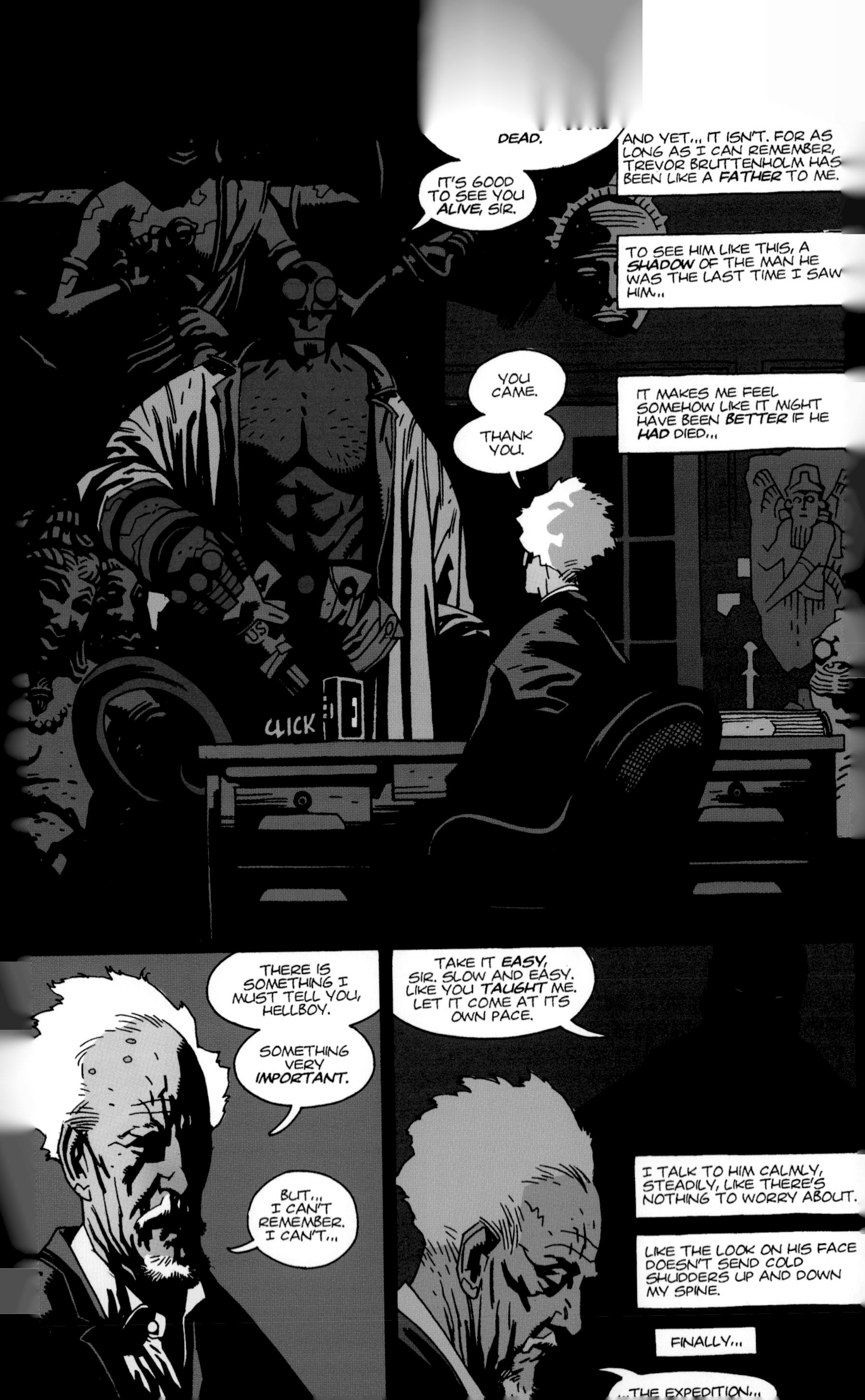
DEAD.
IT'S GOOD TO SEE YOU ALIVE, SIR.
AND YET... IT ISN'T. FOR AS LONG AS I CAN REMEMBER, TREVOR BRUTTENHOLM HAS BEEN LIKE A FATHER TO ME.
TO SEE HIM LIKE THIS, A SHADOW OF THE MAN HE WAS THE LAST TIME I SAW HIM...
YOU CAME.
THANK YOU.
IT MAKES ME FEEL SOMEHOW LIKE IT MIGHT HAVE BEEN BETTER IF HE HAD DIED...
CLICK
THERE IS SOMETHING I MUST TELL YOU, HELLBOY.
SOMETHING VERY IMPORTANT.
BUT... I CAN'T REMEMBER. I CAN'T...
TAKE IT EASY, SIR. SLOW AND EASY. LIKE YOU TAUGHT ME. LET IT COME AT ITS OWN PACE.
I TALK TO HIM CALMLY, STEADILY, LIKE THERE'S NOTHING TO WORRY ABOUT.
LIKE THE LOOK ON HIS FACE DOESN'T SEND COLD SHUDDERS UP AND DOWN MY SPINE.
FINALLY...
...THE EXPEDITION...

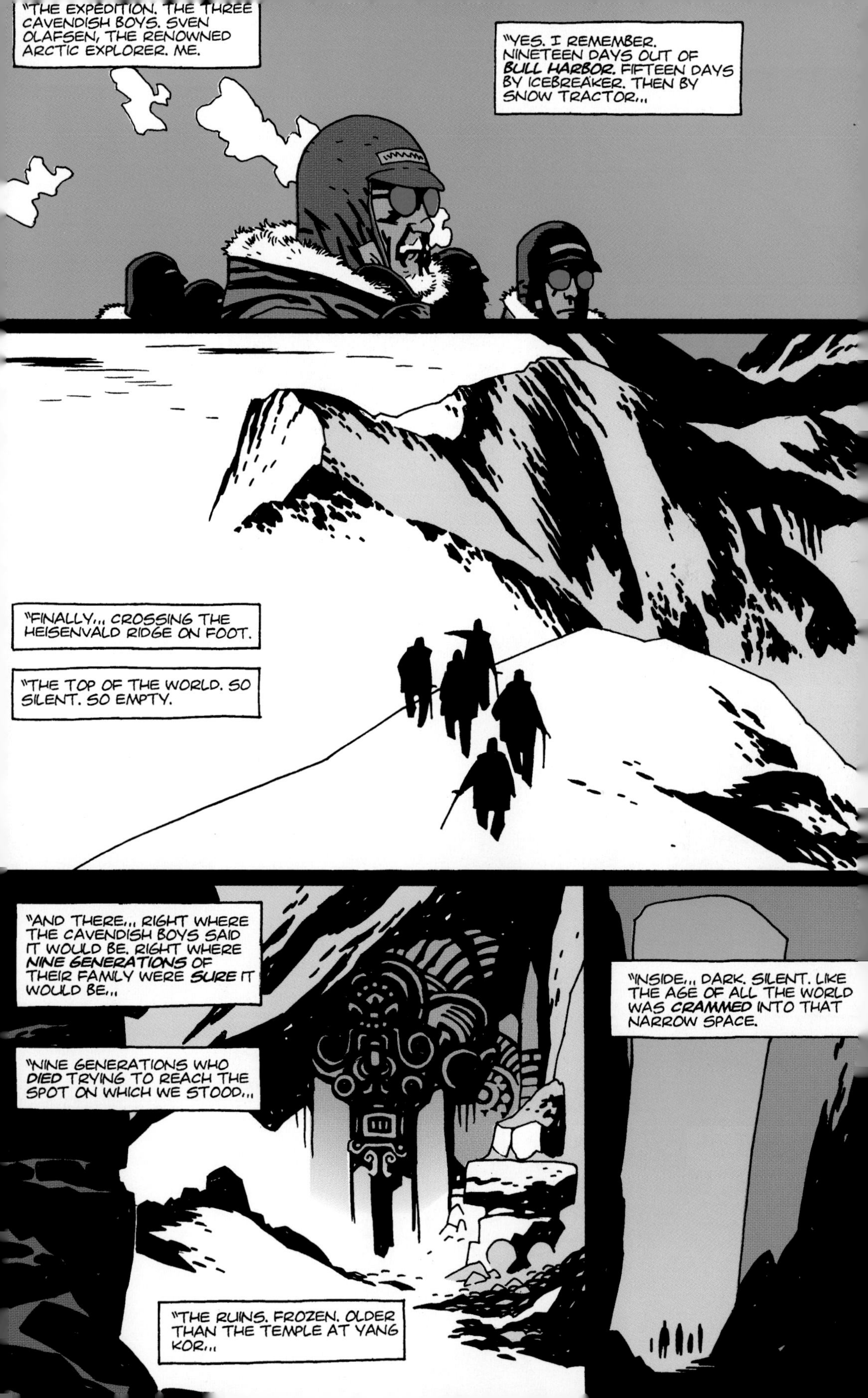
"THE EXPEDITION. THE THREE CAVENDISH BOYS. SVEN OLAFSEN, THE RENOWNED ARCTIC EXPLORER. ME.
"YES. I REMEMBER. NINETEEN DAYS OUT OF BULL HARBOR. FIFTEEN DAYS BY ICEBREAKER. THEN BY SNOW TRACTOR...
"FINALLY... CROSSING THE HEISENVALD RIDGE ON FOOT.
"THE TOP OF THE WORLD. SO SILENT. SO EMPTY.
"AND THERE... RIGHT WHERE THE CAVENDISH BOYS SAID IT WOULD BE. RIGHT WHERE NINE GENERATIONS OF THEIR FAMILY WERE SURE IT WOULD BE...
"NINE GENERATIONS WHO DIED TRYING TO REACH THE SPOT ON WHICH WE STOOD...
"THE RUINS. FROZEN. OLDER THAN THE TEMPLE AT YANG KOR...
"INSIDE... DARK. SILENT. LIKE THE AGE OF ALL THE WORLD WAS CRAMMED INTO THAT NARROW SPACE.

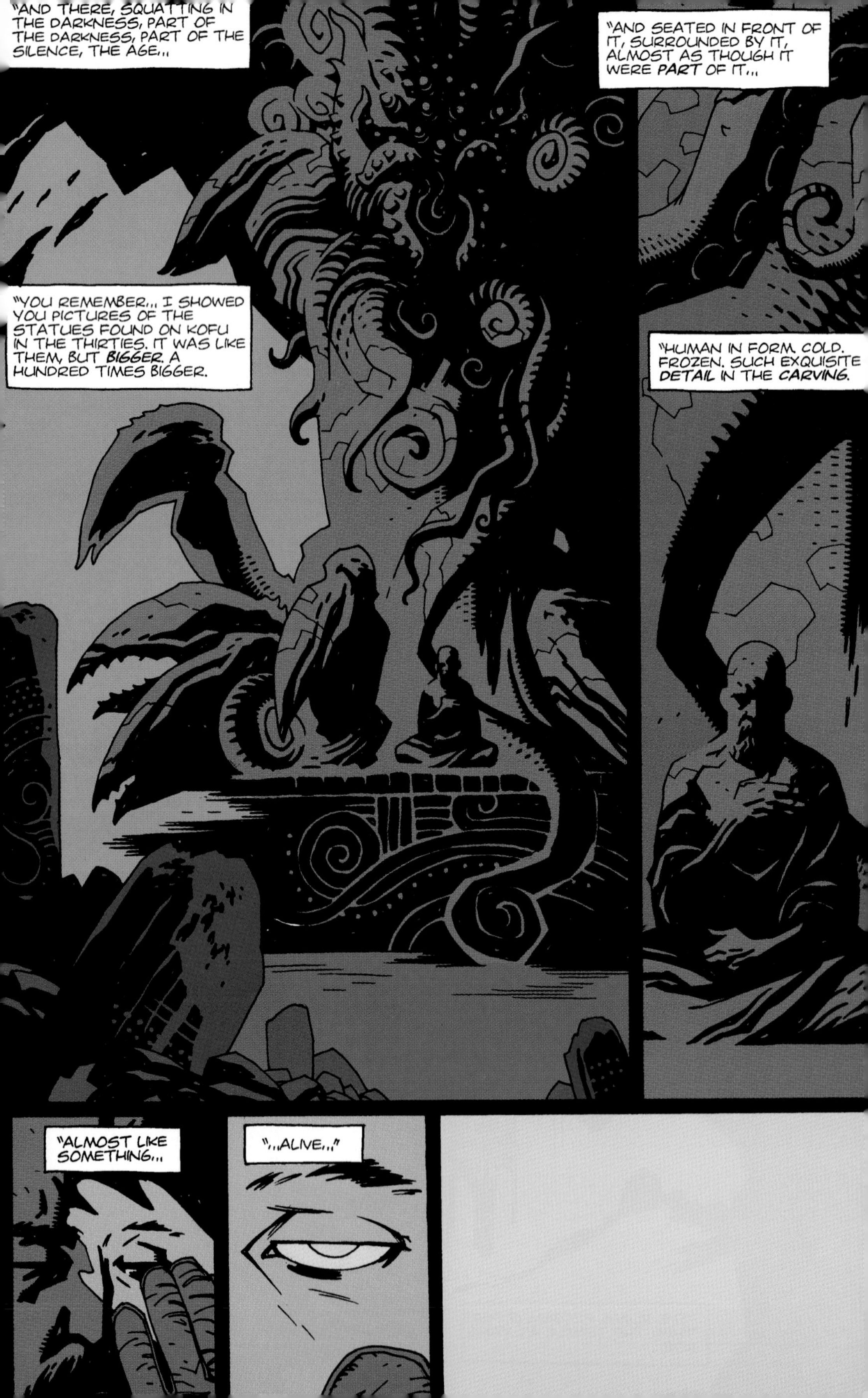
"AND THERE, SQUATTING IN THE DARKNESS, PART OF THE DARKNESS, PART OF THE SILENCE, THE AGE...
"YOU REMEMBER... I SHOWED YOU PICTURES OF THE STATUES FOUND ON KOFU IN THE THIRTIES. IT WAS LIKE THEM, BUT BIGGER. A HUNDRED TIMES BIGGER.
"AND SEATED IN FRONT OF IT, SURROUNDED BY IT, ALMOST AS THOUGH IT WERE PART OF IT...
"HUMAN IN FORM. COLD. FROZEN. SUCH EXQUISITE DETAIL IN THE CARVING.
"ALMOST LIKE SOMETHING...
"...ALIVE..."

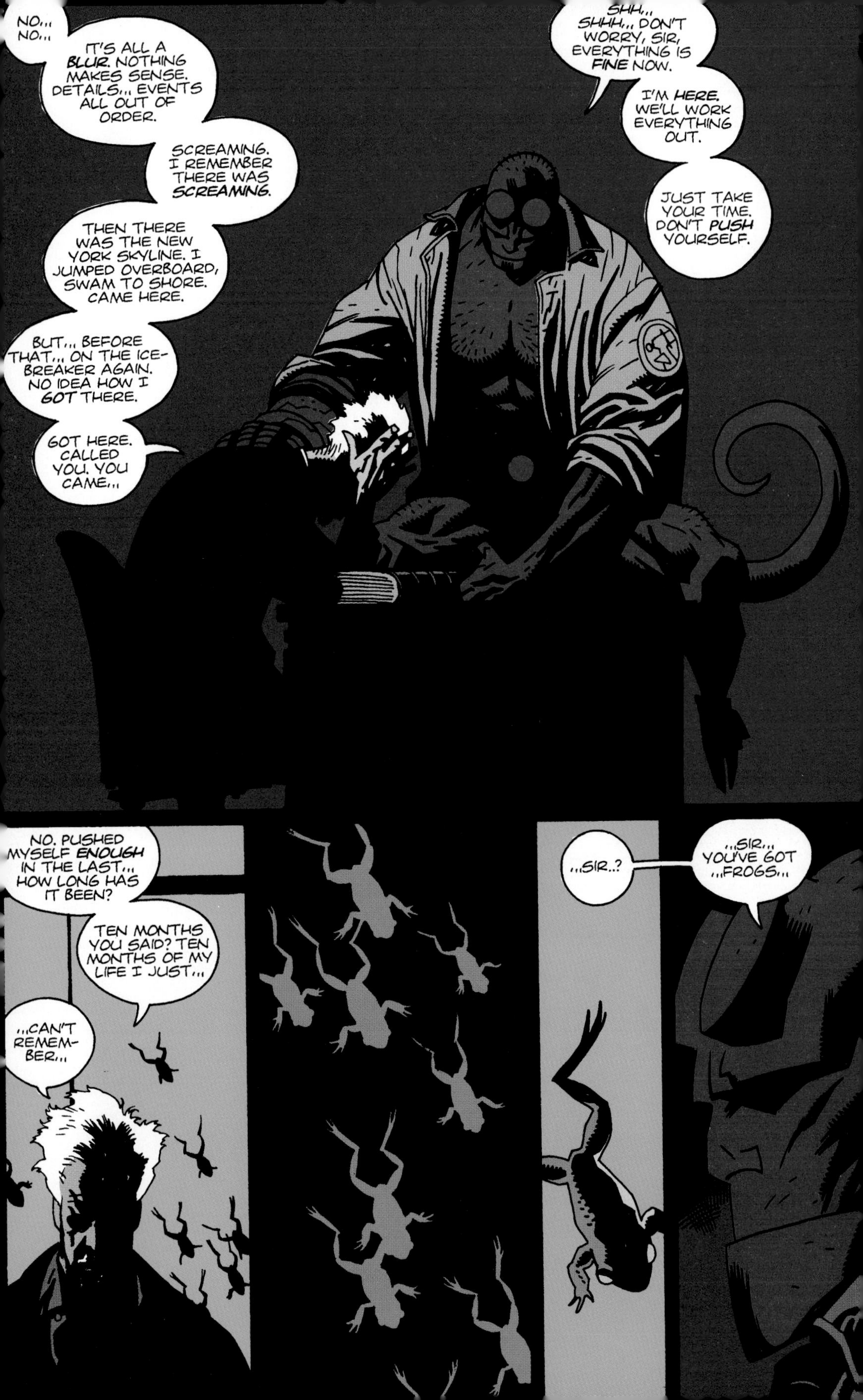
NO... NO...
IT'S ALL A BLUR. NOTHING MAKES SENSE. DETAILS... EVENTS ALL OUT OF ORDER.
SCREAMING. I REMEMBER THERE WAS SCREAMING.
THEN THERE WAS THE NEW YORK SKYLINE. I JUMPED OVERBOARD, SWAM TO SHORE. CAME HERE.
BUT... BEFORE THAT... ON THE ICE-BREAKER AGAIN. NO IDEA HOW I GOT THERE.
GOT HERE. CALLED YOU. YOU CAME...
SHH... SHHH... DON'T WORRY, SIR, EVERYTHING IS FINE NOW.
I'M HERE. WE'LL WORK EVERYTHING OUT.
JUST TAKE YOUR TIME. DON'T PUSH YOURSELF.
NO. PUSHED MYSELF ENOUGH IN THE LAST... HOW LONG HAS IT BEEN?
TEN MONTHS YOU SAID? TEN MONTHS OF MY LIFE I JUST...
...CAN'T REMEM-BER...
...SIR..?
...SIR... YOU'VE GOT ...FROGS...

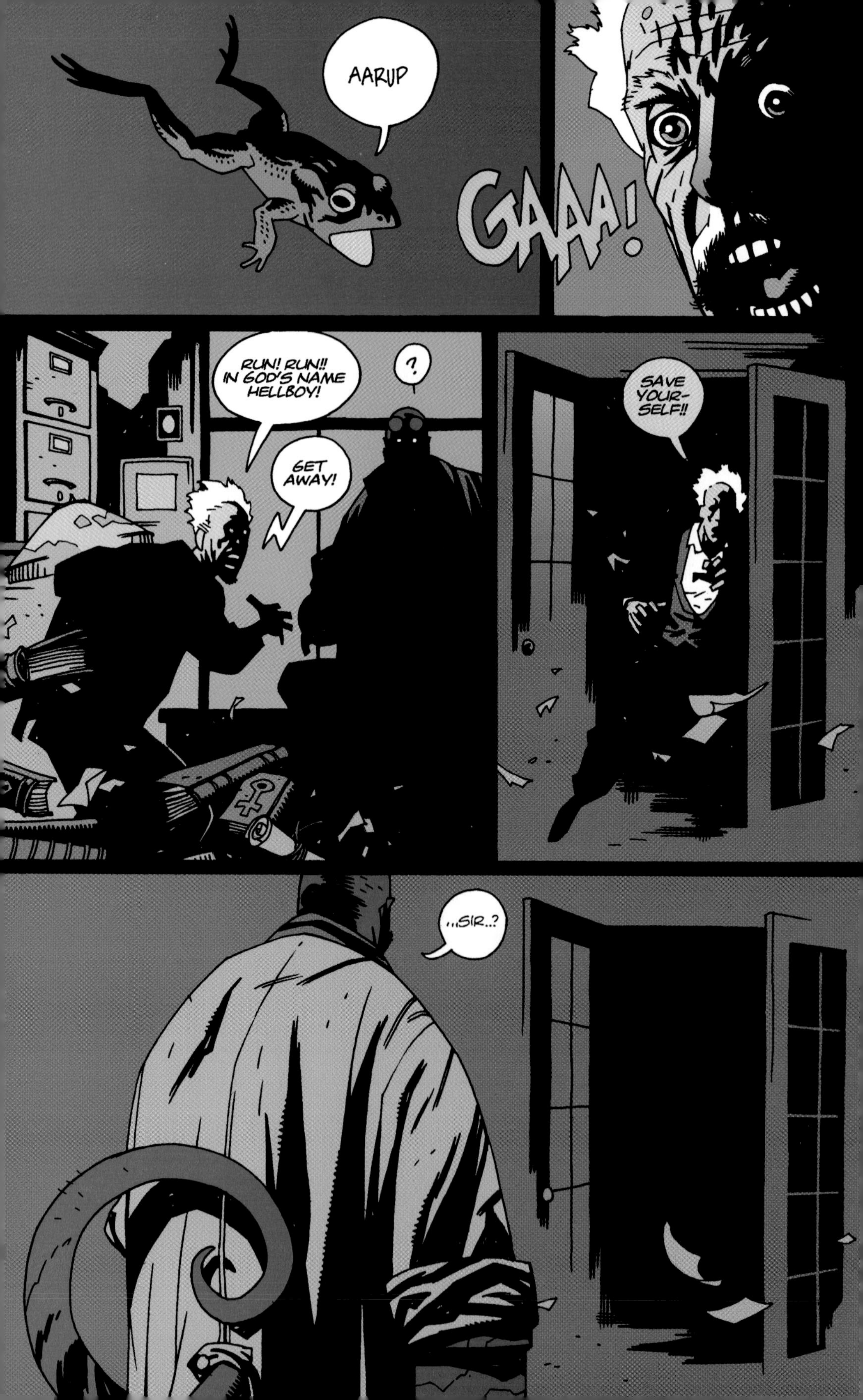
AARUP
GAAA!
RUN! RUN!! IN GOD'S NAME HELLBOY!
?
GET AWAY!
SAVE YOURSELF!!
...SIR..?

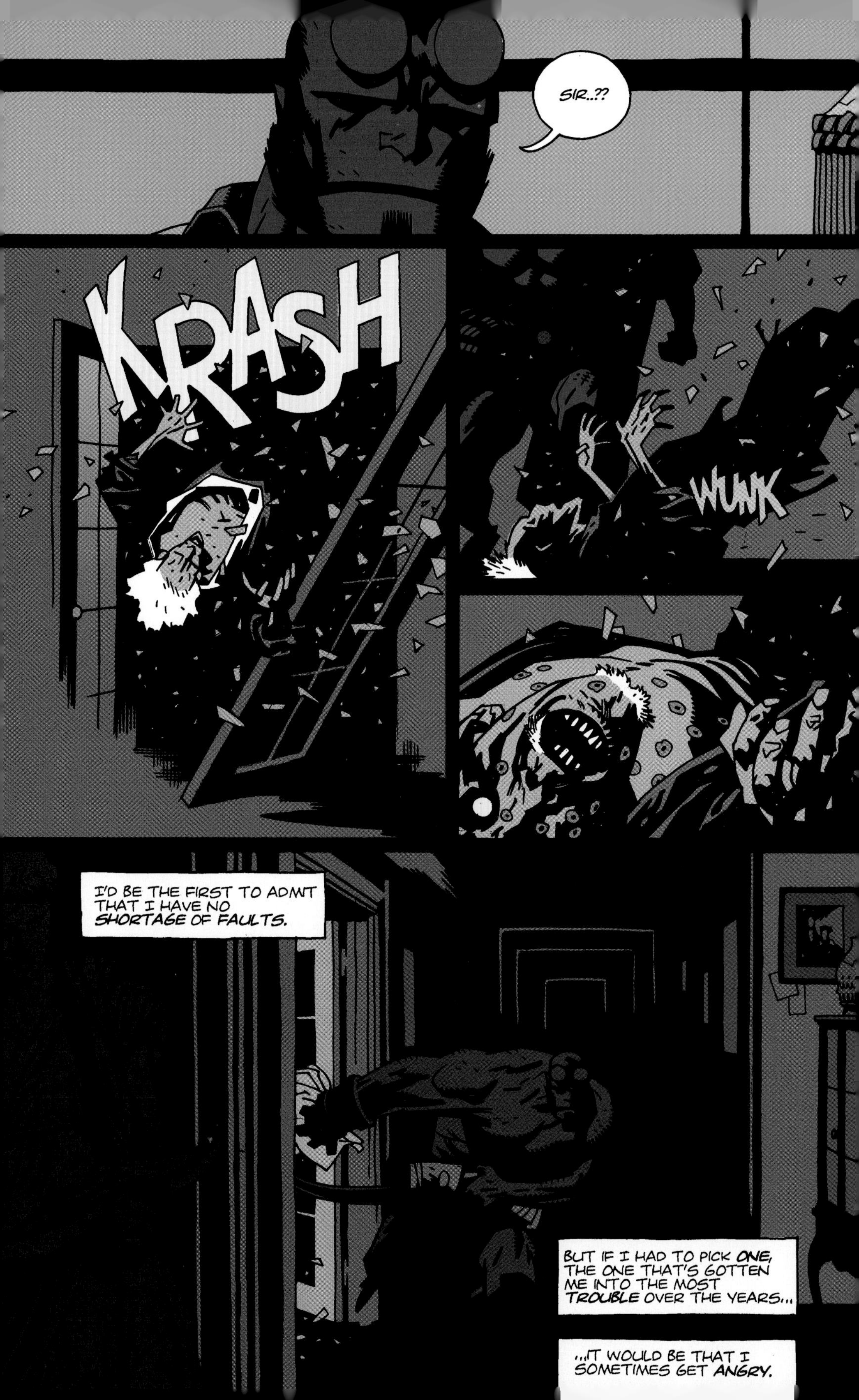
SIR..??
KRASH
WUNK
I'D BE THE FIRST TO ADMIT THAT I HAVE NO SHORTAGE OF FAULTS.
BUT IF I HAD TO PICK ONE, THE ONE THAT'S GOTTEN ME INTO THE MOST TROUBLE OVER THE YEARS...
...IT WOULD BE THAT I SOMETIMES GET ANGRY.

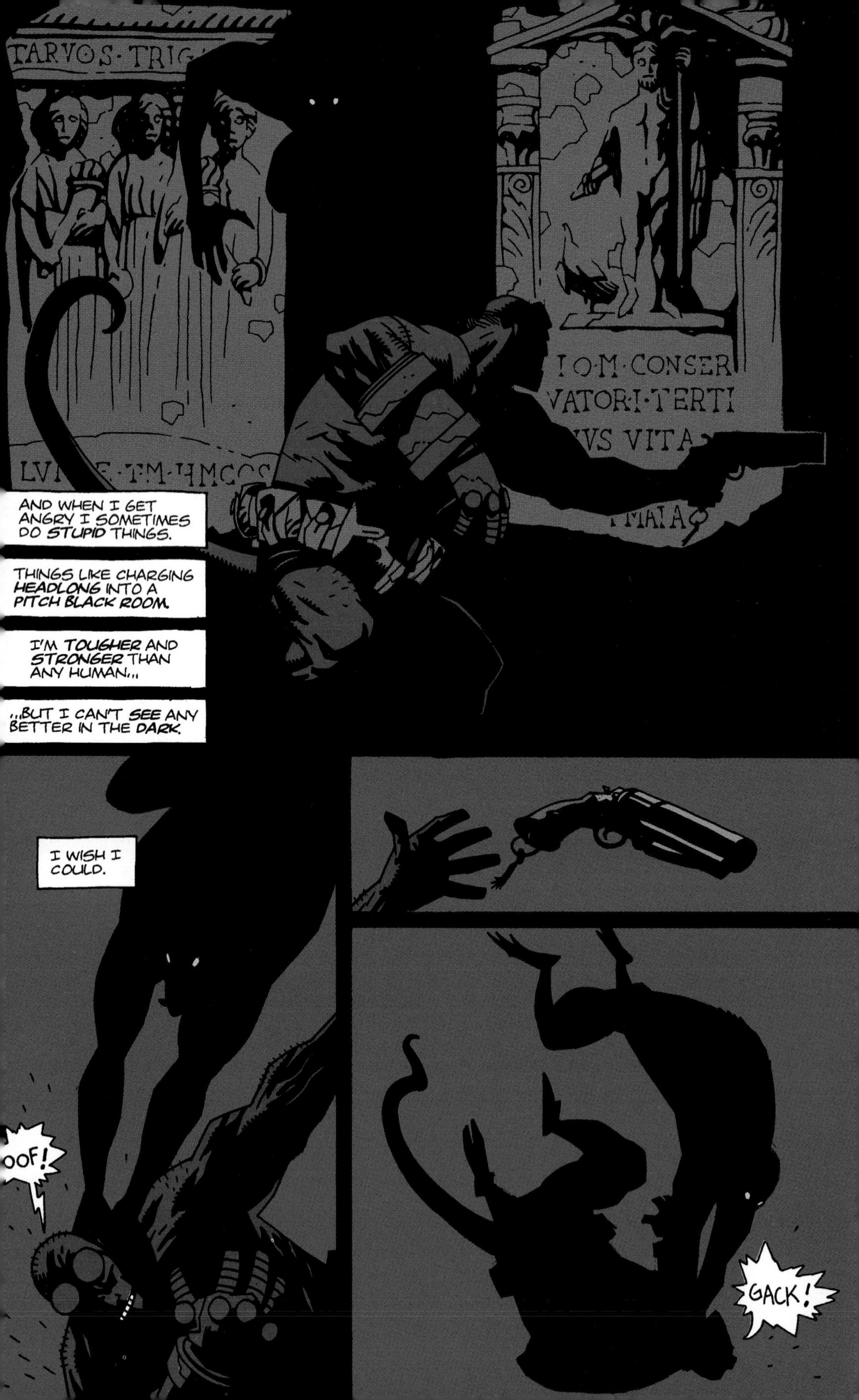
TARVOS·TRIG
I·O·M·CONSER
VATORI·TERTI
AND WHEN I GET ANGRY I SOMETIMES DO STUPID THINGS.
THINGS LIKE CHARGING HEADLONG INTO A PITCH BLACK ROOM.
I'M TOUGHER AND STRONGER THAN ANY HUMAN...
...BUT I CAN'T SEE ANY BETTER IN THE DARK.
I WISH I COULD.
OOF!
GACK!

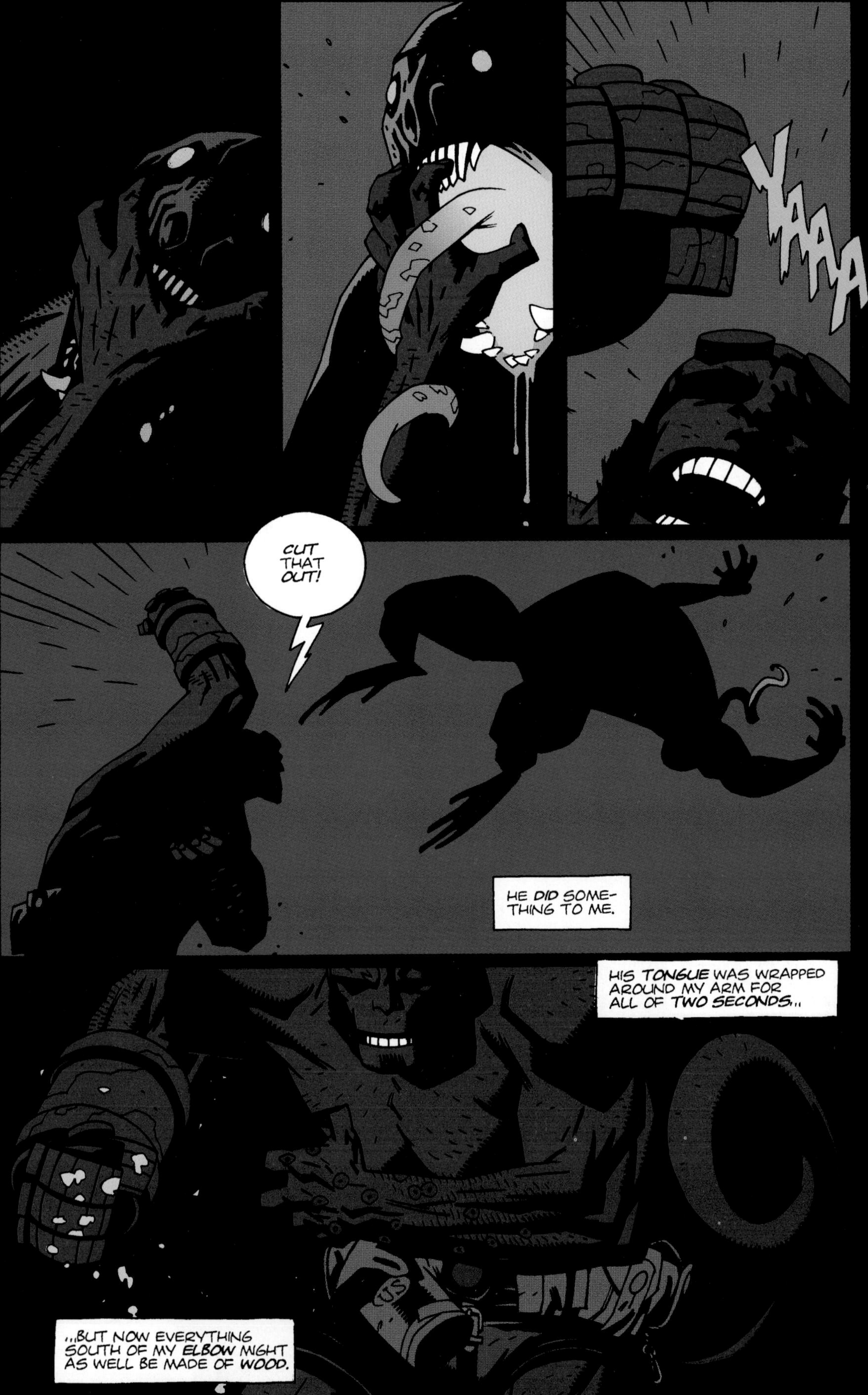
YAAAA
CUT THAT OUT!
HE DID SOME-THING TO ME.
HIS TONGUE WAS WRAPPED AROUND MY ARM FOR ALL OF TWO SECONDS...
...BUT NOW EVERYTHING SOUTH OF MY ELBOW MIGHT AS WELL BE MADE OF WOOD.

AND MY FROG-FACED FRIEND IS COMING BACK TO *FINISH* THE JOB!

HE'S FAST, BUT THIS TIME I'M *FASTER*.

IT'S NOT MY *FLESH AND BLOOD* ARM HE GETS A *HOLD* ON.

I LET HIM GET A *TASTE* OF MY *RIGHT* HAND.

THE HAND THE BEST SCIENTISTS OF THE LAST HALF CENTURY HAVE *TRIED* AND *FAILED* TO *ANALYZE*.

THEY COULDN'T FIND OUT *ANYTHING*...

...BUT AT LEAST I KNOW *ONE THING* ABOUT IT.

IT DOESN'T FEEL *PAIN*.

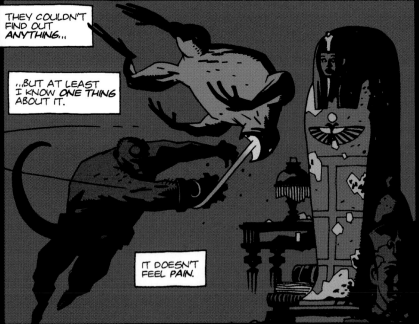

WONDER IF FROGGY DOES?

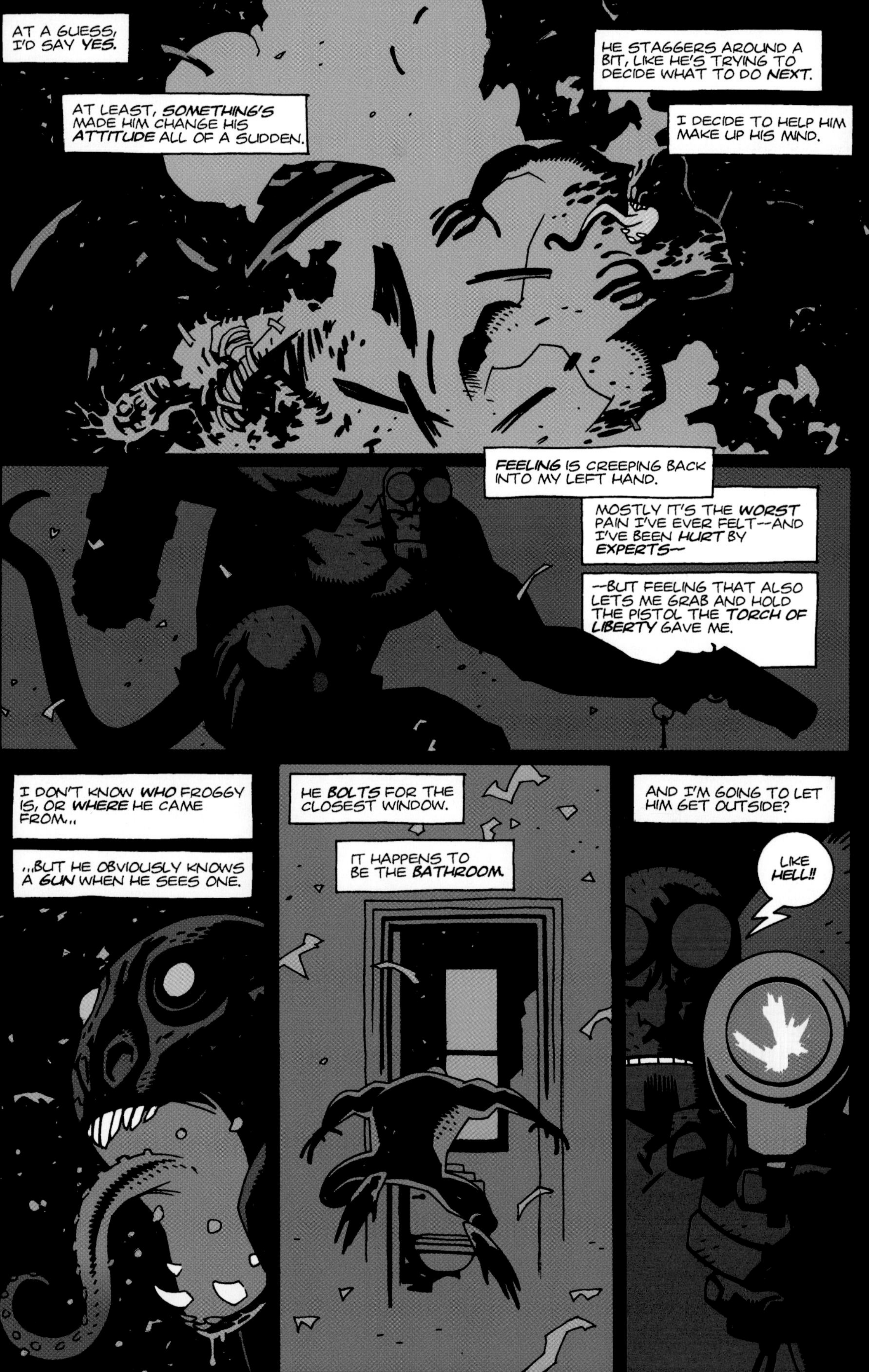
AT A GUESS, I'D SAY YES.
AT LEAST, SOMETHING'S MADE HIM CHANGE HIS ATTITUDE ALL OF A SUDDEN.
HE STAGGERS AROUND A BIT, LIKE HE'S TRYING TO DECIDE WHAT TO DO NEXT.
I DECIDE TO HELP HIM MAKE UP HIS MIND.
FEELING IS CREEPING BACK INTO MY LEFT HAND.
MOSTLY IT'S THE WORST PAIN I'VE EVER FELT--AND I'VE BEEN HURT BY EXPERTS--
--BUT FEELING THAT ALSO LETS ME GRAB AND HOLD THE PISTOL THE TORCH OF LIBERTY GAVE ME.
I DON'T KNOW WHO FROGGY IS, OR WHERE HE CAME FROM...
...BUT HE OBVIOUSLY KNOWS A GUN WHEN HE SEES ONE.
HE BOLTS FOR THE CLOSEST WINDOW.
IT HAPPENS TO BE THE BATHROOM.
AND I'M GOING TO LET HIM GET OUTSIDE?
LIKE HELL!!

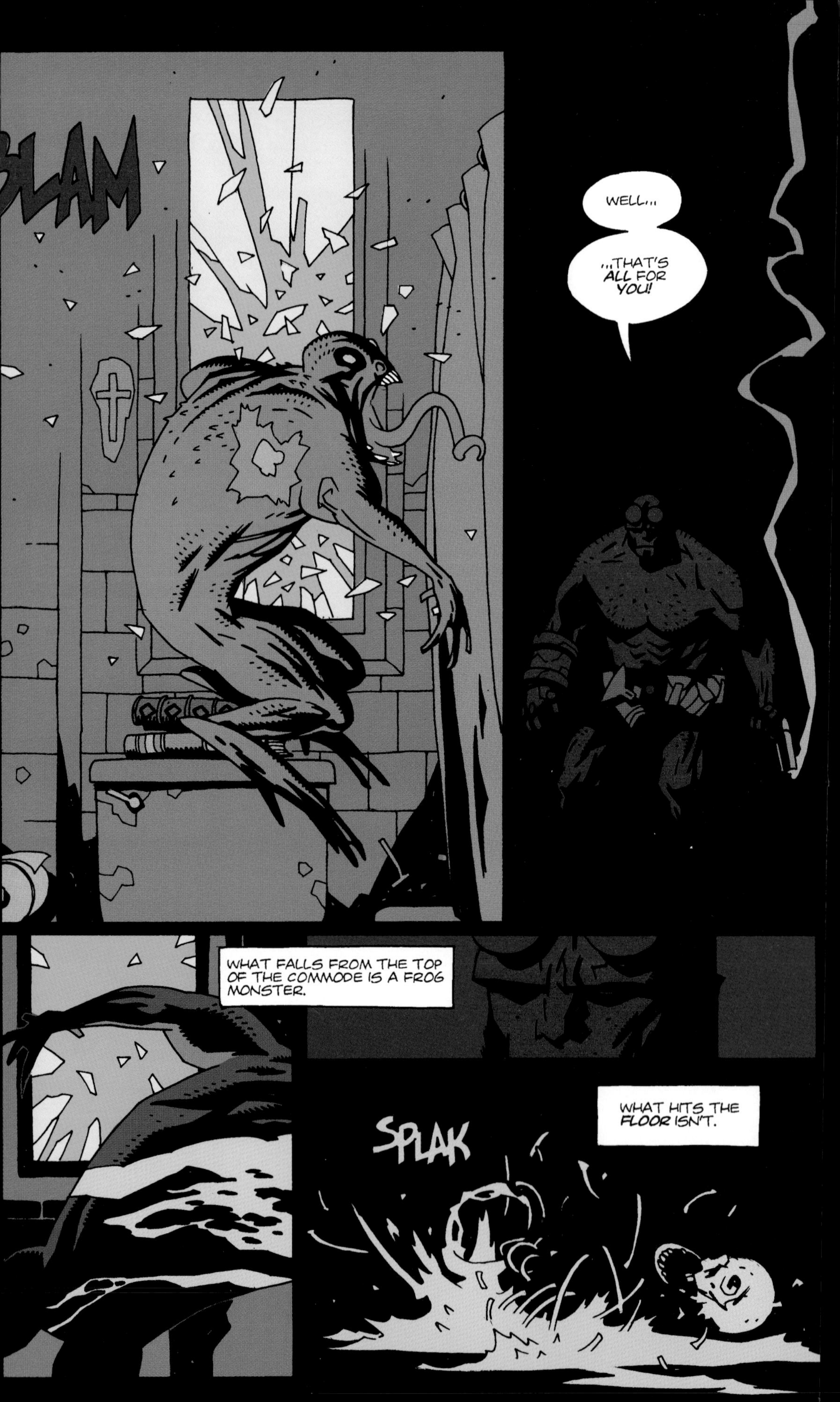
BLAM
WELL...
...THAT'S ALL FOR YOU!
WHAT FALLS FROM THE TOP OF THE COMMODE IS A FROG MONSTER.
WHAT HITS THE FLOOR ISN'T.
SPLAK

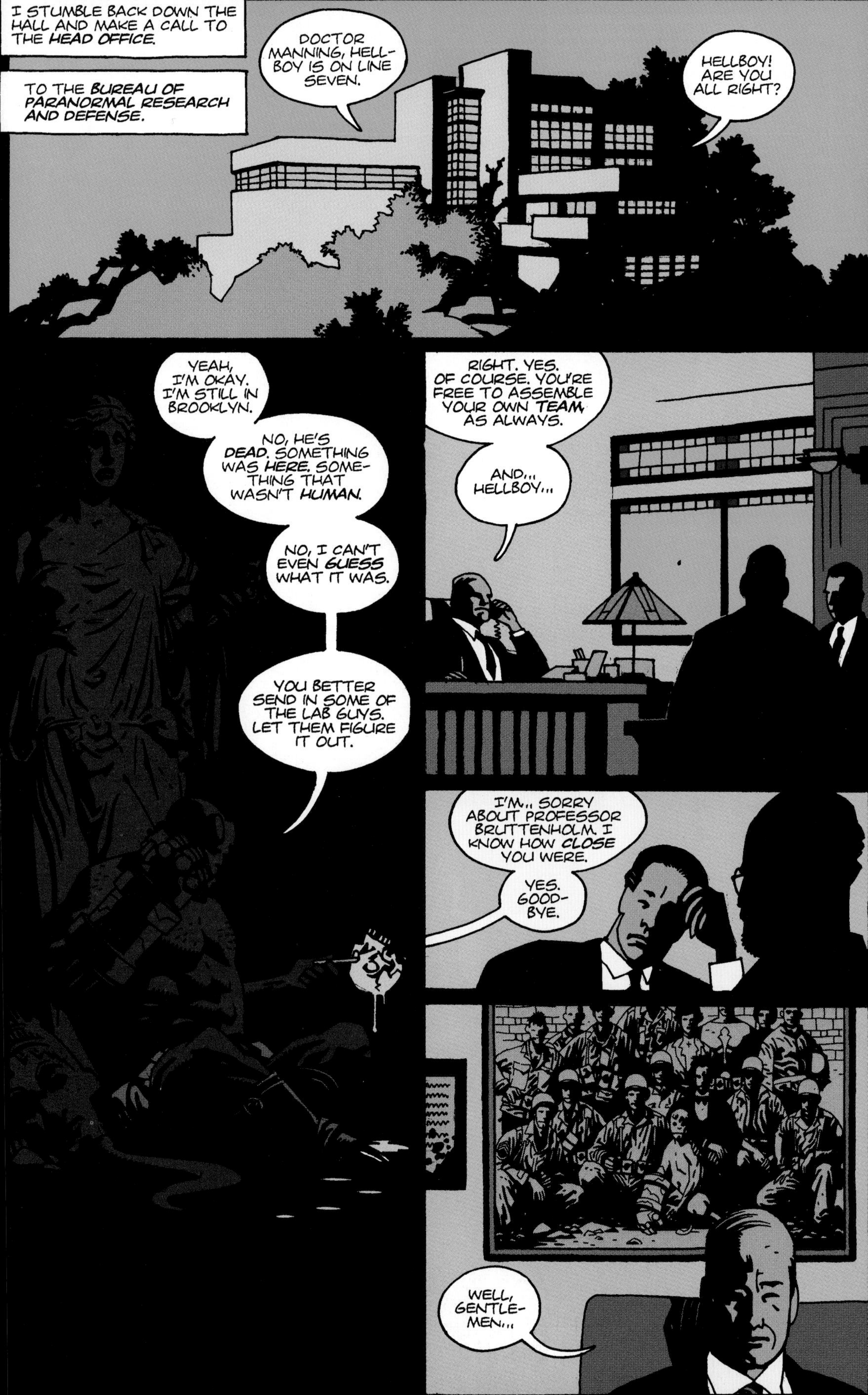
I STUMBLE BACK DOWN THE HALL AND MAKE A CALL TO THE HEAD OFFICE.
TO THE BUREAU OF PARANORMAL RESEARCH AND DEFENSE.
DOCTOR MANNING, HELL-BOY IS ON LINE SEVEN.
HELLBOY! ARE YOU ALL RIGHT?
YEAH, I'M OKAY. I'M STILL IN BROOKLYN.
NO, HE'S DEAD. SOMETHING WAS HERE. SOME-THING THAT WASN'T HUMAN.
NO, I CAN'T EVEN GUESS WHAT IT WAS.
YOU BETTER SEND IN SOME OF THE LAB GUYS. LET THEM FIGURE IT OUT.
RIGHT. YES. OF COURSE. YOU'RE FREE TO ASSEMBLE YOUR OWN TEAM AS ALWAYS.
AND... HELLBOY...
I'M... SORRY ABOUT PROFESSOR BRUTTENHOLM. I KNOW HOW CLOSE YOU WERE.
YES. GOOD-BYE.
WELL, GENTLE-MEN...

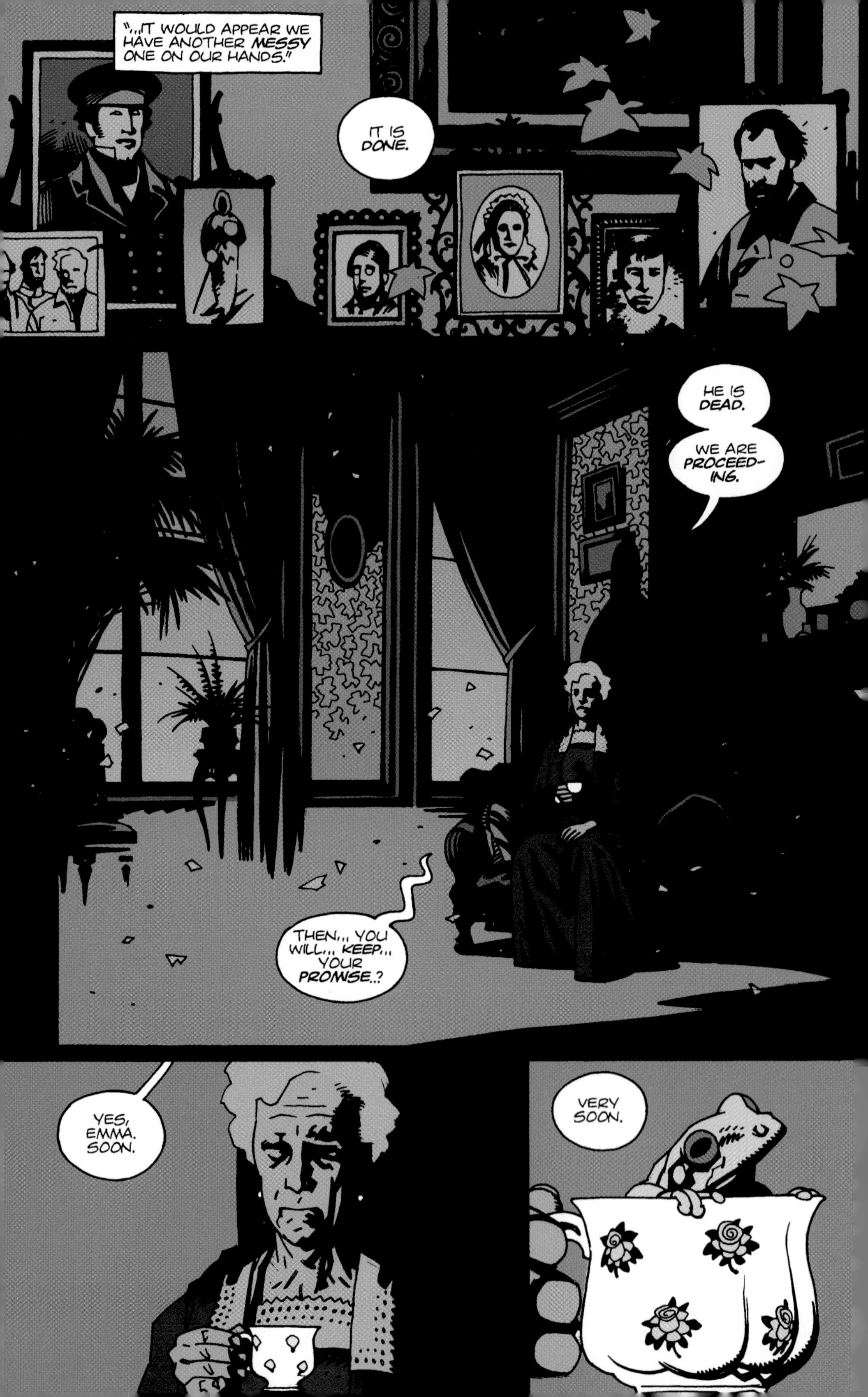
"...IT WOULD APPEAR WE HAVE ANOTHER MESSY ONE ON OUR HANDS."
IT IS DONE.
HE IS DEAD.
WE ARE PROCEED-ING.
THEN... YOU WILL... KEEP... YOUR PROMISE..?
YES, EMMA. SOON.
VERY SOON.

BUREAU FOR PARANORMAL RESEARCH AND DEFENSE

File #267999 (9/16/48)

Re: Nazi "Project Ragna Rok" (The Fatal Destiny)

To the best determination of the assigned investigative team, "Ragna Rok" was one of Hitler's many "Doomsday" projects initiated in the closing days of World War Two.

Principally there were known to be five individuals (see photos below) involved at key steps of the project, and so far as has been determined all five were present in the final moments. The project was apparently headed by General Klaus Werner von Krupt (see addendum under photo.)

The culmination of several years' work by the individuals, the ritual performed on Tarmagant Island (see map, pg. 162) on 23 Dec. 1944 corresponds precisely with the manifestation of the creature now code named "Hellboy" (see File #25891), the so-called "HELLBOY INCIDENT."

Professor Trevor Bruttenholm and his staff have examined both "Hellboy" and the site on Tarmagant Island extensively, and although no physical evidence can be found to link the events it seems unlikely their temporal juxtaposition is merely a coincidence.

VON KRUPT, KLAUS WERNER
(Photo taken 12/2/45) Committed to Eisenvalt Sanitarium. Died 6 months later. Body discovered to be infested with beetles of unknown species. No explanation.

Leopold Kurtz
(b 10/11/15)
whereabouts unknown

Ilsa Haupstein
(b 6/7/19)
whereabouts unknown

Professor Doctor Karl
Ruprect Kroenen
(b unknown)
whereabouts unknown

Name Unknown
(b unknown)
whereabouts unknown

B.P. R.D.

FROGS

Frogs, like snakes, scorpions, ravens, and black cats, are traditionally considered harbingers of doom, witnessed by the following tale.

AN AFRICAN MYTH ABOUT A FROG

ON A DAY when little water was to be found, Man spent awhile in thought and realized that he might one day die, never to rise again. Man sent Dog to God to ask that he might come back to life again, like the flowering plant, after death.

Dog went off and followed his nose toward God. He was soon distracted by the smell of soup, and followed his hunger toward the source. Leaning close to watch it boil, Dog was content and forgot his mission.

Seeing that Dog was lost, Frog took it upon himself to go to God and tell him that Man did not want to live again. If Man were to be reborn, thought Frog, he would soon muddy the rivers and destroy the birthplaces of frogs.

Dog finally arrived to tell God Man's message. Leaning low, he crooned Man's need for rebirth in the song of his howl. God was touched by the devotion of Dog for Man.

But God granted the frog's wish, because he got there first.

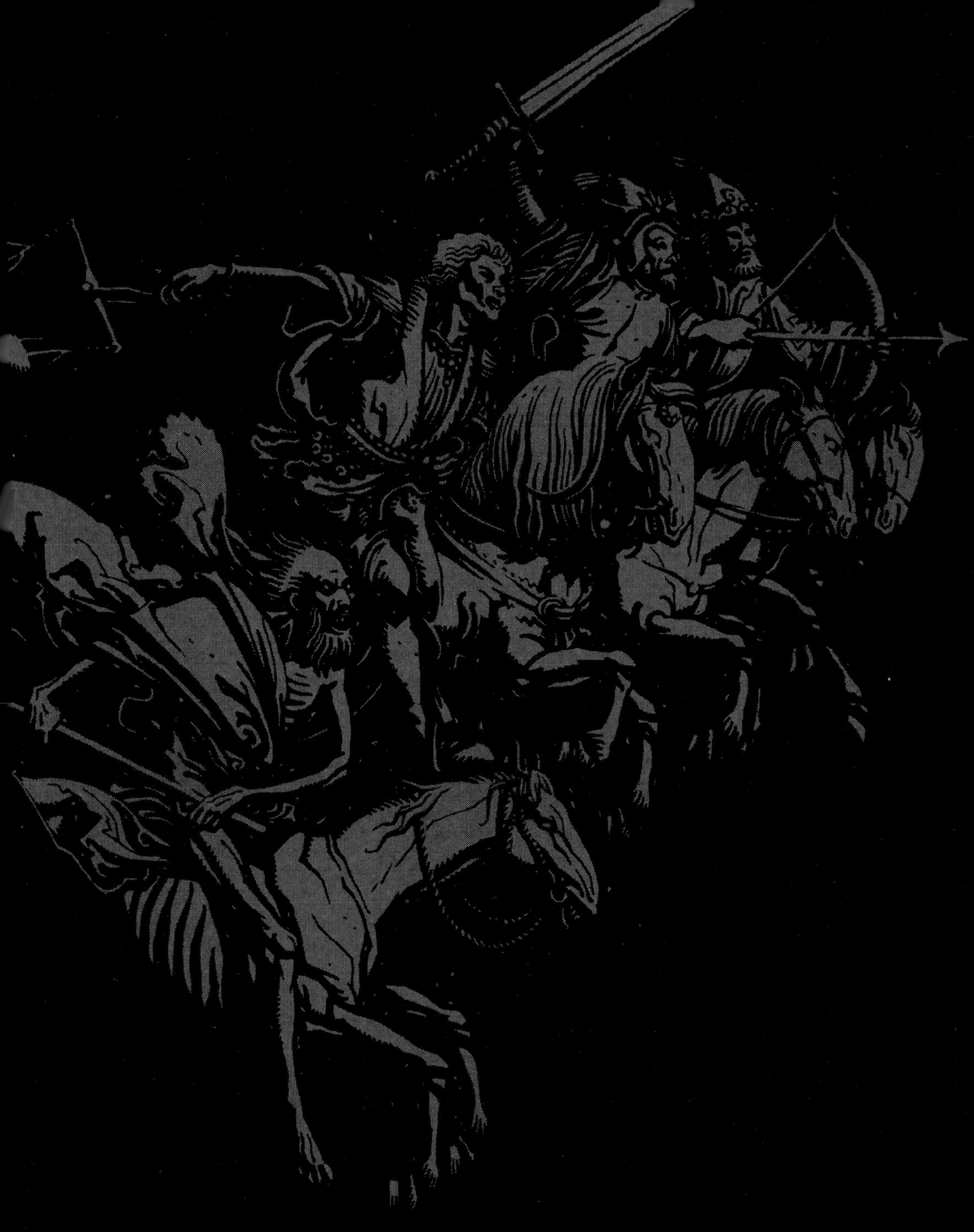

CHAPTER TWO

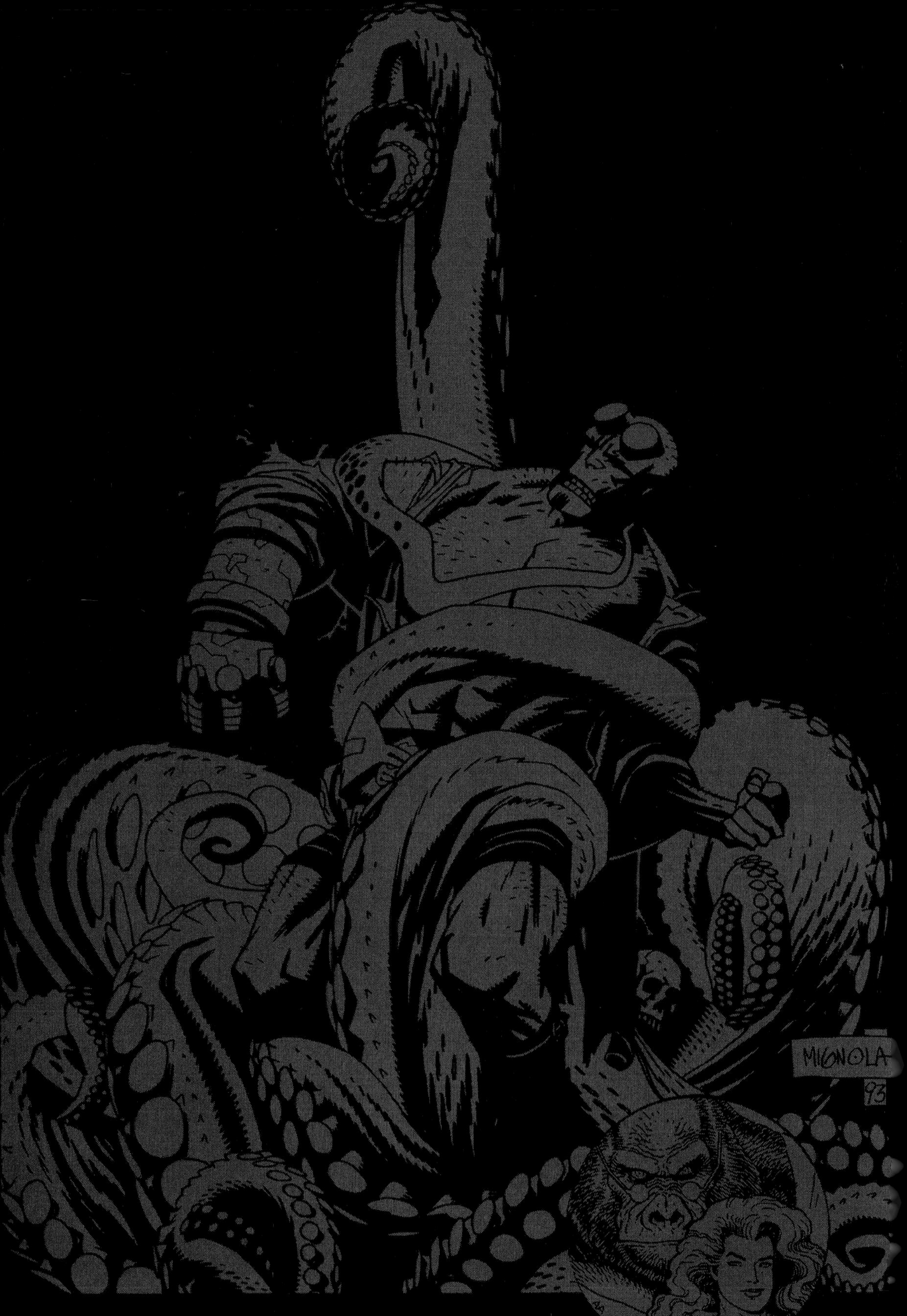
MIGNOLA
93

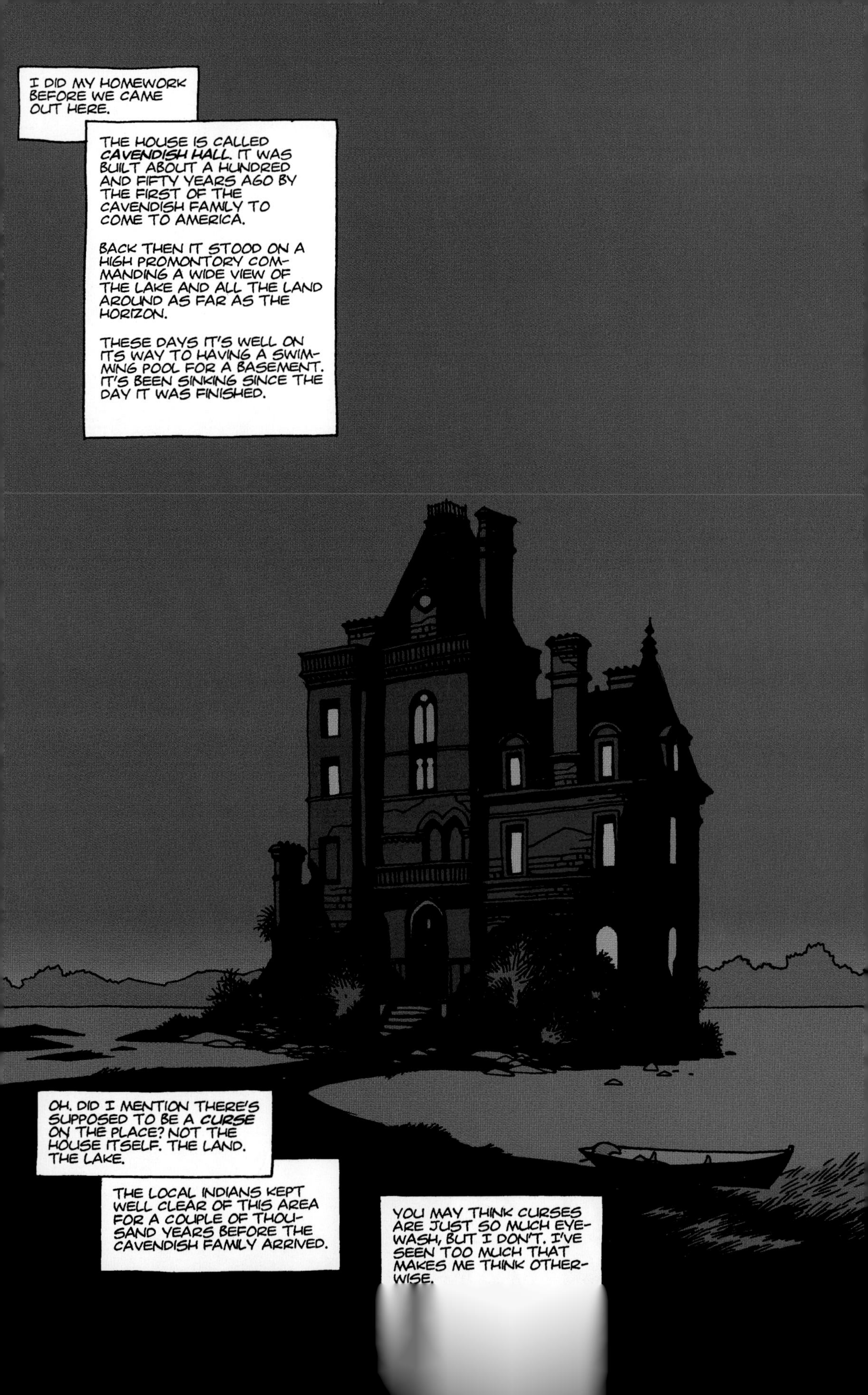
I DID MY HOMEWORK BEFORE WE CAME OUT HERE.
THE HOUSE IS CALLED *CAVENDISH HALL*. IT WAS BUILT ABOUT A HUNDRED AND FIFTY YEARS AGO BY THE FIRST OF THE CAVENDISH FAMILY TO COME TO AMERICA.
BACK THEN IT STOOD ON A HIGH PROMONTORY COMMANDING A WIDE VIEW OF THE LAKE AND ALL THE LAND AROUND AS FAR AS THE HORIZON.
THESE DAYS IT'S WELL ON ITS WAY TO HAVING A SWIMMING POOL FOR A BASEMENT. IT'S BEEN SINKING SINCE THE DAY IT WAS FINISHED.
OH, DID I MENTION THERE'S SUPPOSED TO BE A *CURSE* ON THE PLACE? NOT THE HOUSE ITSELF. THE LAND. THE LAKE.
THE LOCAL INDIANS KEPT WELL CLEAR OF THIS AREA FOR A COUPLE OF THOUSAND YEARS BEFORE THE CAVENDISH FAMILY ARRIVED.
YOU MAY THINK CURSES ARE JUST SO MUCH EYEWASH, BUT I DON'T. I'VE SEEN TOO MUCH THAT MAKES ME THINK OTHERWISE.

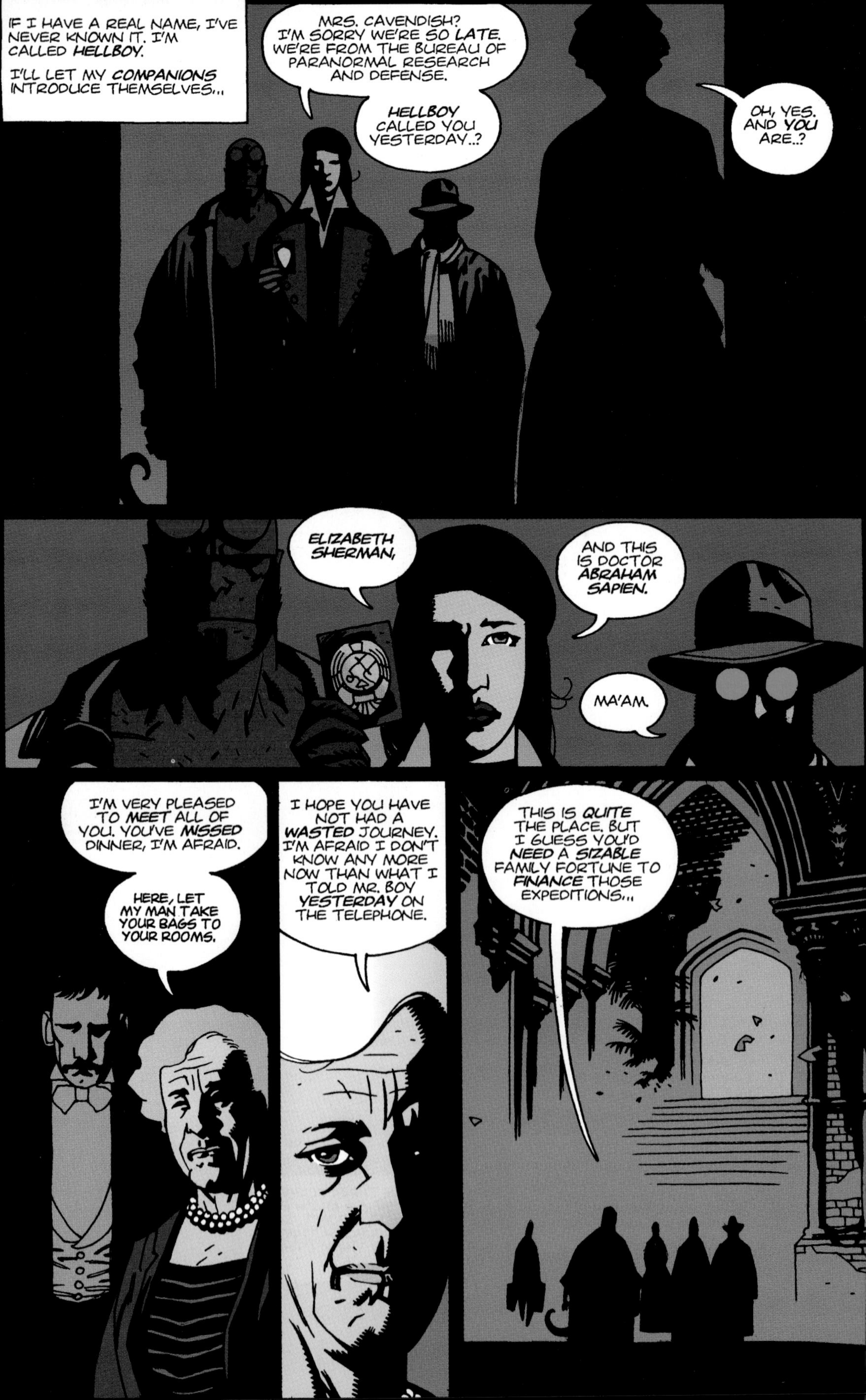
IF I HAVE A REAL NAME, I'VE NEVER KNOWN IT. I'M CALLED HELLBOY.
I'LL LET MY COMPANIONS INTRODUCE THEMSELVES...
MRS. CAVENDISH? I'M SORRY WE'RE SO LATE. WE'RE FROM THE BUREAU OF PARANORMAL RESEARCH AND DEFENSE.
HELLBOY CALLED YOU YESTERDAY..?
OH, YES. AND YOU ARE..?
ELIZABETH SHERMAN,
AND THIS IS DOCTOR ABRAHAM SAPIEN.
MA'AM.
I'M VERY PLEASED TO MEET ALL OF YOU. YOU'VE MISSED DINNER, I'M AFRAID.
HERE, LET MY MAN TAKE YOUR BAGS TO YOUR ROOMS.
I HOPE YOU HAVE NOT HAD A WASTED JOURNEY. I'M AFRAID I DON'T KNOW ANY MORE NOW THAN WHAT I TOLD MR. BOY YESTERDAY ON THE TELEPHONE.
THIS IS QUITE THE PLACE. BUT I GUESS YOU'D NEED A SIZABLE FAMILY FORTUNE TO FINANCE THOSE EXPEDITIONS...

THE EXPEDITIONS. NINE GENERATIONS OF THE CAVENDISH FAMILY BELIEVED THERE WAS *SOMETHING* AT THE TOP OF THE WORLD.

I DON'T KNOW HOW MANY OF THEM *DIED* TRYING TO FIND IT. BUT THE LAST TIME THEY TOOK *TREVOR BRUTTENHOLM* WITH THEM.

THE MAN I CALLED MY FATHER.

AND NOW HE'S *DEAD.*

AND... YOU DON'T KNOW ANYTHING ABOUT... FROGS..?

HELL-BOY...

QUITE ALL RIGHT, MY DEAR. I DON'T MIND *DIRECT QUESTIONS,* EVEN WHEN I DON'T *UNDER-STAND* THEM.

YOUR *SONS,* THEN.

YOU HEARD *NOTHING* FROM THEM AFTER THE EXPEDITION LEFT *BULL HARBOR?*

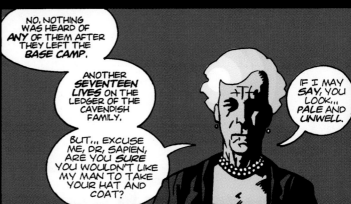

NO. NOTHING WAS HEARD OF *ANY* OF THEM AFTER THEY LEFT THE *BASE CAMP.*

ANOTHER *SEVENTEEN LIVES* ON THE LEDGER OF THE *CAVENDISH* FAMILY.

BUT... EXCUSE ME, DR. SAPIEN, ARE YOU *SURE* YOU WOULDN'T LIKE MY MAN TO TAKE YOUR HAT AND COAT?

IF I MAY *SAY,* YOU LOOK... *PALE* AND *UNWELL.*

NO, MA'AM, I'M *FINE,* THANK YOU.

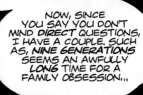

DR. SAPIEN DOESN'T CARE MUCH FOR TRAVELING.

NOW, SINCE YOU SAY YOU DON'T MIND *DIRECT QUESTIONS,* I HAVE A COUPLE. SUCH AS, *NINE GENERATIONS* SEEMS AN AWFULLY *LONG* TIME FOR A FAMILY OBSESSION...

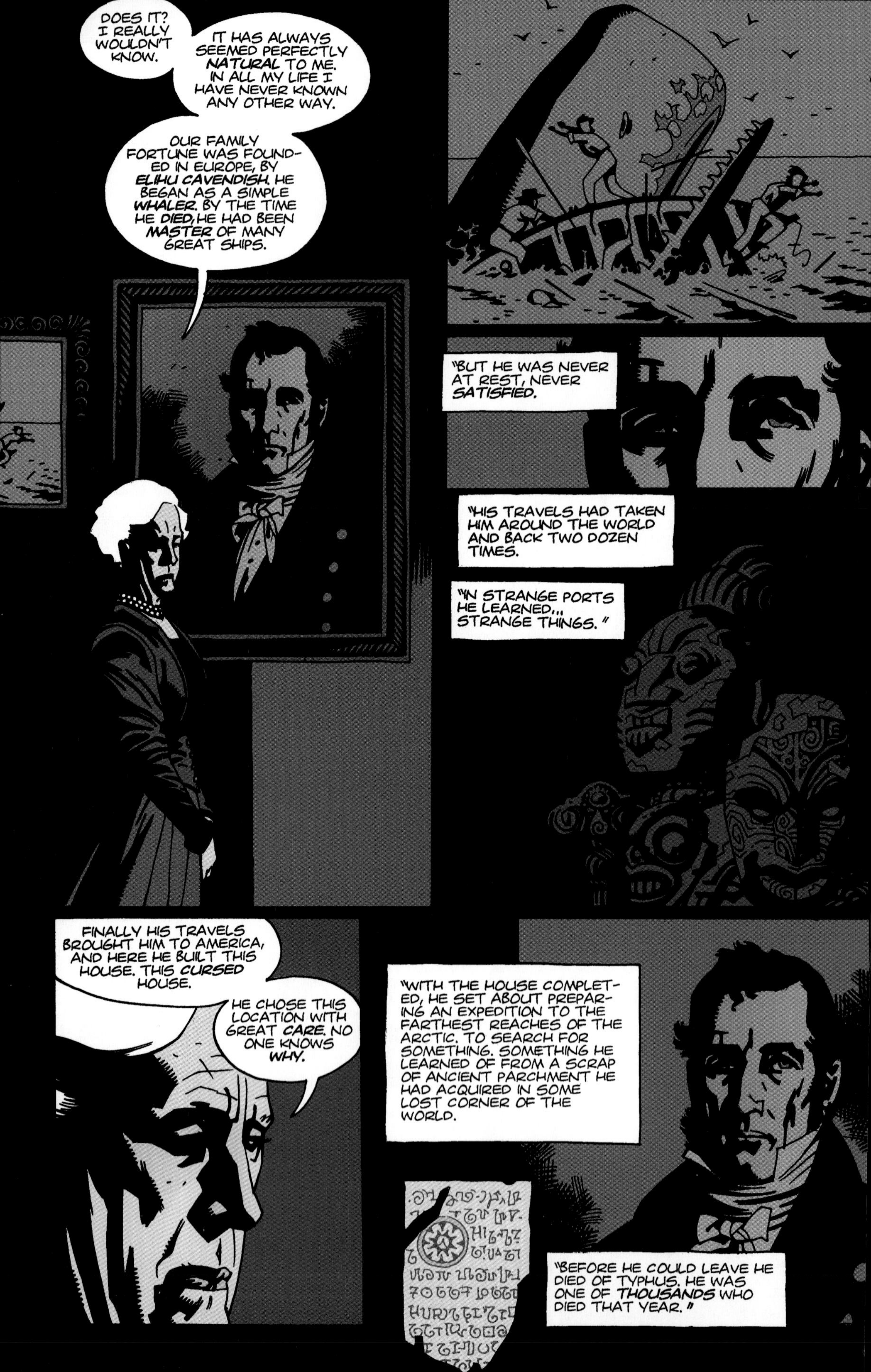
DOES IT? I REALLY WOULDN'T KNOW.
IT HAS ALWAYS SEEMED PERFECTLY NATURAL TO ME. IN ALL MY LIFE I HAVE NEVER KNOWN ANY OTHER WAY.
OUR FAMILY FORTUNE WAS FOUNDED IN EUROPE, BY ELIHU CAVENDISH. HE BEGAN AS A SIMPLE WHALER. BY THE TIME HE DIED, HE HAD BEEN MASTER OF MANY GREAT SHIPS.
"BUT HE WAS NEVER AT REST, NEVER SATISFIED.
"HIS TRAVELS HAD TAKEN HIM AROUND THE WORLD AND BACK TWO DOZEN TIMES.
"IN STRANGE PORTS HE LEARNED... STRANGE THINGS."
FINALLY HIS TRAVELS BROUGHT HIM TO AMERICA, AND HERE HE BUILT THIS HOUSE. THIS CURSED HOUSE.
HE CHOSE THIS LOCATION WITH GREAT CARE. NO ONE KNOWS WHY.
"WITH THE HOUSE COMPLETED, HE SET ABOUT PREPARING AN EXPEDITION TO THE FARTHEST REACHES OF THE ARCTIC. TO SEARCH FOR SOMETHING. SOMETHING HE LEARNED OF FROM A SCRAP OF ANCIENT PARCHMENT HE HAD ACQUIRED IN SOME LOST CORNER OF THE WORLD.
"BEFORE HE COULD LEAVE HE DIED OF TYPHUS. HE WAS ONE OF THOUSANDS WHO DIED THAT YEAR."

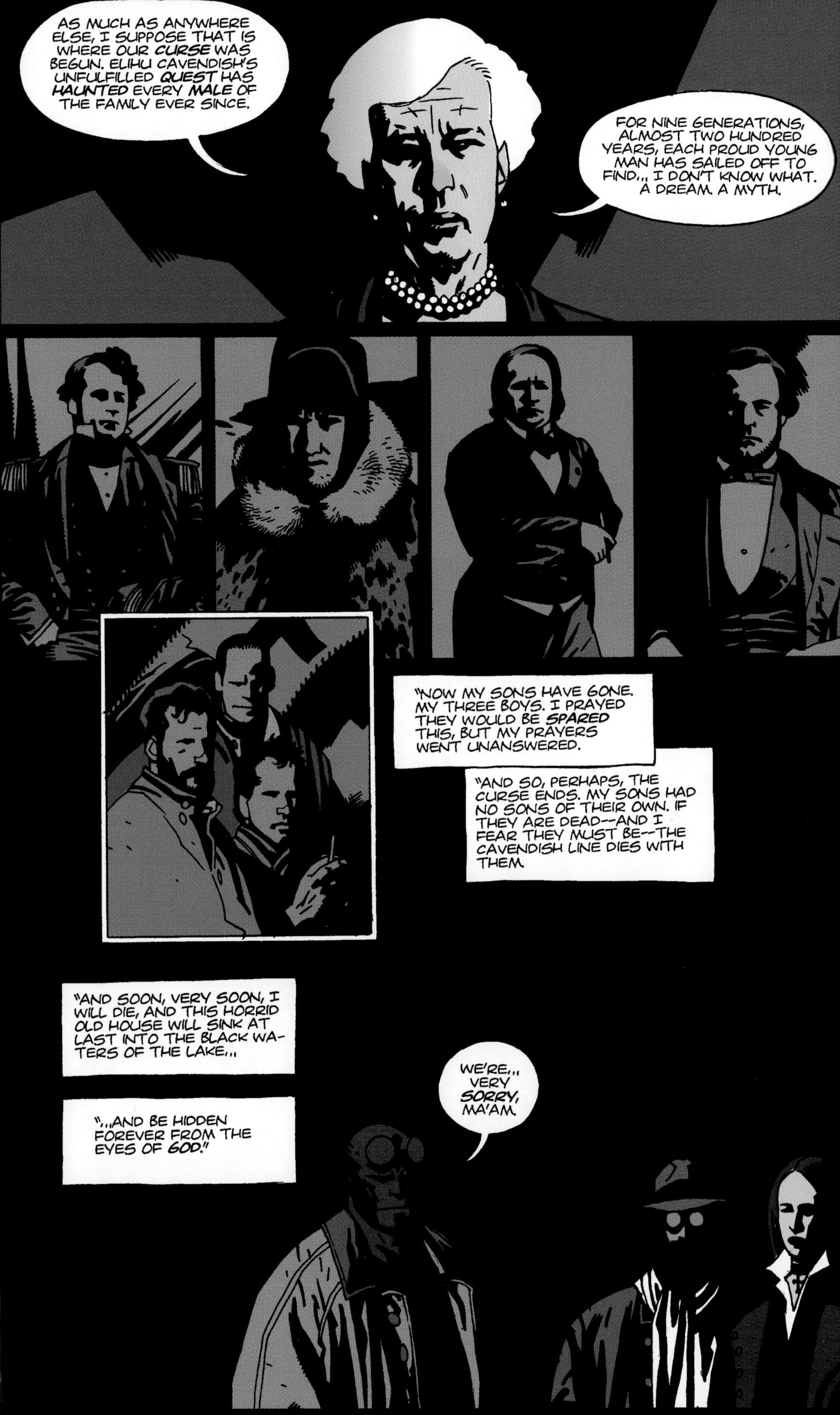
AS MUCH AS ANYWHERE ELSE, I SUPPOSE THAT IS WHERE OUR CURSE WAS BEGUN. ELIHU CAVENDISH'S UNFULFILLED QUEST HAS HAUNTED EVERY MALE OF THE FAMILY EVER SINCE.
FOR NINE GENERATIONS, ALMOST TWO HUNDRED YEARS, EACH PROUD YOUNG MAN HAS SAILED OFF TO FIND... I DON'T KNOW WHAT. A DREAM. A MYTH.
"NOW MY SONS HAVE GONE. MY THREE BOYS. I PRAYED THEY WOULD BE SPARED THIS, BUT MY PRAYERS WENT UNANSWERED.
"AND SO, PERHAPS, THE CURSE ENDS. MY SONS HAD NO SONS OF THEIR OWN. IF THEY ARE DEAD--AND I FEAR THEY MUST BE--THE CAVENDISH LINE DIES WITH THEM.
"AND SOON, VERY SOON, I WILL DIE, AND THIS HORRID OLD HOUSE WILL SINK AT LAST INTO THE BLACK WATERS OF THE LAKE...
"...AND BE HIDDEN FOREVER FROM THE EYES OF GOD."
WE'RE... VERY SORRY, MA'AM.

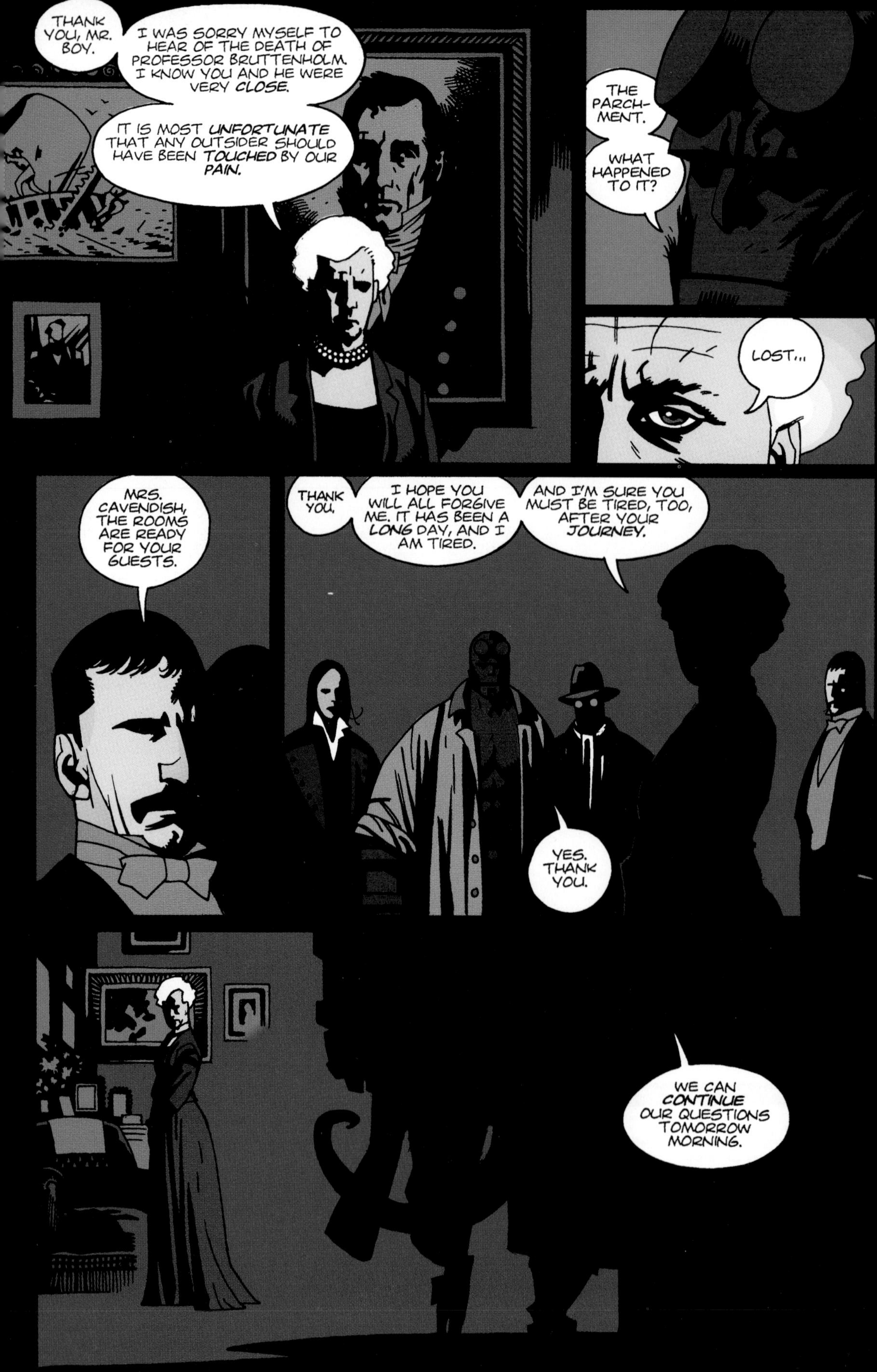
THANK YOU, MR. BOY.
I WAS SORRY MYSELF TO HEAR OF THE DEATH OF PROFESSOR BRUTTENHOLM. I KNOW YOU AND HE WERE VERY CLOSE.
IT IS MOST UNFORTUNATE THAT ANY OUTSIDER SHOULD HAVE BEEN TOUCHED BY OUR PAIN.
THE PARCHMENT.
WHAT HAPPENED TO IT?
LOST...
MRS. CAVENDISH, THE ROOMS ARE READY FOR YOUR GUESTS.
THANK YOU.
I HOPE YOU WILL ALL FORGIVE ME. IT HAS BEEN A LONG DAY, AND I AM TIRED.
AND I'M SURE YOU MUST BE TIRED, TOO, AFTER YOUR JOURNEY.
YES. THANK YOU.
WE CAN CONTINUE OUR QUESTIONS TOMORROW MORNING.

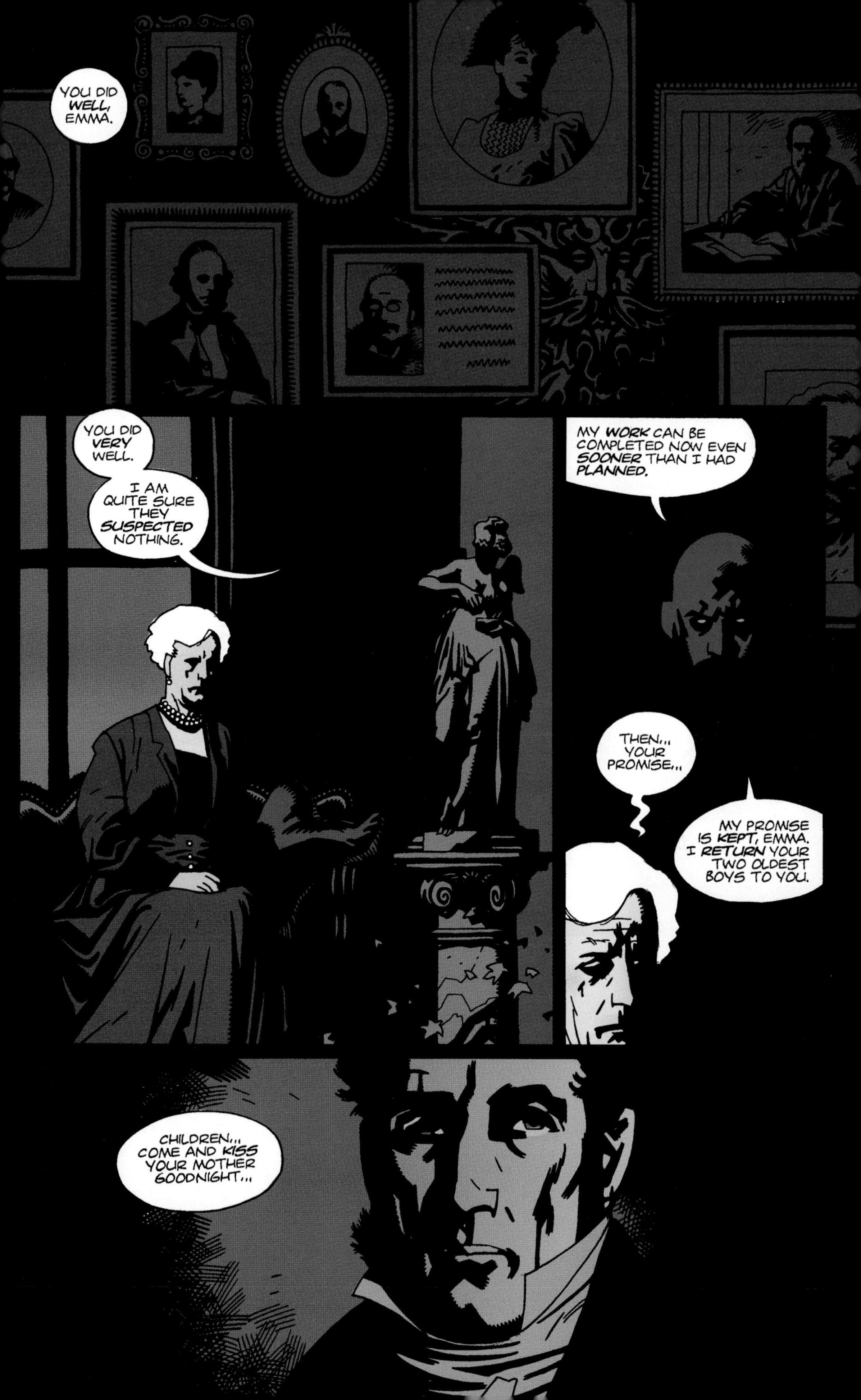
YOU DID WELL, EMMA.
YOU DID VERY WELL.
I AM QUITE SURE THEY SUSPECTED NOTHING.
MY WORK CAN BE COMPLETED NOW EVEN SOONER THAN I HAD PLANNED.
THEN... YOUR PROMISE...
MY PROMISE IS KEPT, EMMA. I RETURN YOUR TWO OLDEST BOYS TO YOU.
CHILDREN... COME AND KISS YOUR MOTHER GOODNIGHT...

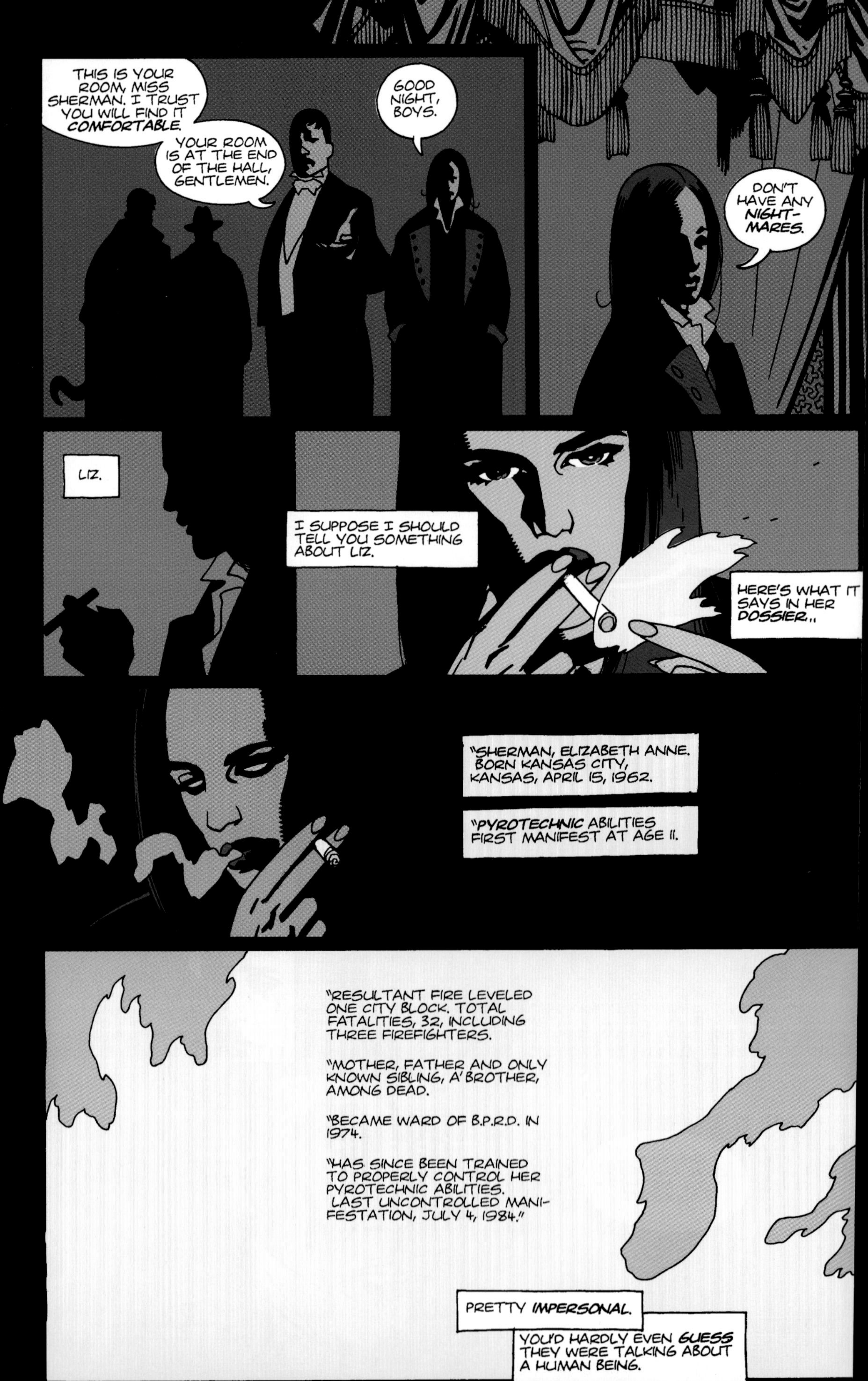
THIS IS YOUR ROOM, MISS SHERMAN. I TRUST YOU WILL FIND IT COMFORTABLE.
YOUR ROOM IS AT THE END OF THE HALL, GENTLEMEN.
GOOD NIGHT, BOYS.
DON'T HAVE ANY NIGHT-MARES.
LIZ.
I SUPPOSE I SHOULD TELL YOU SOMETHING ABOUT LIZ.
HERE'S WHAT IT SAYS IN HER DOSSIER..
"SHERMAN, ELIZABETH ANNE. BORN KANSAS CITY, KANSAS, APRIL 15, 1962.
"PYROTECHNIC ABILITIES FIRST MANIFEST AT AGE 11.
"RESULTANT FIRE LEVELED ONE CITY BLOCK. TOTAL FATALITIES, 32, INCLUDING THREE FIREFIGHTERS.
"MOTHER, FATHER AND ONLY KNOWN SIBLING, A BROTHER, AMONG DEAD.
"BECAME WARD OF B.P.R.D. IN 1974.
"HAS SINCE BEEN TRAINED TO PROPERLY CONTROL HER PYROTECHNIC ABILITIES. LAST UNCONTROLLED MANI-FESTATION, JULY 4, 1984."
PRETTY IMPERSONAL.
YOU'D HARDLY EVEN GUESS THEY WERE TALKING ABOUT A HUMAN BEING.

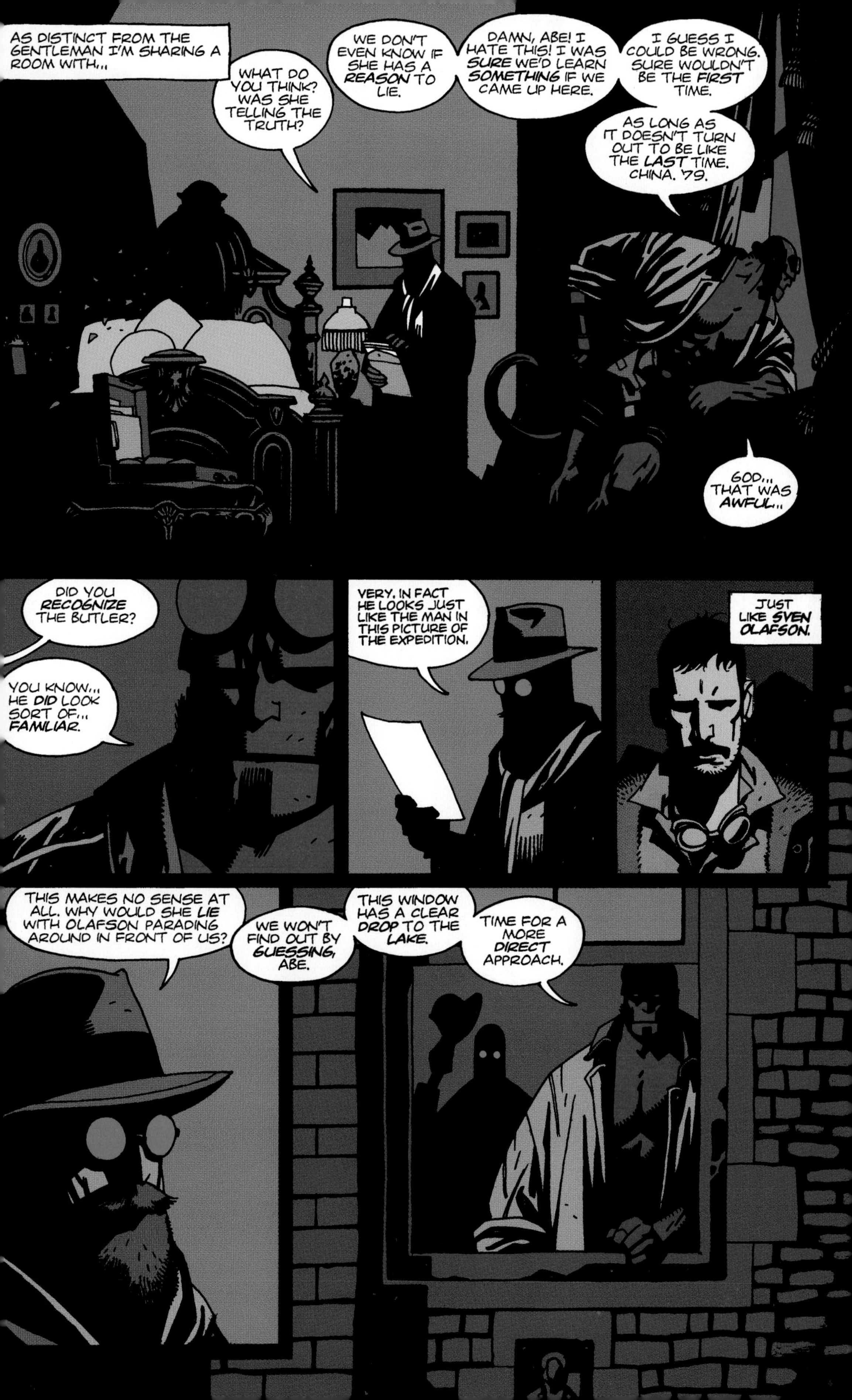

AS DISTINCT FROM THE GENTLEMAN I'M SHARING A ROOM WITH...
WHAT DO YOU THINK? WAS SHE TELLING THE TRUTH?
WE DON'T EVEN KNOW IF SHE HAS A REASON TO LIE.
DAMN, ABE! I HATE THIS! I WAS SURE WE'D LEARN SOMETHING IF WE CAME UP HERE.
I GUESS I COULD BE WRONG. SURE WOULDN'T BE THE FIRST TIME.
AS LONG AS IT DOESN'T TURN OUT TO BE LIKE THE LAST TIME. CHINA. '79.
GOD... THAT WAS AWFUL...
DID YOU RECOGNIZE THE BUTLER?
YOU KNOW... HE DID LOOK SORT OF... FAMILIAR.
VERY. IN FACT HE LOOKS JUST LIKE THE MAN IN THIS PICTURE OF THE EXPEDITION.
JUST LIKE SVEN OLAFSON.
THIS MAKES NO SENSE AT ALL. WHY WOULD SHE LIE WITH OLAFSON PARADING AROUND IN FRONT OF US?
WE WON'T FIND OUT BY GUESSING, ABE.
THIS WINDOW HAS A CLEAR DROP TO THE LAKE.
TIME FOR A MORE DIRECT APPROACH.

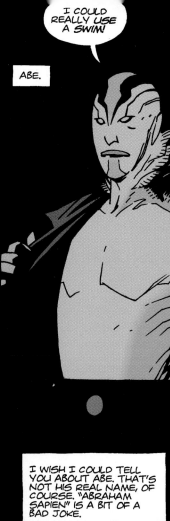

TIME FOR YOU TO GET WET!

AND NOT A MOMENT TOO SOON! THIS BEARD WAS STARTING TO MAKE ME FEEL CLAUSTROPHOBIC.

I COULD REALLY *USE* A *SWIM!*

ABE.

I WISH I COULD TELL YOU ABOUT ABE. THAT'S NOT HIS REAL NAME, OF COURSE. "ABRAHAM SAPIEN" IS A BIT OF A BAD JOKE.

HE WAS DISCOVERED WHEN PLUMBERS WORKING IN THE BASEMENT OF *ST. TRINIAN'S HOSPITAL* IN WASHINGTON, D.C., BROKE OPEN A SEALED DOOR AND DISCOVERED A LONG-FORGOTTEN CHAMBER.

ICTHYO SAPIEN

APRIL 14 1865

THE BUREAU TOOK HIS NAME FROM THE INSCRIPTION ON A SCRAP OF PAPER PINNED UP NEAR THE TUBE... THE DAY PRESIDENT *LINCOLN* DIED.

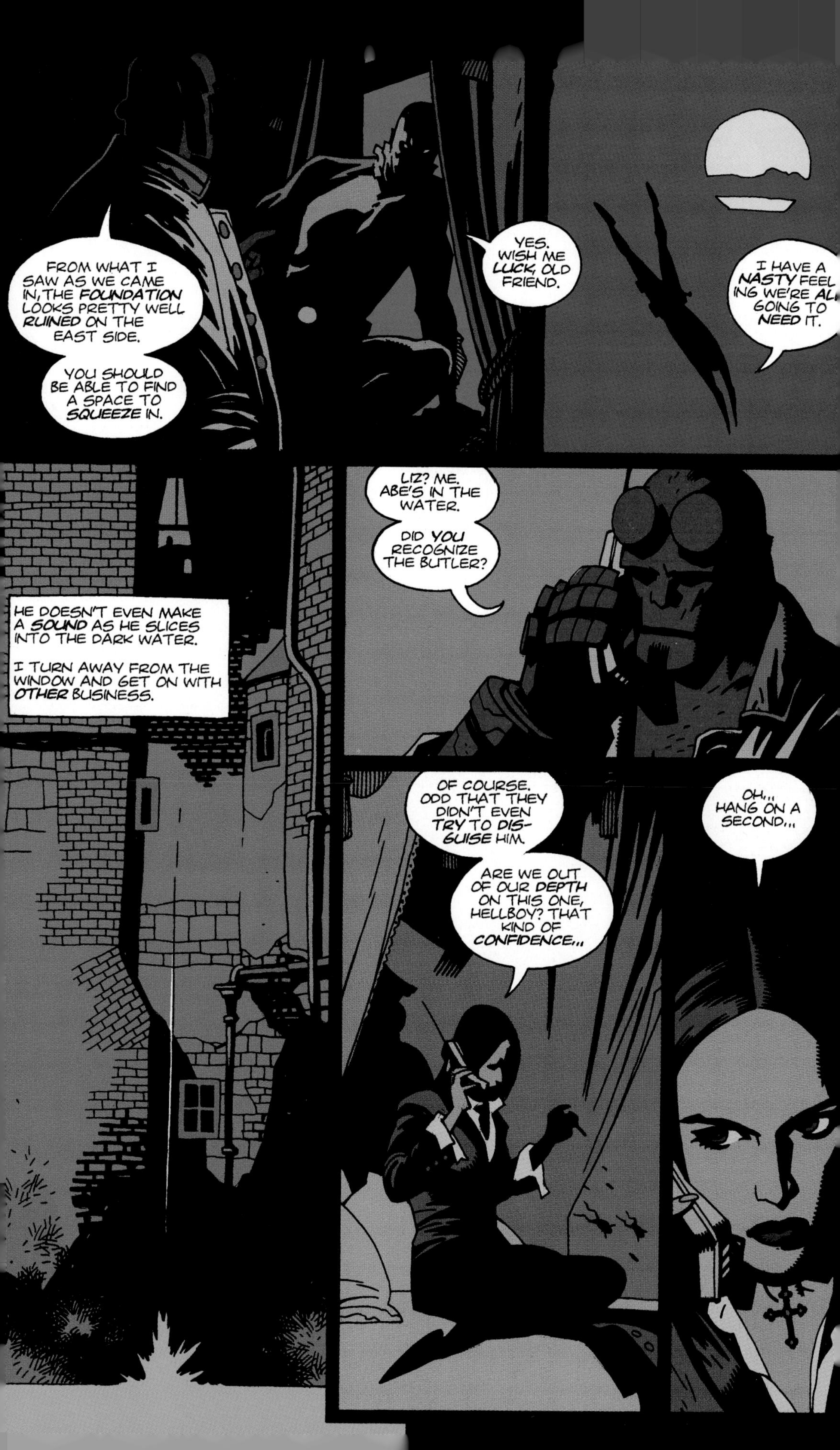

FROM WHAT I SAW AS WE CAME IN, THE FOUNDATION LOOKS PRETTY WELL RUINED ON THE EAST SIDE.
YOU SHOULD BE ABLE TO FIND A SPACE TO SQUEEZE IN.
YES. WISH ME LUCK, OLD FRIEND.
I HAVE A NASTY FEEL ING WE'RE ALL GOING TO NEED IT.
HE DOESN'T EVEN MAKE A SOUND AS HE SLICES INTO THE DARK WATER.
I TURN AWAY FROM THE WINDOW AND GET ON WITH OTHER BUSINESS.
LIZ? ME. ABE'S IN THE WATER.
DID YOU RECOGNIZE THE BUTLER?
OF COURSE. ODD THAT THEY DIDN'T EVEN TRY TO DIS-GUISE HIM.
ARE WE OUT OF OUR DEPTH ON THIS ONE, HELLBOY? THAT KIND OF CONFIDENCE...
OH... HANG ON A SECOND...

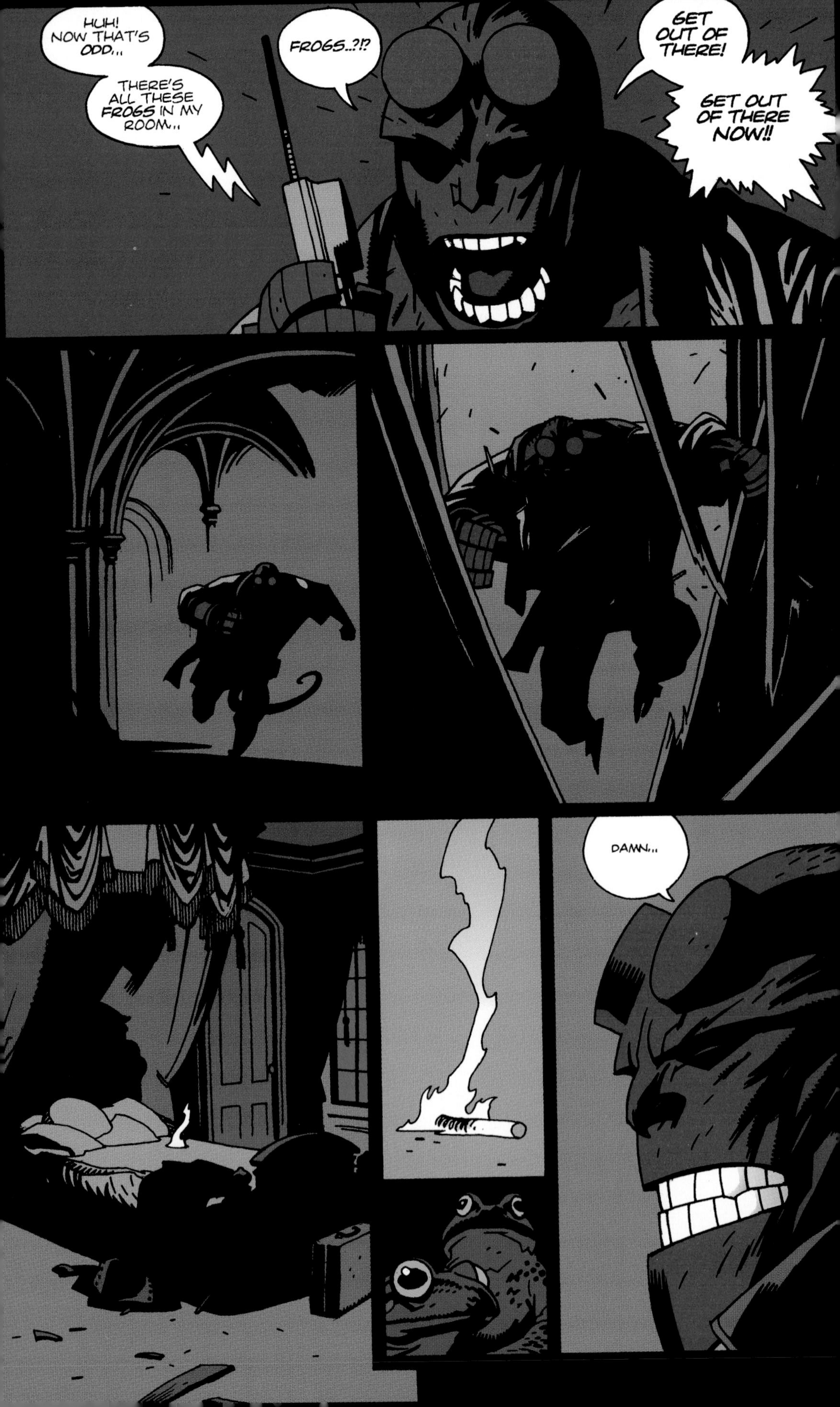
HUH! NOW THAT'S ODD...
THERE'S ALL THESE FROGS IN MY ROOM...
FROGS..?!?
GET OUT OF THERE!
GET OUT OF THERE NOW!!
DAMN...

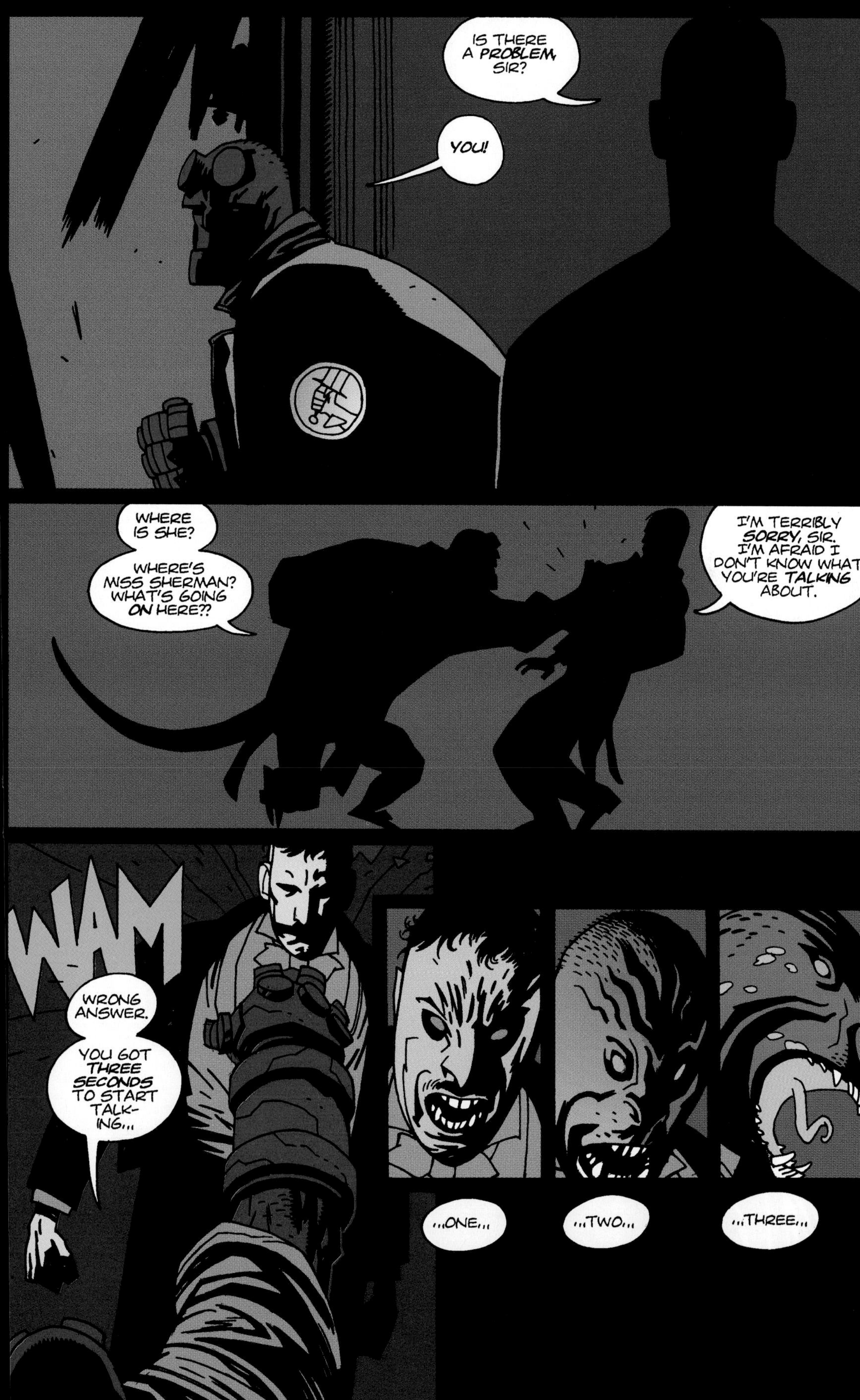

IS THERE A PROBLEM, SIR?
YOU!
WHERE IS SHE?
WHERE'S MISS SHERMAN? WHAT'S GOING ON HERE??
I'M TERRIBLY SORRY, SIR. I'M AFRAID I DON'T KNOW WHAT YOU'RE TALKING ABOUT.
WAM
WRONG ANSWER.
YOU GOT THREE SECONDS TO START TALK-ING...
...ONE...
...TWO...
...THREE...

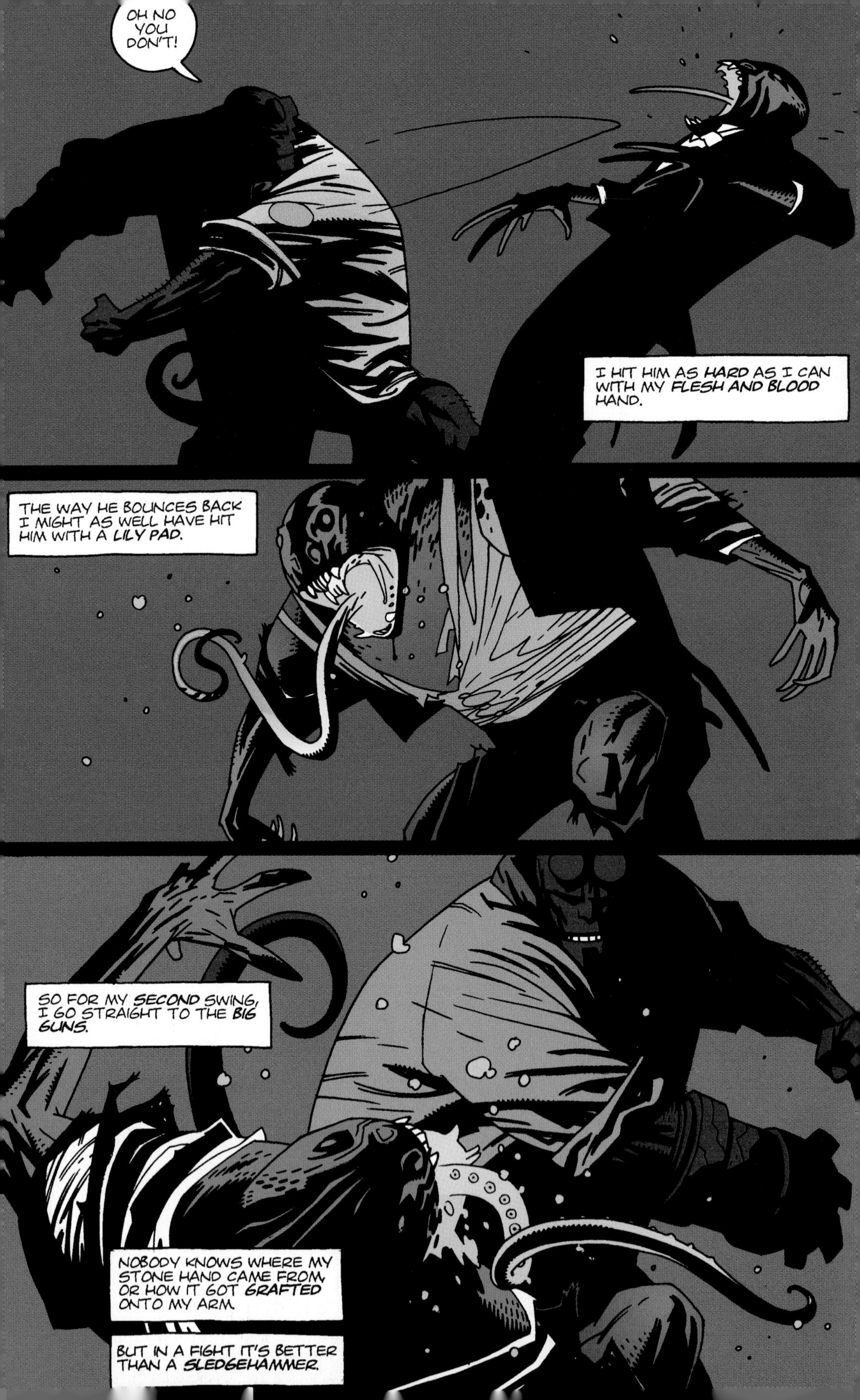
OH NO YOU DON'T!
I HIT HIM AS HARD AS I CAN WITH MY FLESH AND BLOOD HAND.
THE WAY HE BOUNCES BACK I MIGHT AS WELL HAVE HIT HIM WITH A LILY PAD.
SO FOR MY SECOND SWING, I GO STRAIGHT TO THE BIG GUNS.
NOBODY KNOWS WHERE MY STONE HAND CAME FROM, OR HOW IT GOT GRAFTED ONTO MY ARM.
BUT IN A FIGHT IT'S BETTER THAN A SLEDGEHAMMER.

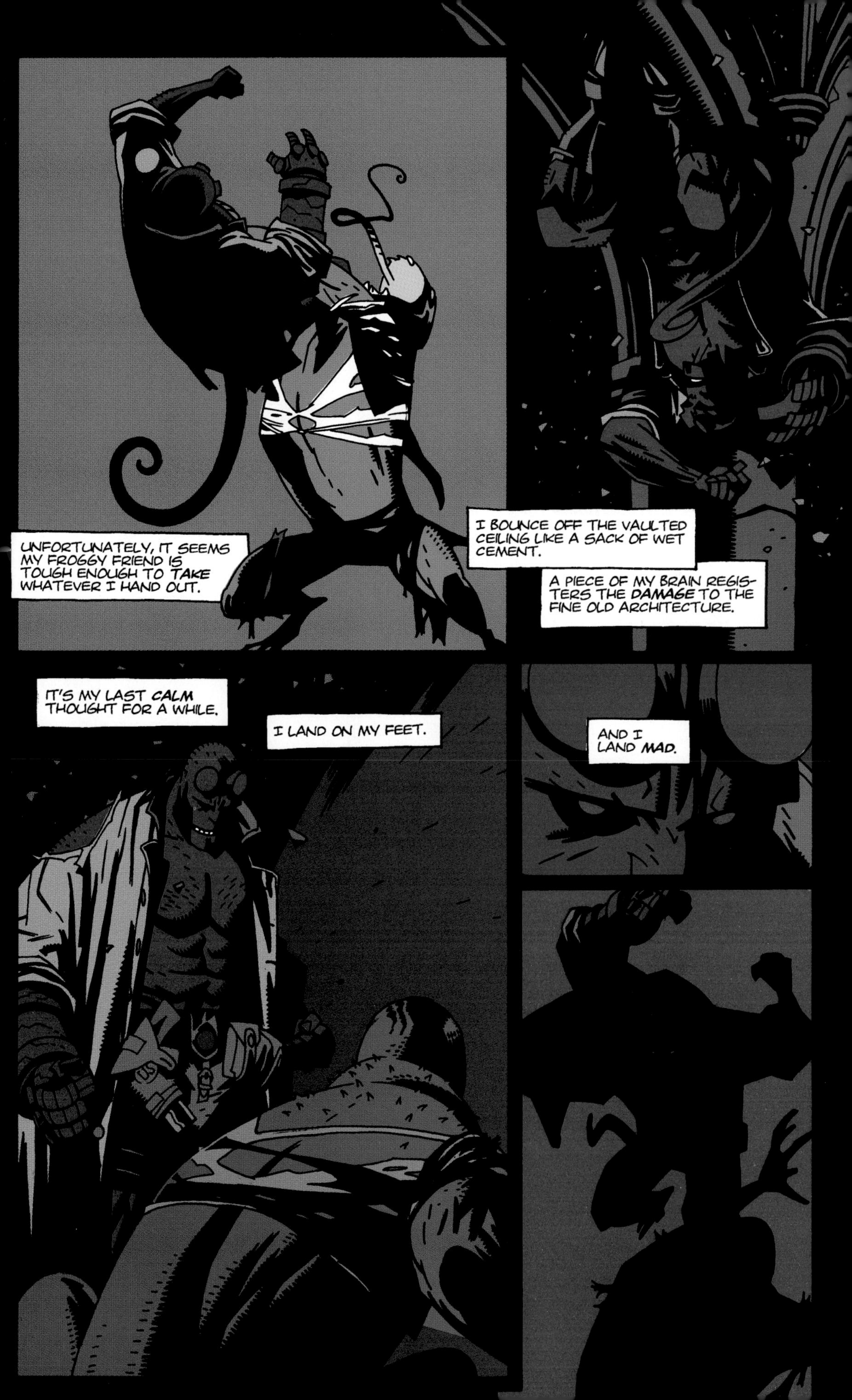
UNFORTUNATELY, IT SEEMS MY FROGGY FRIEND IS TOUGH ENOUGH TO TAKE WHATEVER I HAND OUT.
I BOUNCE OFF THE VAULTED CEILING LIKE A SACK OF WET CEMENT.
A PIECE OF MY BRAIN REGISTERS THE DAMAGE TO THE FINE OLD ARCHITECTURE.
IT'S MY LAST CALM THOUGHT FOR A WHILE.
I LAND ON MY FEET.
AND I LAND MAD.

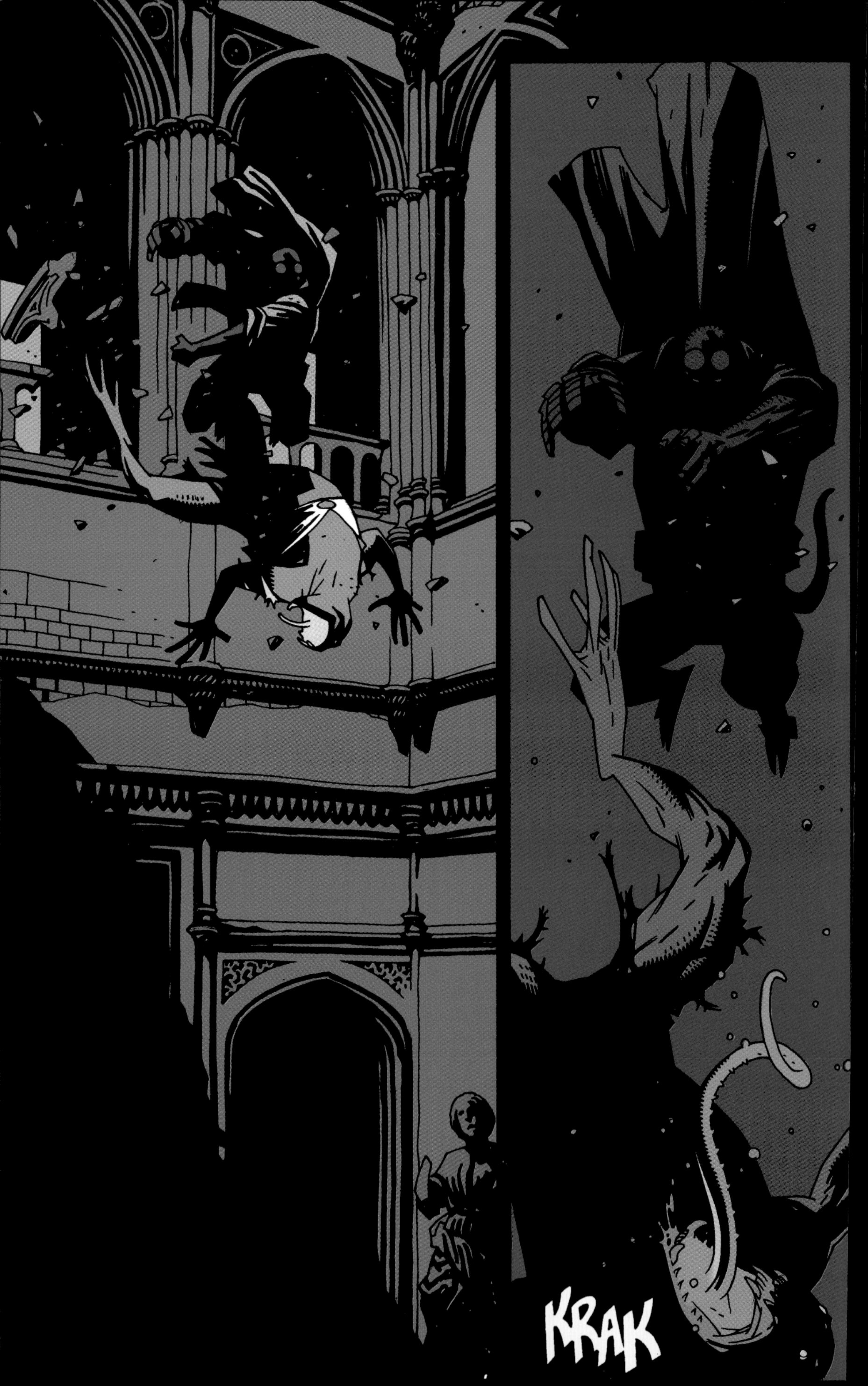
KRAK

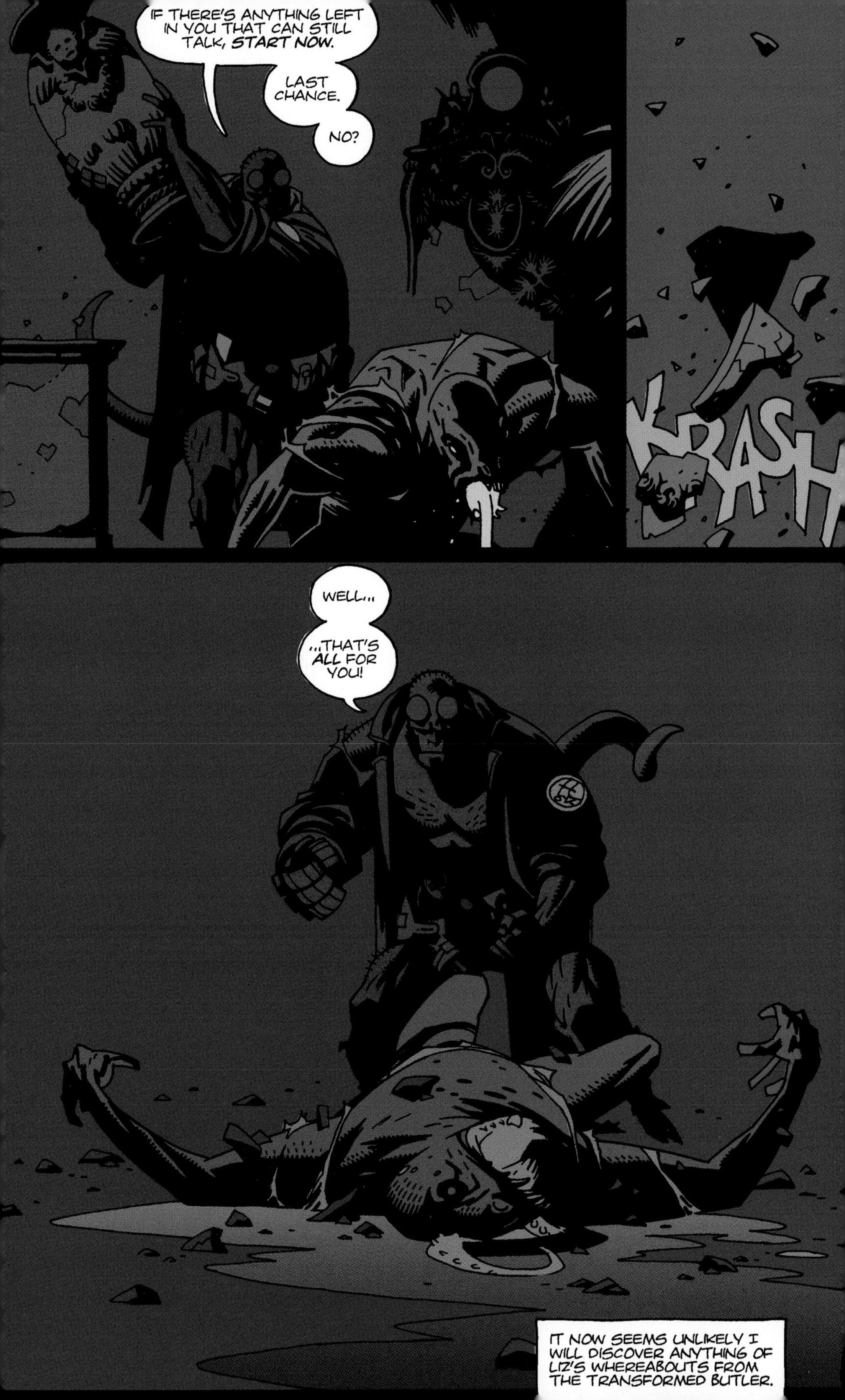
IF THERE'S ANYTHING LEFT IN YOU THAT CAN STILL TALK, **START NOW.**
LAST CHANCE.
NO?
KRASH
WELL...
...THAT'S **ALL** FOR YOU!
IT NOW SEEMS UNLIKELY I WILL DISCOVER ANYTHING OF LIZ'S WHEREABOUTS FROM THE TRANSFORMED BUTLER.

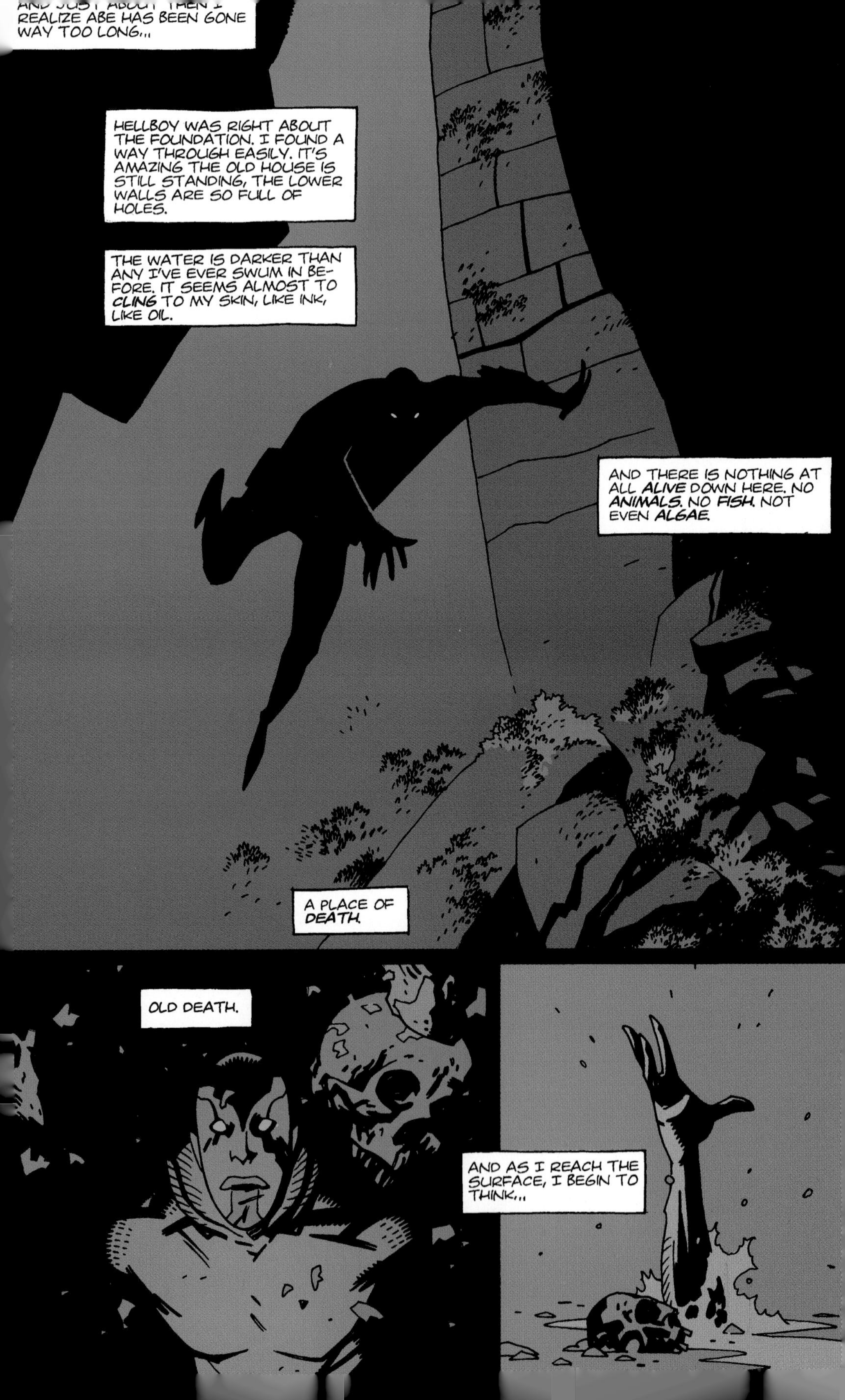
REALIZE ABE HAS BEEN GONE WAY TOO LONG...
HELLBOY WAS RIGHT ABOUT THE FOUNDATION. I FOUND A WAY THROUGH EASILY. IT'S AMAZING THE OLD HOUSE IS STILL STANDING, THE LOWER WALLS ARE SO FULL OF HOLES.
THE WATER IS DARKER THAN ANY I'VE EVER SWUM IN BE-FORE. IT SEEMS ALMOST TO CLING TO MY SKIN, LIKE INK, LIKE OIL.
AND THERE IS NOTHING AT ALL ALIVE DOWN HERE. NO ANIMALS. NO FISH. NOT EVEN ALGAE.
A PLACE OF DEATH.
OLD DEATH.
AND AS I REACH THE SURFACE, I BEGIN TO THINK...

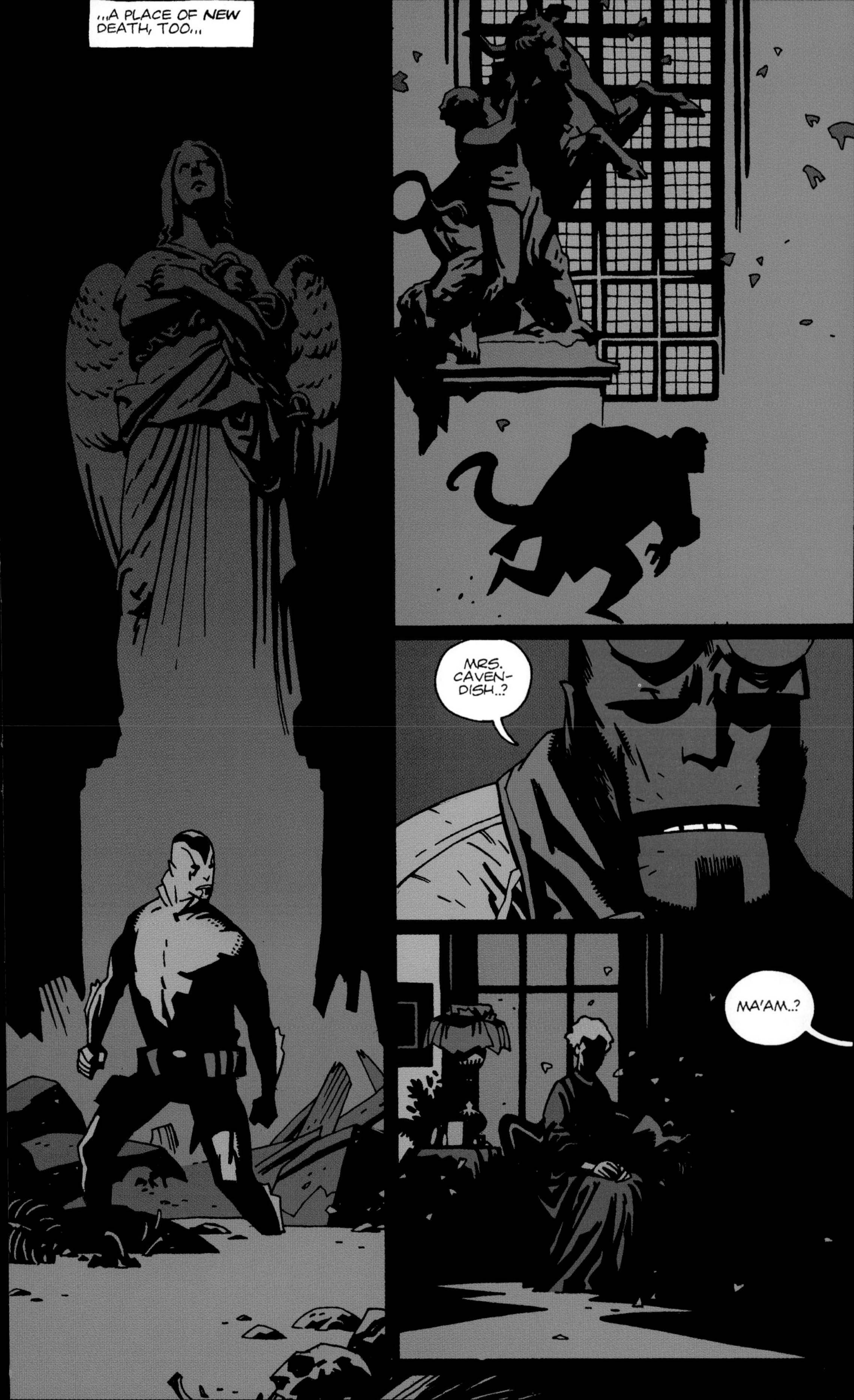
...A PLACE OF NEW DEATH, TOO...
MRS. CAVEN-DISH..?
MA'AM..?

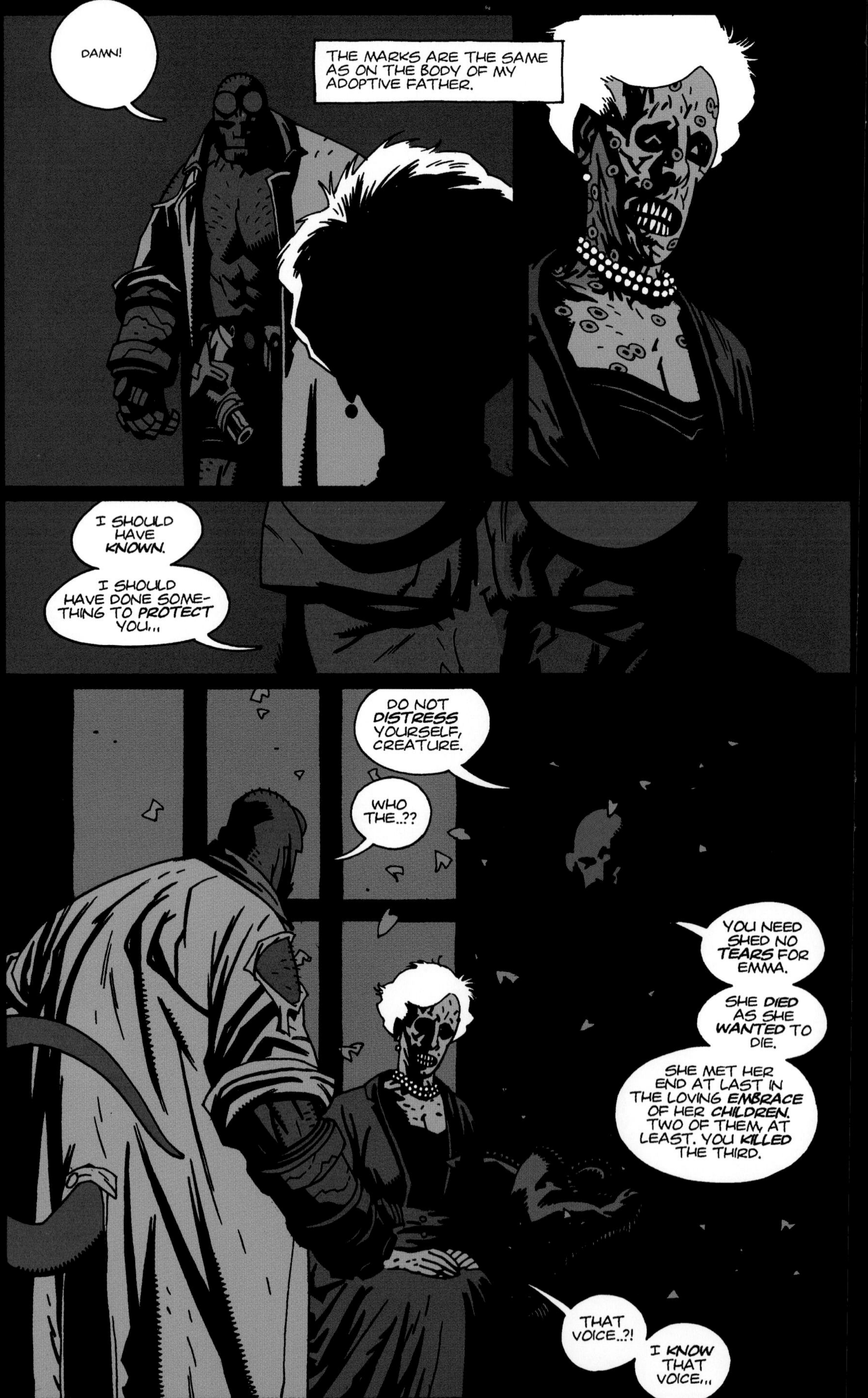
DAMN!
THE MARKS ARE THE SAME AS ON THE BODY OF MY ADOPTIVE FATHER.
I SHOULD HAVE KNOWN.
I SHOULD HAVE DONE SOME-THING TO PROTECT YOU...
DO NOT DISTRESS YOURSELF, CREATURE.
WHO THE..??
YOU NEED SHED NO TEARS FOR EMMA.
SHE DIED AS SHE WANTED TO DIE.
SHE MET HER END AT LAST IN THE LOVING EMBRACE OF HER CHILDREN. TWO OF THEM, AT LEAST. YOU KILLED THE THIRD.
THAT VOICE..?!
I KNOW THAT VOICE...

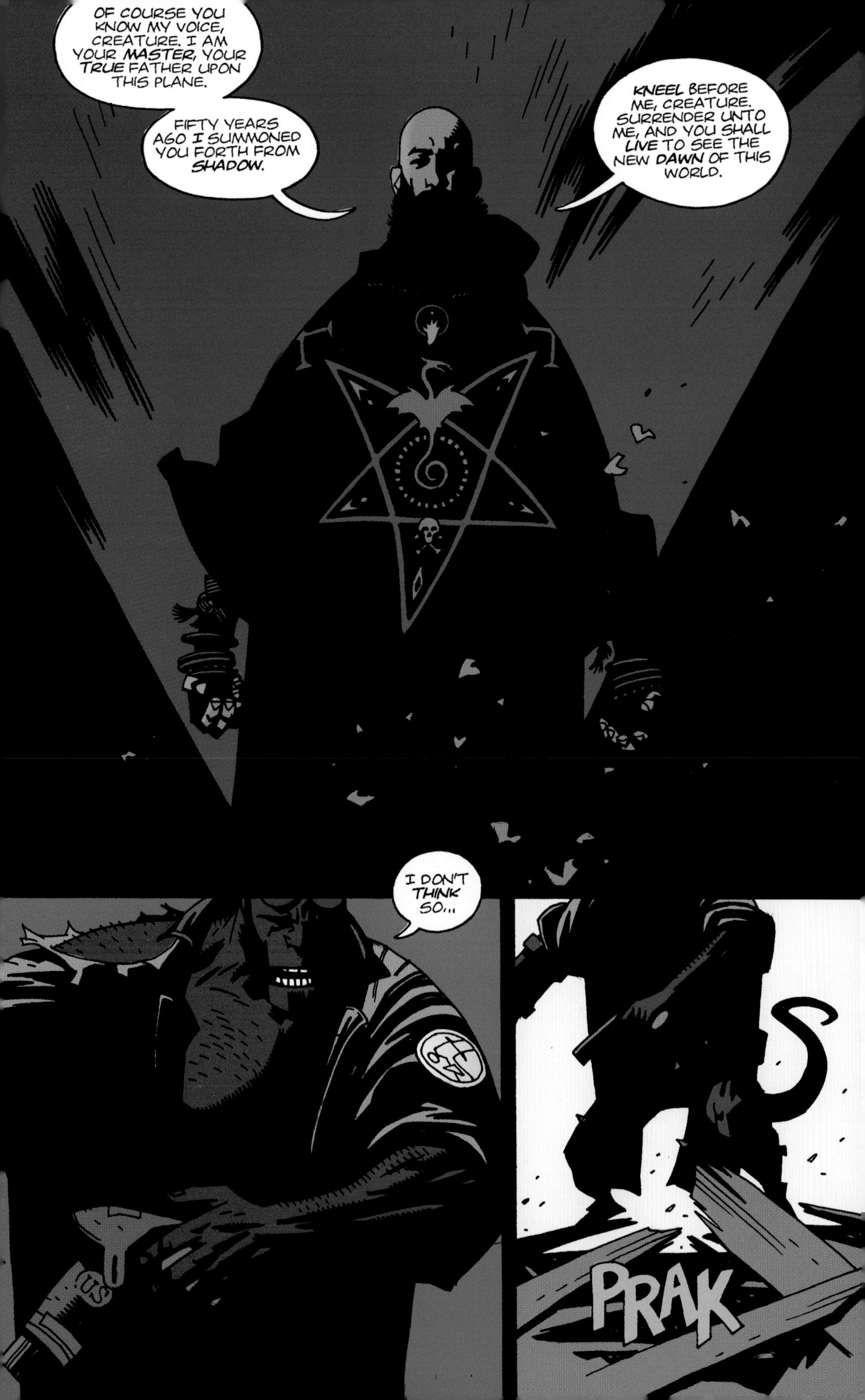
OF COURSE YOU KNOW MY VOICE, CREATURE. I AM YOUR MASTER, YOUR TRUE FATHER UPON THIS PLANE.
FIFTY YEARS AGO I SUMMONED YOU FORTH FROM SHADOW.
KNEEL BEFORE ME, CREATURE. SURRENDER UNTO ME, AND YOU SHALL LIVE TO SEE THE NEW DAWN OF THIS WORLD.
I DON'T THINK SO...
PRAK

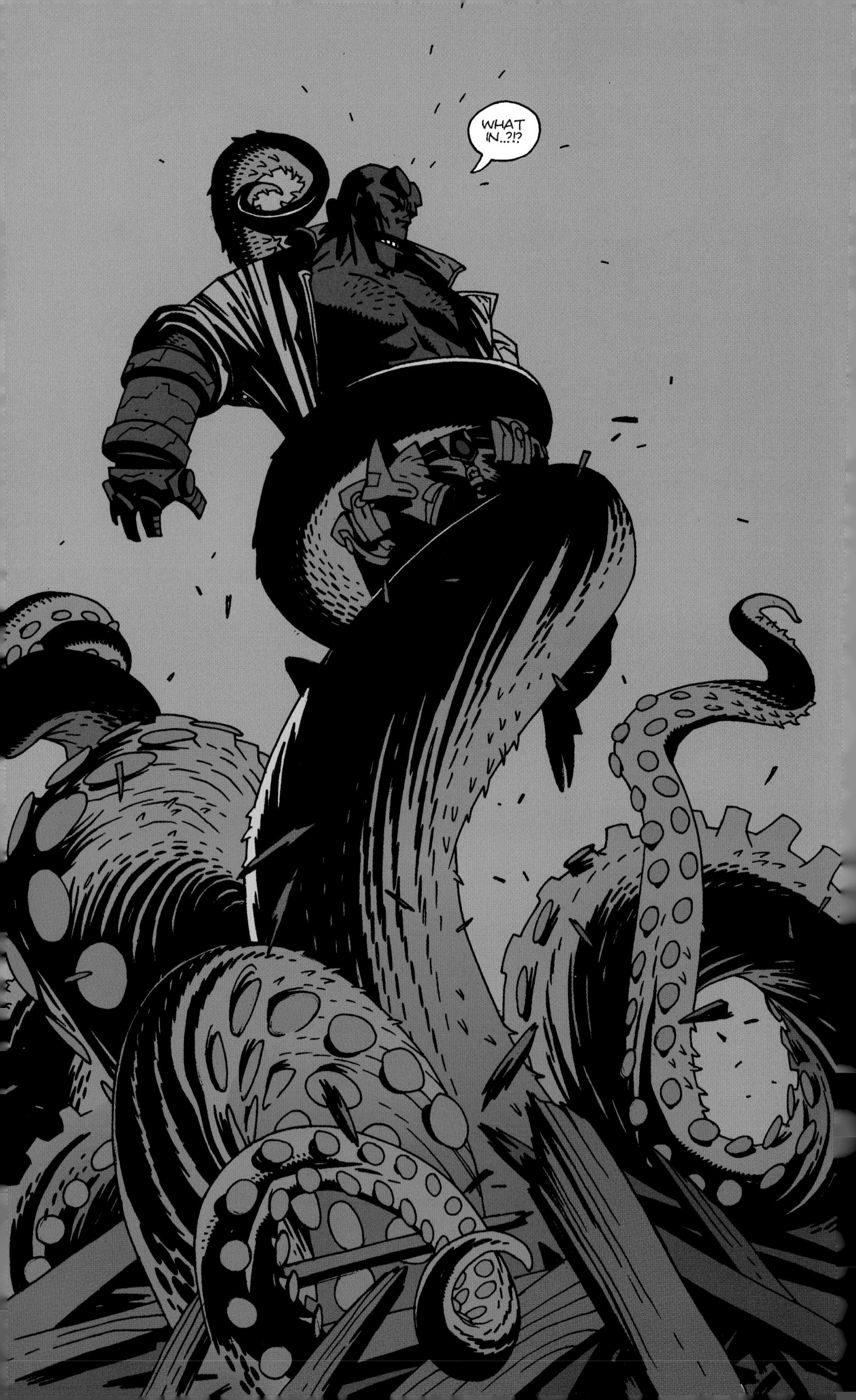
WHAT IN..?!?

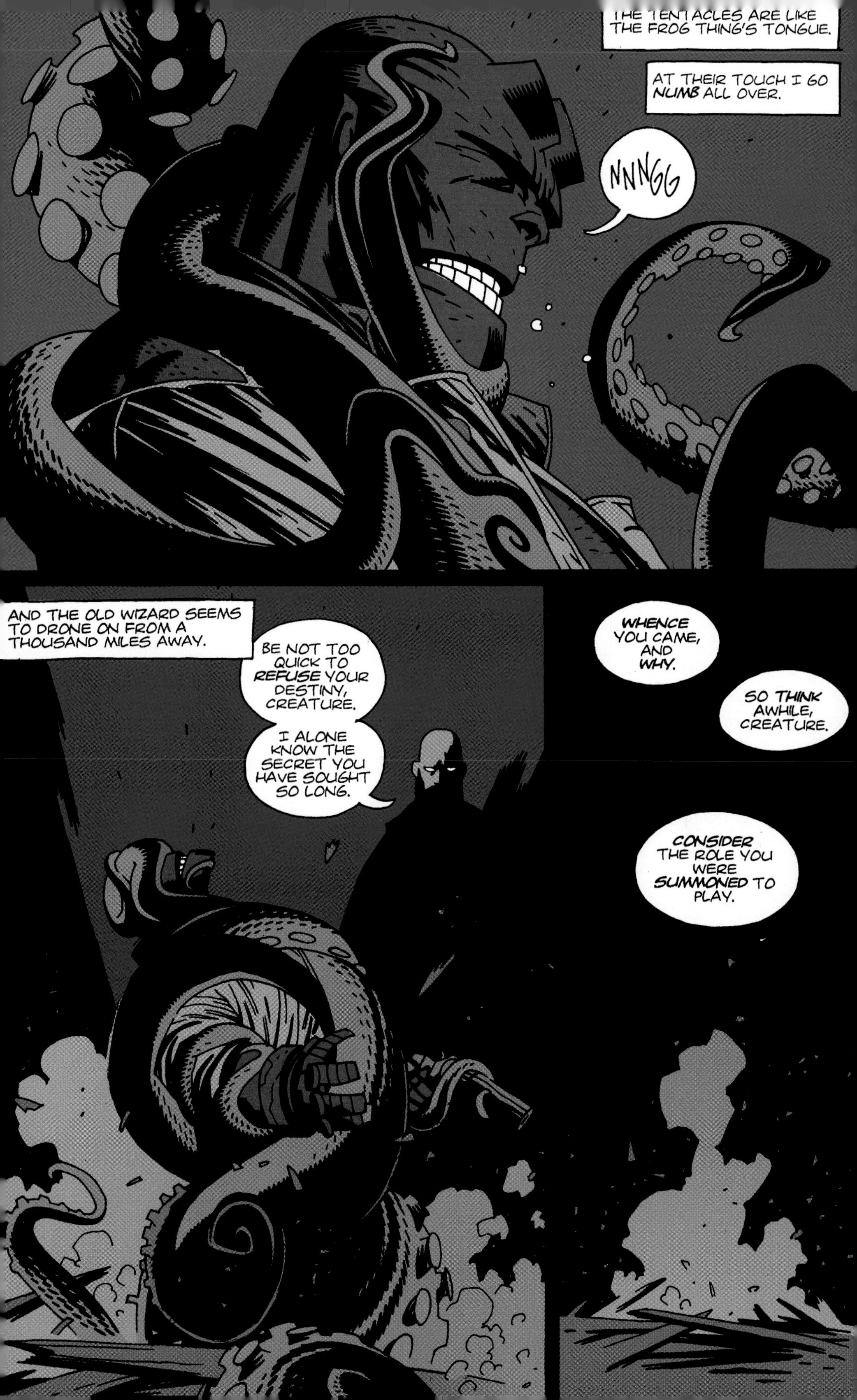
THE TENTACLES ARE LIKE THE FROG THING'S TONGUE.
AT THEIR TOUCH I GO NUMB ALL OVER.
NNNGG
AND THE OLD WIZARD SEEMS TO DRONE ON FROM A THOUSAND MILES AWAY.
BE NOT TOO QUICK TO REFUSE YOUR DESTINY, CREATURE.
I ALONE KNOW THE SECRET YOU HAVE SOUGHT SO LONG.
WHENCE YOU CAME, AND WHY.
SO THINK AWHILE, CREATURE.
CONSIDER THE ROLE YOU WERE SUMMONED TO PLAY.

STAND BESIDE ME. LET ME HARNESS THE POWER YOU HOLD UNKNOWING IN YOUR RIGHT HAND...
...OR DIE.

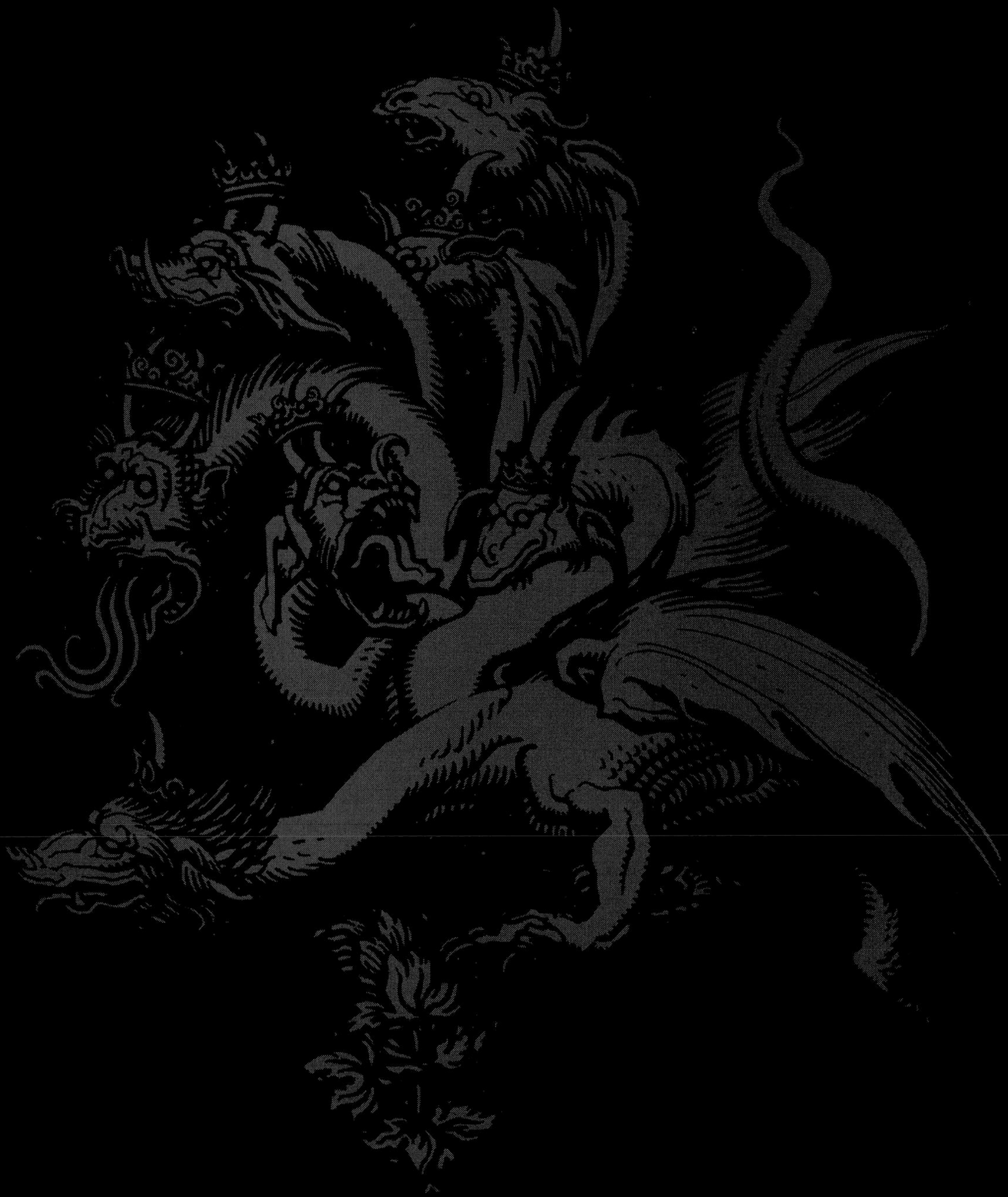

CHAPTER THREE

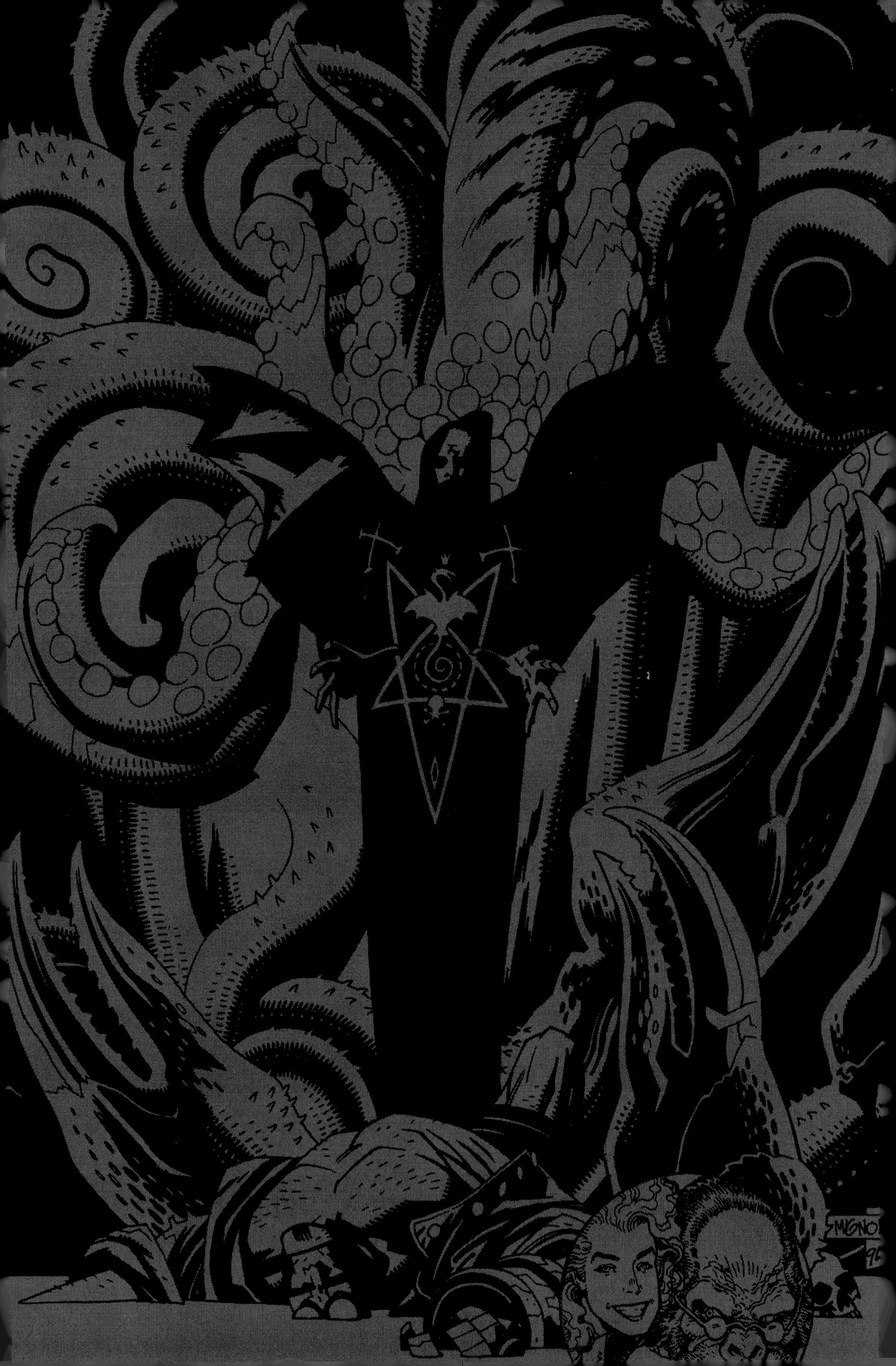

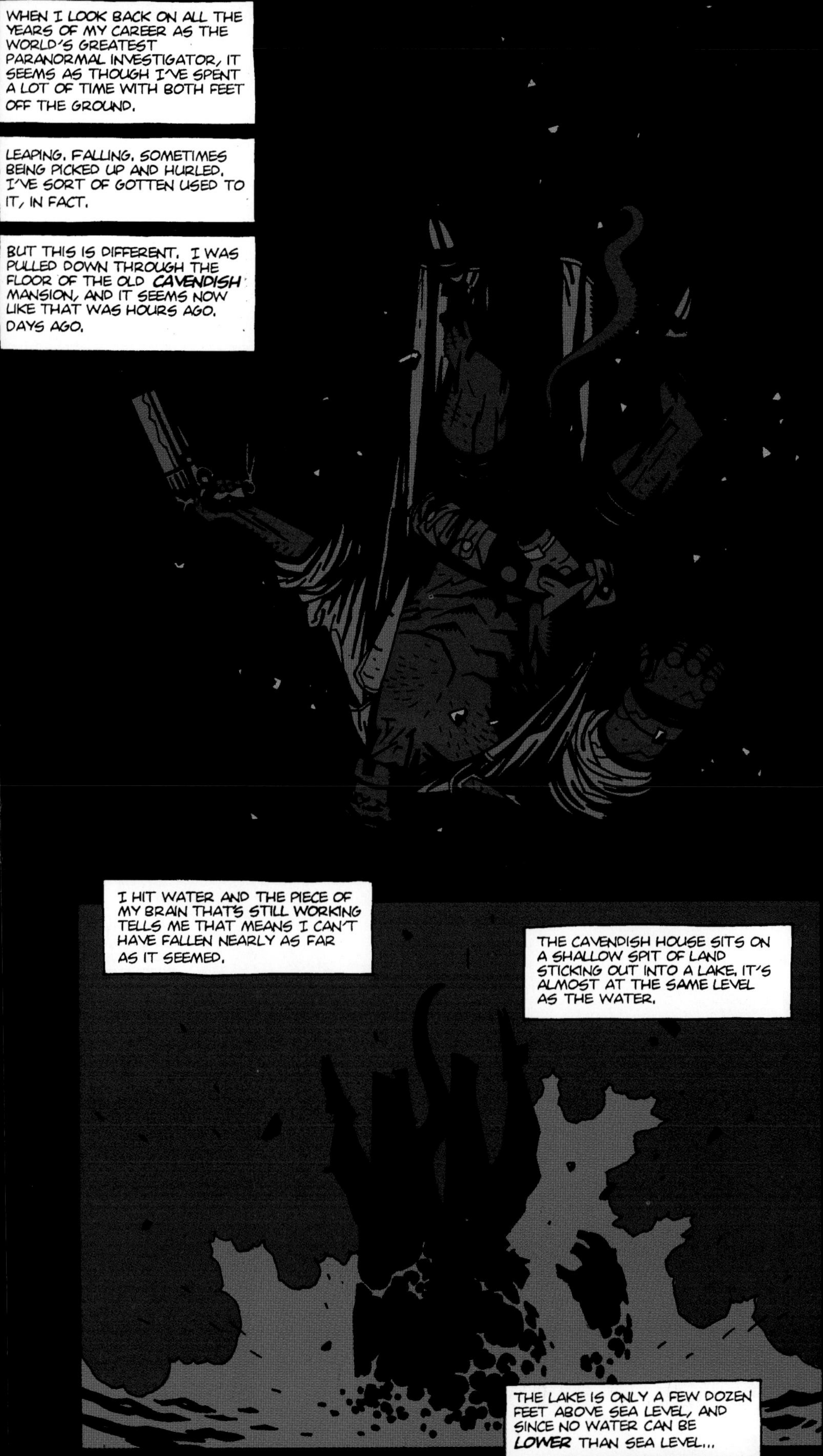
WHEN I LOOK BACK ON ALL THE YEARS OF MY CAREER AS THE WORLD'S GREATEST PARANORMAL INVESTIGATOR, IT SEEMS AS THOUGH I'VE SPENT A LOT OF TIME WITH BOTH FEET OFF THE GROUND.
LEAPING. FALLING. SOMETIMES BEING PICKED UP AND HURLED. I'VE SORT OF GOTTEN USED TO IT, IN FACT.
BUT THIS IS DIFFERENT. I WAS PULLED DOWN THROUGH THE FLOOR OF THE OLD CAVENDISH MANSION, AND IT SEEMS NOW LIKE THAT WAS HOURS AGO. DAYS AGO.
I HIT WATER AND THE PIECE OF MY BRAIN THAT'S STILL WORKING TELLS ME THAT MEANS I CAN'T HAVE FALLEN NEARLY AS FAR AS IT SEEMED.
THE CAVENDISH HOUSE SITS ON A SHALLOW SPIT OF LAND STICKING OUT INTO A LAKE. IT'S ALMOST AT THE SAME LEVEL AS THE WATER.
THE LAKE IS ONLY A FEW DOZEN FEET ABOVE SEA LEVEL, AND SINCE NO WATER CAN BE LOWER THAN SEA LEVEL...

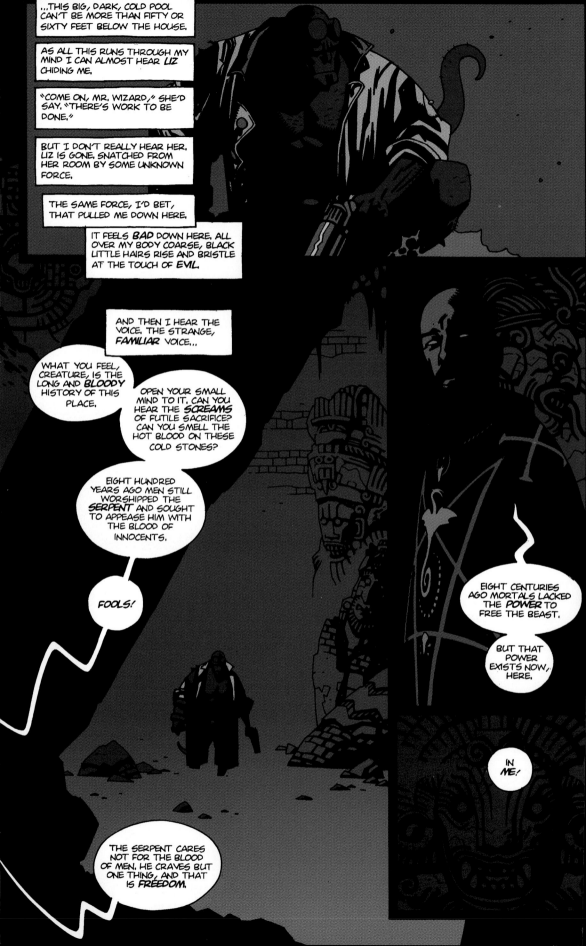

...THIS BIG, DARK, COLD POOL CAN'T BE MORE THAN FIFTY OR SIXTY FEET BELOW THE HOUSE.

AS ALL THIS RUNS THROUGH MY MIND I CAN ALMOST HEAR *LIZ* CHIDING ME.

"COME ON, MR. WIZARD," SHE'D SAY. "THERE'S WORK TO BE DONE."

BUT I DON'T REALLY HEAR HER. LIZ IS GONE, SNATCHED FROM HER ROOM BY SOME UNKNOWN FORCE.

THE SAME FORCE, I'D BET, THAT PULLED ME DOWN HERE.

IT FEELS *BAD* DOWN HERE. ALL OVER MY BODY COARSE, BLACK LITTLE HAIRS RISE AND BRISTLE AT THE TOUCH OF *EVIL*.

AND THEN I HEAR THE VOICE. THE STRANGE, *FAMILIAR* VOICE...

WHAT YOU FEEL, CREATURE, IS THE LONG AND *BLOODY* HISTORY OF THIS PLACE.

OPEN YOUR SMALL MIND TO IT. CAN YOU HEAR THE *SCREAMS* OF FUTILE SACRIFICE? CAN YOU SMELL THE HOT BLOOD ON THESE COLD STONES?

EIGHT HUNDRED YEARS AGO MEN STILL WORSHIPPED THE *SERPENT* AND SOUGHT TO APPEASE HIM WITH THE BLOOD OF INNOCENTS.

FOOLS!

EIGHT CENTURIES AGO MORTALS LACKED THE *POWER* TO FREE THE BEAST.

BUT THAT POWER EXISTS NOW, HERE.

IN *ME!*

THE SERPENT CARES NOT FOR THE BLOOD OF MEN. HE CRAVES BUT ONE THING, AND THAT IS *FREEDOM*.

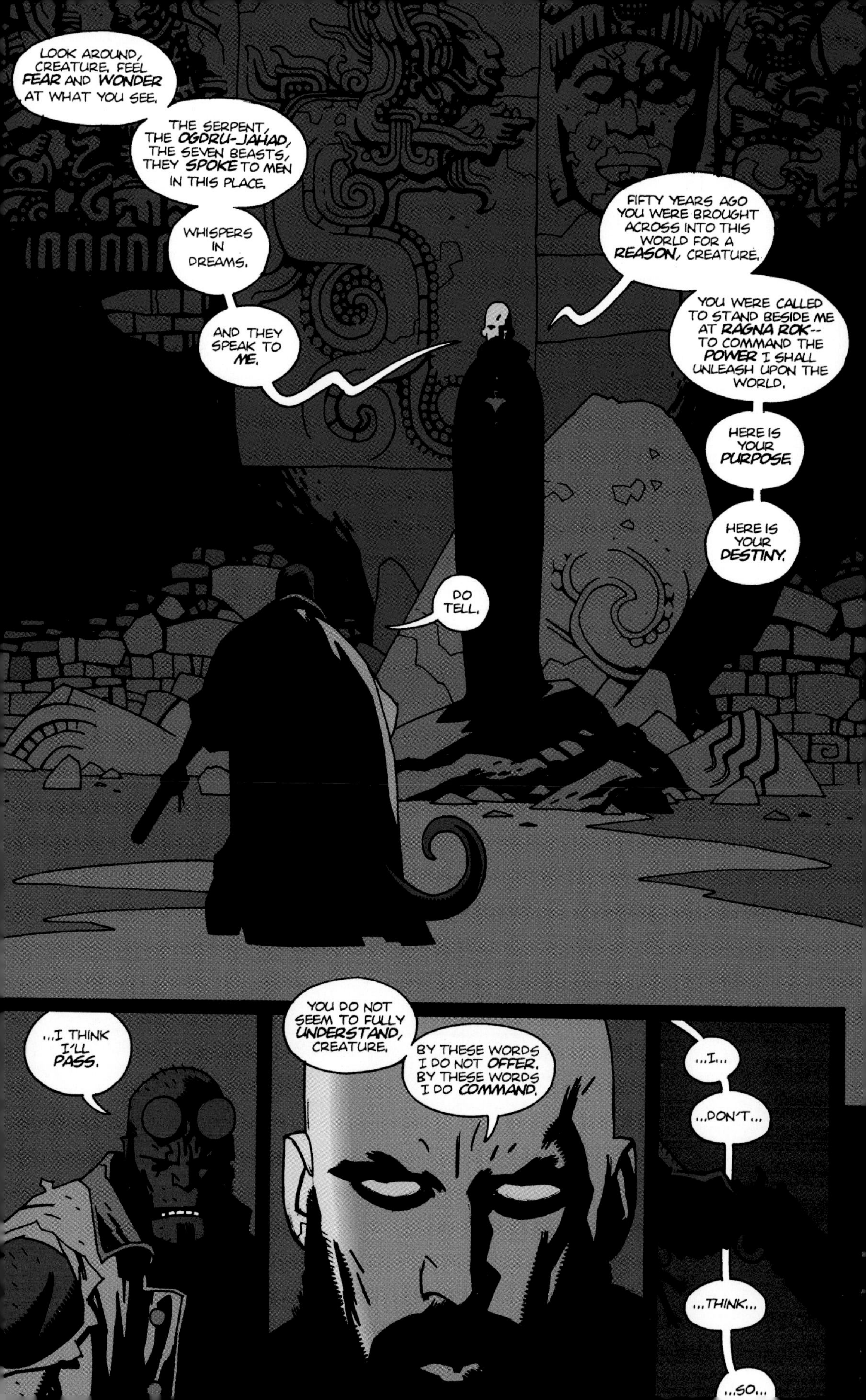
LOOK AROUND, CREATURE. FEEL FEAR AND WONDER AT WHAT YOU SEE.
THE SERPENT, THE OGDRU-JAHAD, THE SEVEN BEASTS, THEY SPOKE TO MEN IN THIS PLACE.
WHISPERS IN DREAMS.
AND THEY SPEAK TO ME.
FIFTY YEARS AGO YOU WERE BROUGHT ACROSS INTO THIS WORLD FOR A REASON, CREATURE.
YOU WERE CALLED TO STAND BESIDE ME AT RAGNA ROK-- TO COMMAND THE POWER I SHALL UNLEASH UPON THE WORLD.
HERE IS YOUR PURPOSE.
HERE IS YOUR DESTINY.
DO TELL.
...I THINK I'LL PASS.
YOU DO NOT SEEM TO FULLY UNDERSTAND, CREATURE.
BY THESE WORDS I DO NOT OFFER. BY THESE WORDS I DO COMMAND.
...I...
...DON'T...
...THINK...
...SO...

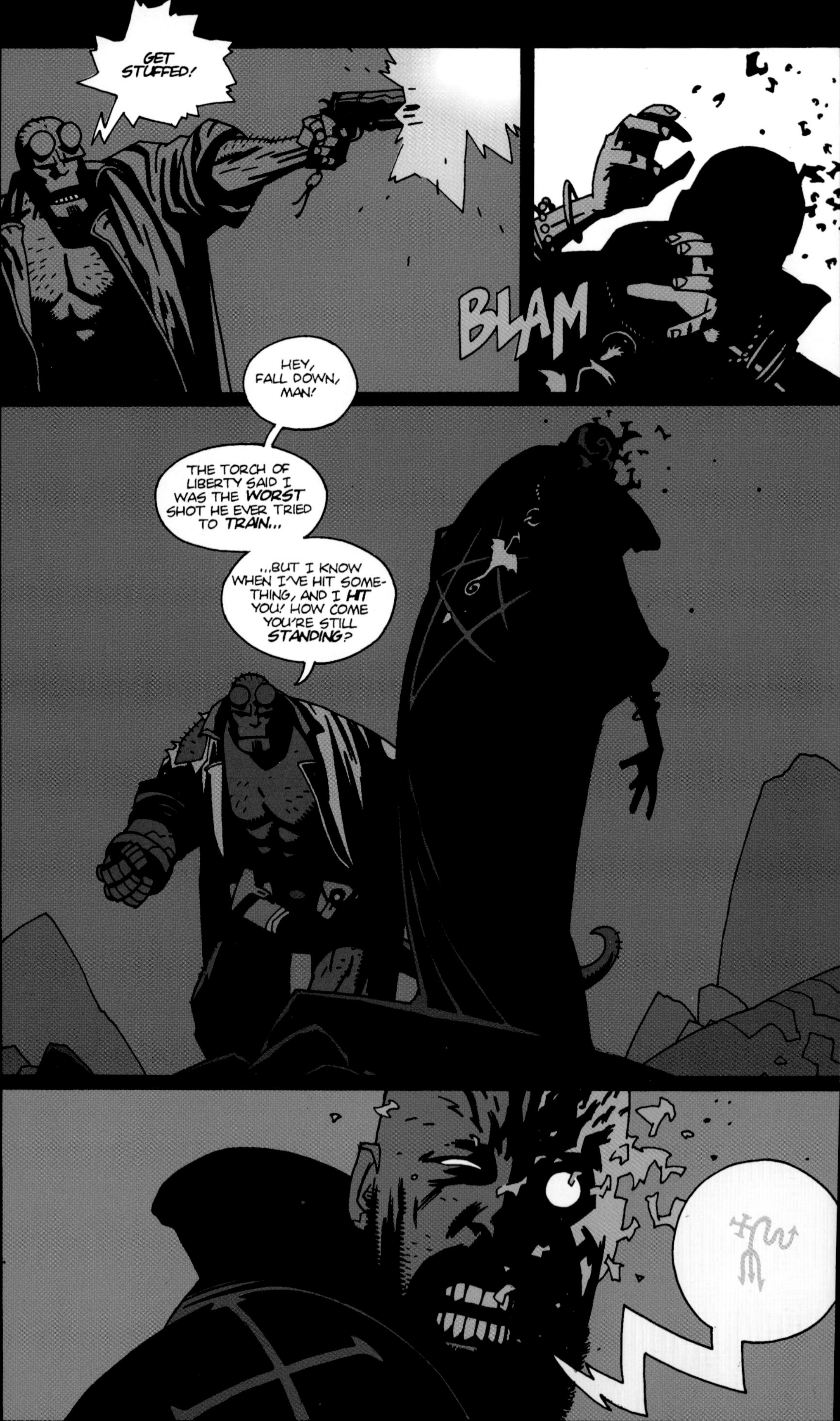
GET STUFFED!
BLAM
HEY, FALL DOWN, MAN!
THE TORCH OF LIBERTY SAID I WAS THE WORST SHOT HE EVER TRIED TO TRAIN...
...BUT I KNOW WHEN I'VE HIT SOME-THING, AND I HIT YOU! HOW COME YOU'RE STILL STANDING?

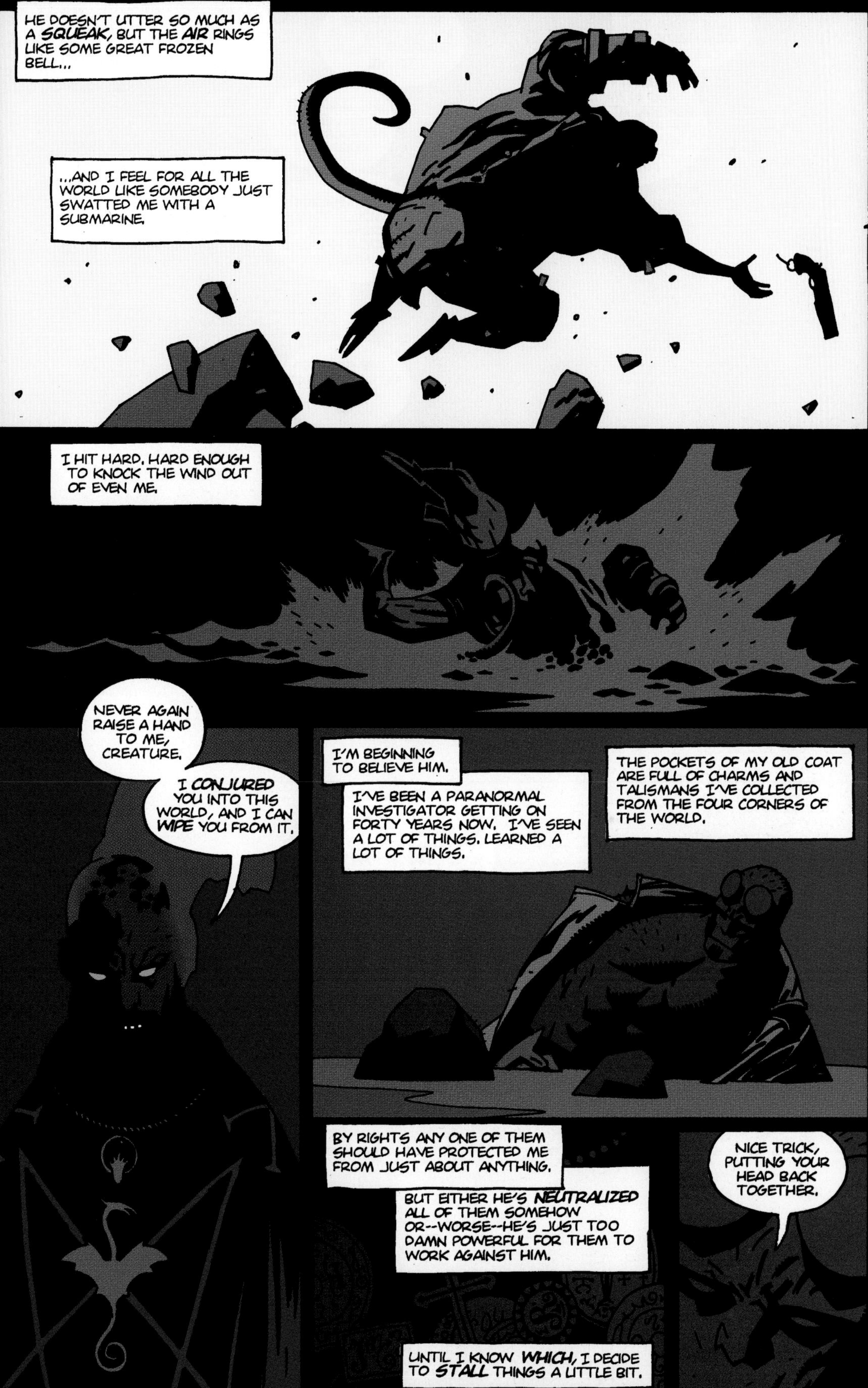
HE DOESN'T UTTER SO MUCH AS A SQUEAK, BUT THE AIR RINGS LIKE SOME GREAT FROZEN BELL...
...AND I FEEL FOR ALL THE WORLD LIKE SOMEBODY JUST SWATTED ME WITH A SUBMARINE.
I HIT HARD. HARD ENOUGH TO KNOCK THE WIND OUT OF EVEN ME.
NEVER AGAIN RAISE A HAND TO ME, CREATURE.
I CONJURED YOU INTO THIS WORLD, AND I CAN WIPE YOU FROM IT.
I'M BEGINNING TO BELIEVE HIM.
I'VE BEEN A PARANORMAL INVESTIGATOR GETTING ON FORTY YEARS NOW. I'VE SEEN A LOT OF THINGS. LEARNED A LOT OF THINGS.
THE POCKETS OF MY OLD COAT ARE FULL OF CHARMS AND TALISMANS I'VE COLLECTED FROM THE FOUR CORNERS OF THE WORLD.
BY RIGHTS ANY ONE OF THEM SHOULD HAVE PROTECTED ME FROM JUST ABOUT ANYTHING.
BUT EITHER HE'S NEUTRALIZED ALL OF THEM SOMEHOW OR--WORSE--HE'S JUST TOO DAMN POWERFUL FOR THEM TO WORK AGAINST HIM.
UNTIL I KNOW WHICH, I DECIDE TO STALL THINGS A LITTLE BIT.
NICE TRICK, PUTTING YOUR HEAD BACK TOGETHER.

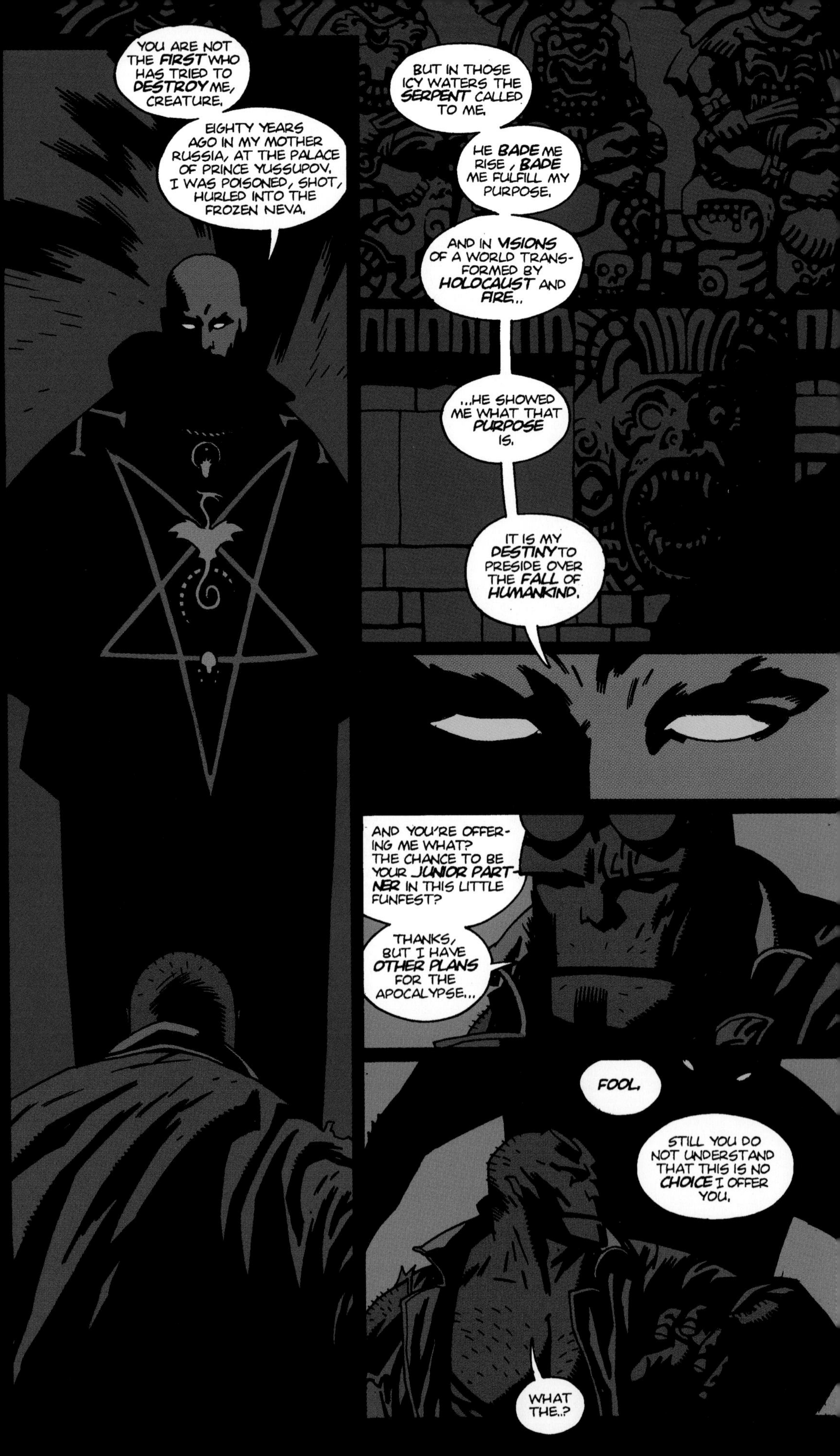
YOU ARE NOT THE FIRST WHO HAS TRIED TO DESTROY ME, CREATURE.
EIGHTY YEARS AGO IN MY MOTHER RUSSIA, AT THE PALACE OF PRINCE YUSSUPOV, I WAS POISONED, SHOT, HURLED INTO THE FROZEN NEVA.
BUT IN THOSE ICY WATERS THE SERPENT CALLED TO ME.
HE BADE ME RISE, BADE ME FULFILL MY PURPOSE.
AND IN VISIONS OF A WORLD TRANS-FORMED BY HOLOCAUST AND FIRE...
...HE SHOWED ME WHAT THAT PURPOSE IS.
IT IS MY DESTINY TO PRESIDE OVER THE FALL OF HUMANKIND.
AND YOU'RE OFFER-ING ME WHAT? THE CHANCE TO BE YOUR JUNIOR PART-NER IN THIS LITTLE FUNFEST?
THANKS, BUT I HAVE OTHER PLANS FOR THE APOCALYPSE...
FOOL.
STILL YOU DO NOT UNDERSTAND THAT THIS IS NO CHOICE I OFFER YOU.
WHAT THE..?

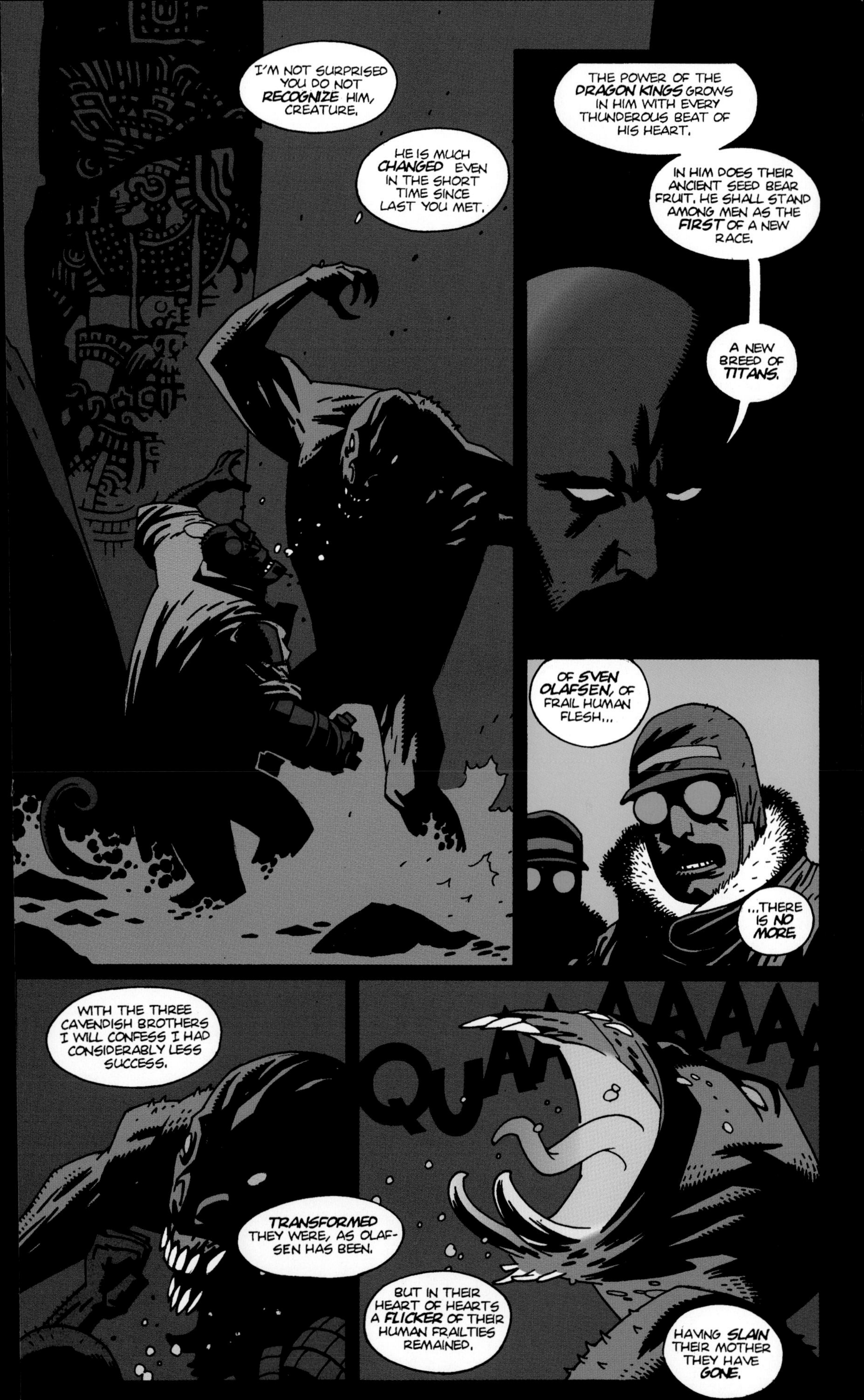
I'M NOT SURPRISED YOU DO NOT RECOGNIZE HIM, CREATURE.
HE IS MUCH CHANGED EVEN IN THE SHORT TIME SINCE LAST YOU MET.
THE POWER OF THE DRAGON KINGS GROWS IN HIM WITH EVERY THUNDEROUS BEAT OF HIS HEART.
IN HIM DOES THEIR ANCIENT SEED BEAR FRUIT. HE SHALL STAND AMONG MEN AS THE FIRST OF A NEW RACE.
A NEW BREED OF TITANS.
OF SVEN OLAFSEN, OF FRAIL HUMAN FLESH...
...THERE IS NO MORE.
WITH THE THREE CAVENDISH BROTHERS I WILL CONFESS I HAD CONSIDERABLY LESS SUCCESS.
QUAAAAAAA
TRANSFORMED THEY WERE, AS OLAFSEN HAS BEEN.
BUT IN THEIR HEART OF HEARTS A FLICKER OF THEIR HUMAN FRAILTIES REMAINED.
HAVING SLAIN THEIR MOTHER THEY HAVE GONE.

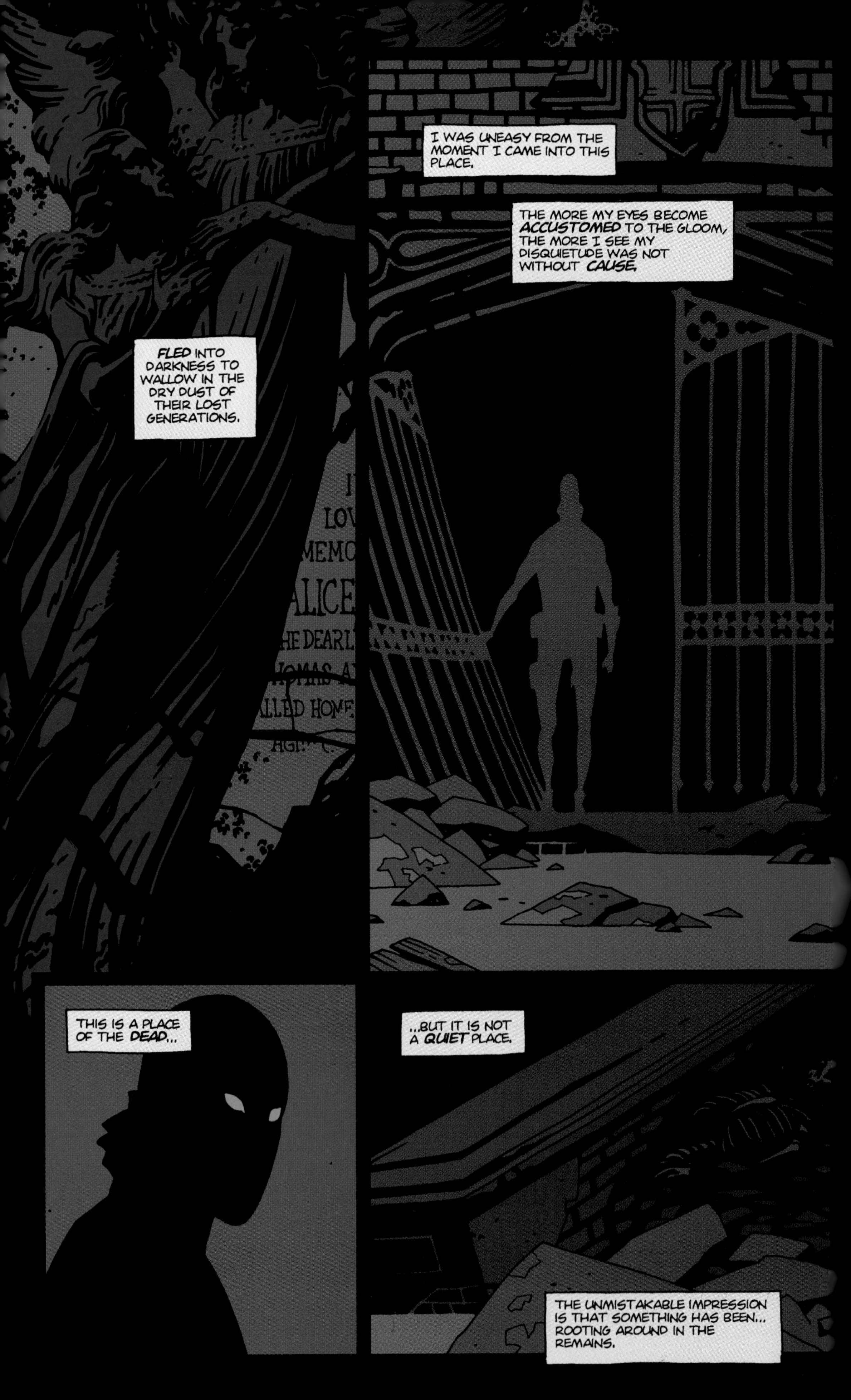
FLED INTO DARKNESS TO WALLOW IN THE DRY DUST OF THEIR LOST GENERATIONS.
I WAS UNEASY FROM THE MOMENT I CAME INTO THIS PLACE.
THE MORE MY EYES BECOME ACCUSTOMED TO THE GLOOM, THE MORE I SEE MY DISQUIETUDE WAS NOT WITHOUT CAUSE.
THIS IS A PLACE OF THE DEAD...
...BUT IT IS NOT A QUIET PLACE.
THE UNMISTAKABLE IMPRESSION IS THAT SOMETHING HAS BEEN... ROOTING AROUND IN THE REMAINS.

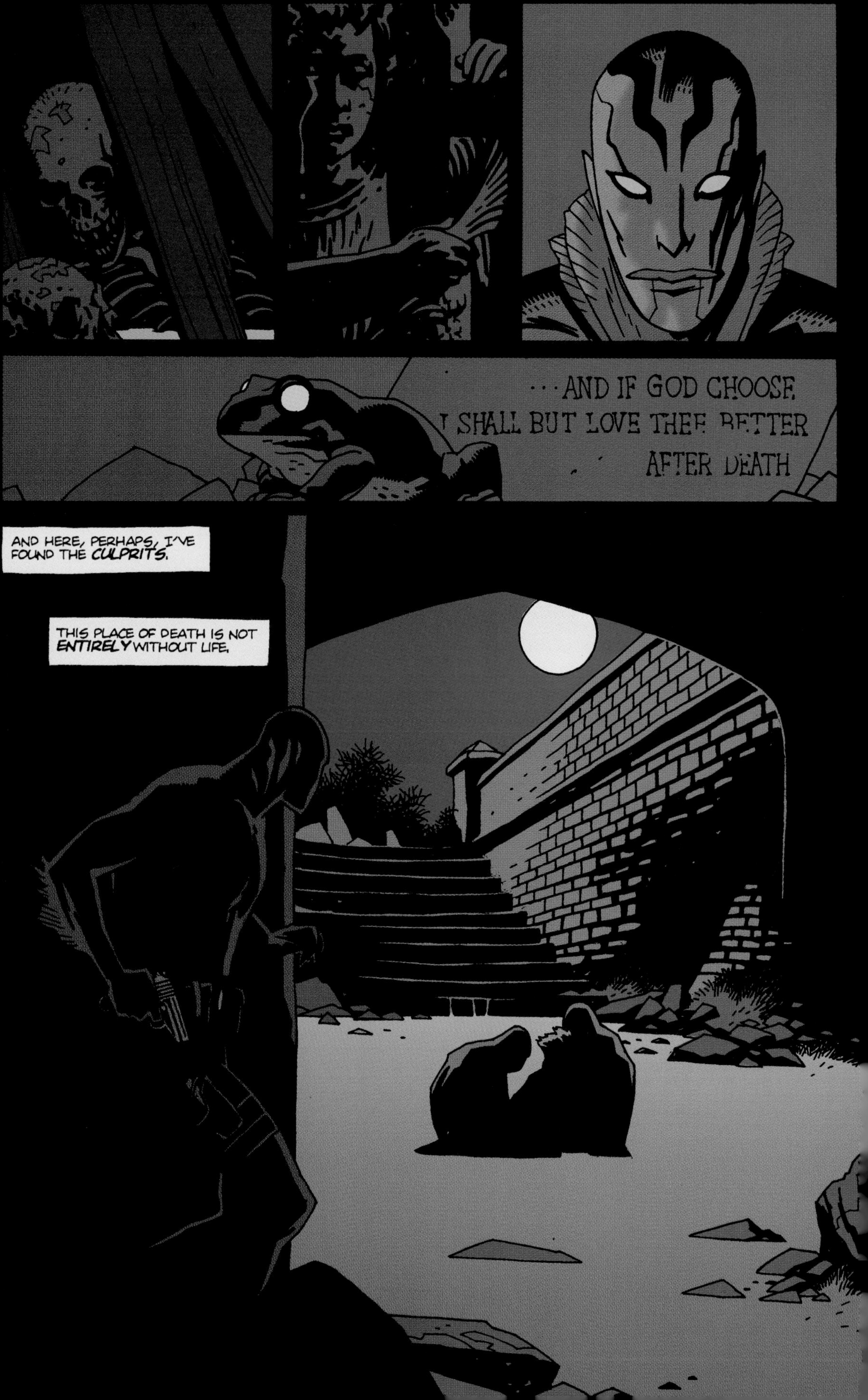
...AND IF GOD CHOOSE
I SHALL BUT LOVE THEE BETTER
AFTER DEATH
AND HERE, PERHAPS, I'VE FOUND THE CULPRITS.
THIS PLACE OF DEATH IS NOT ENTIRELY WITHOUT LIFE.

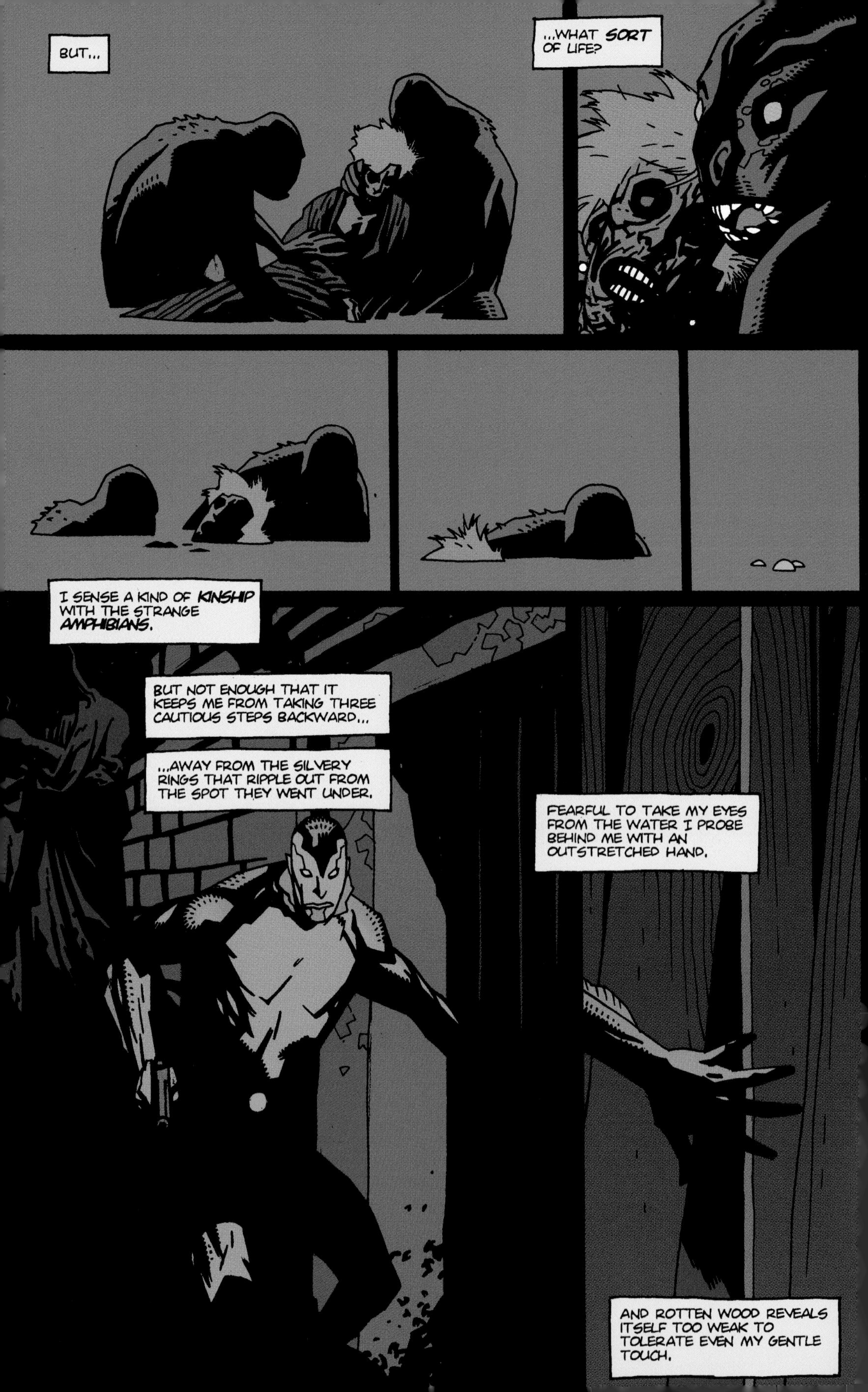
BUT...
...WHAT SORT OF LIFE?
I SENSE A KIND OF KINSHIP WITH THE STRANGE AMPHIBIANS.
BUT NOT ENOUGH THAT IT KEEPS ME FROM TAKING THREE CAUTIOUS STEPS BACKWARD...
...AWAY FROM THE SILVERY RINGS THAT RIPPLE OUT FROM THE SPOT THEY WENT UNDER.
FEARFUL TO TAKE MY EYES FROM THE WATER I PROBE BEHIND ME WITH AN OUTSTRETCHED HAND.
AND ROTTEN WOOD REVEALS ITSELF TOO WEAK TO TOLERATE EVEN MY GENTLE TOUCH.

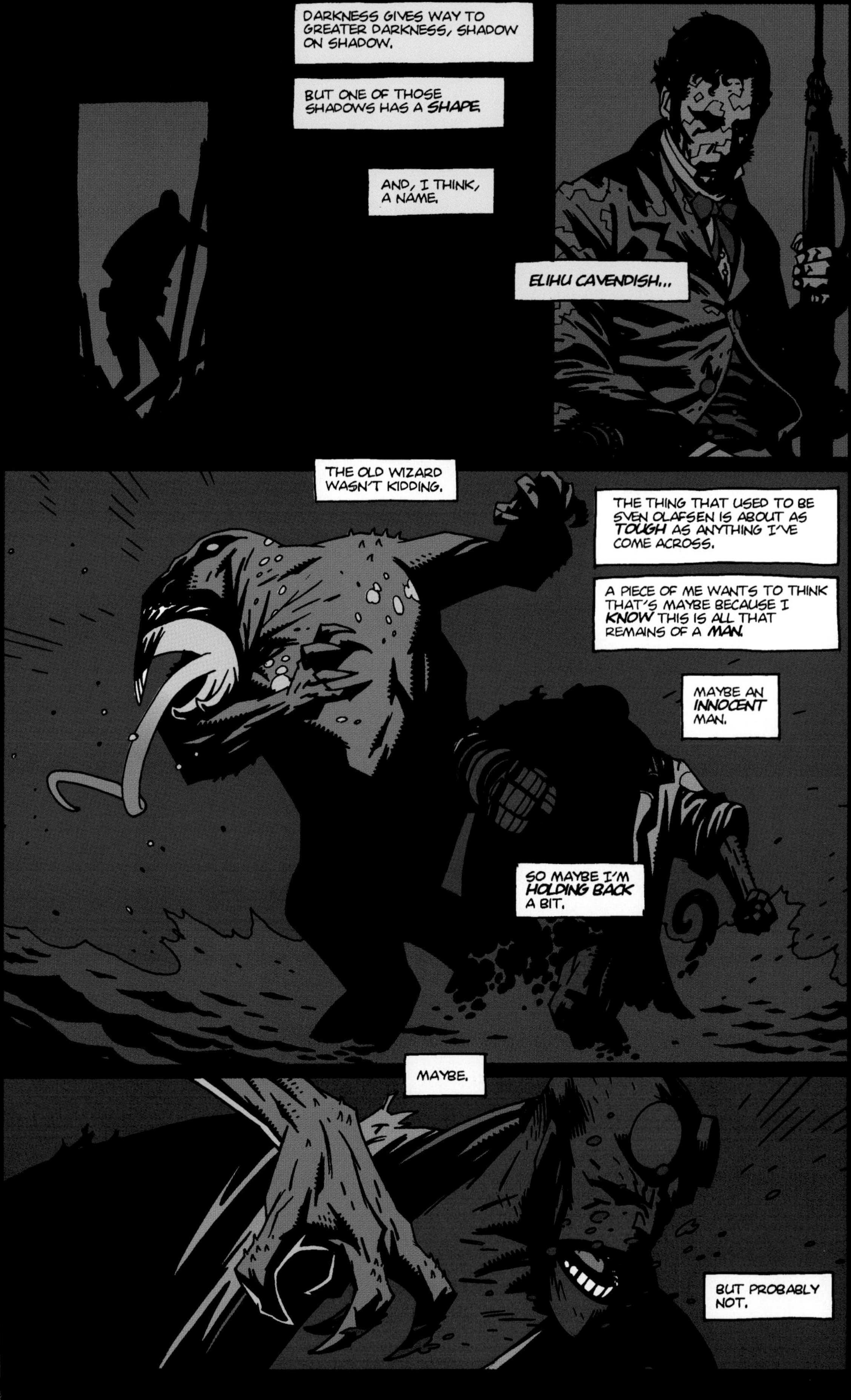
DARKNESS GIVES WAY TO GREATER DARKNESS, SHADOW ON SHADOW.
BUT ONE OF THOSE SHADOWS HAS A SHAPE.
AND, I THINK, A NAME.
ELIHU CAVENDISH...
THE OLD WIZARD WASN'T KIDDING.
THE THING THAT USED TO BE SVEN OLAFSEN IS ABOUT AS TOUGH AS ANYTHING I'VE COME ACROSS.
A PIECE OF ME WANTS TO THINK THAT'S MAYBE BECAUSE I KNOW THIS IS ALL THAT REMAINS OF A MAN.
MAYBE AN INNOCENT MAN.
SO MAYBE I'M HOLDING BACK A BIT.
MAYBE.
BUT PROBABLY NOT.

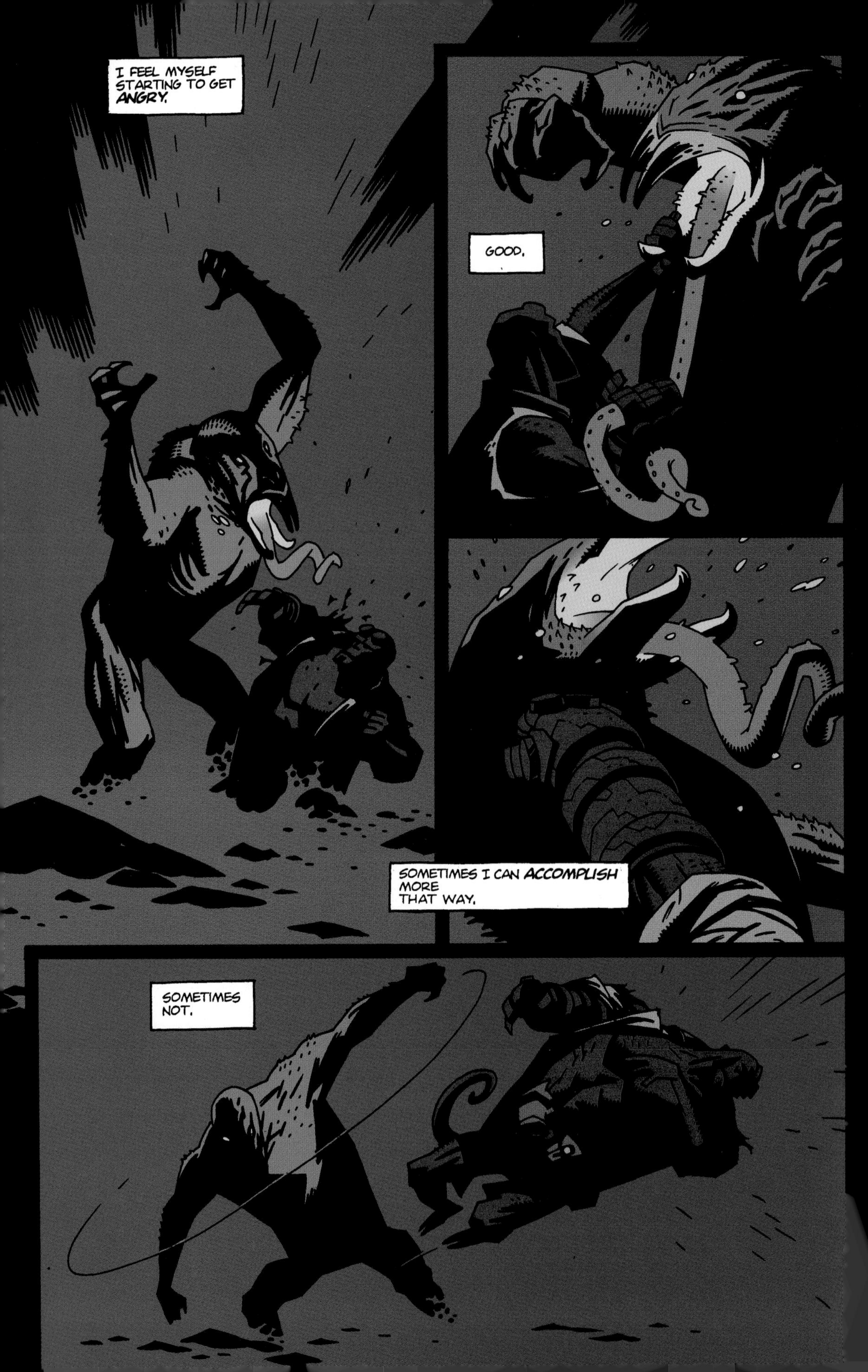
I FEEL MYSELF STARTING TO GET ANGRY.
GOOD.
SOMETIMES I CAN ACCOMPLISH MORE THAT WAY.
SOMETIMES NOT.

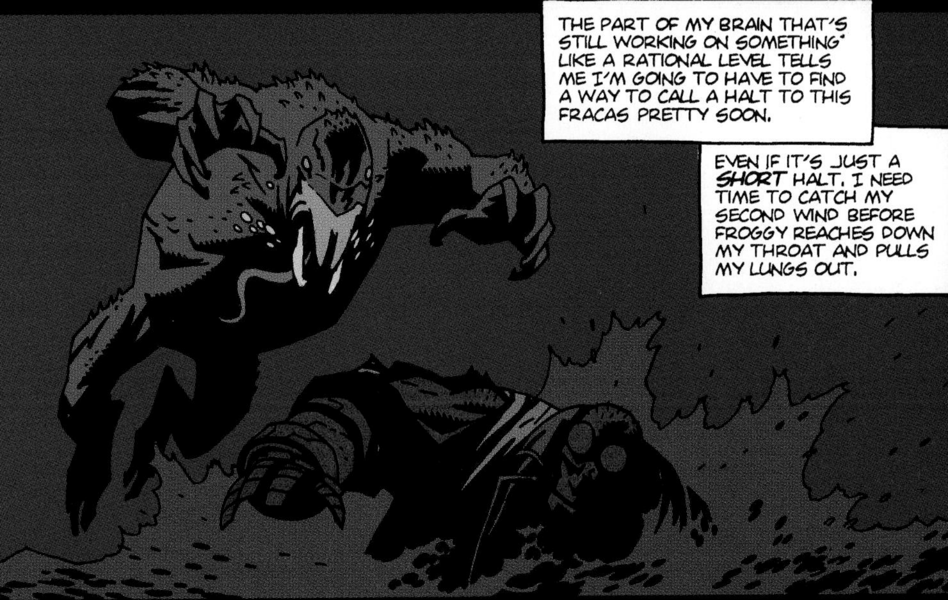
THE PART OF MY BRAIN THAT'S STILL WORKING ON SOMETHING LIKE A RATIONAL LEVEL TELLS ME I'M GOING TO HAVE TO FIND A WAY TO CALL A HALT TO THIS FRACAS PRETTY SOON.
EVEN IF IT'S JUST A SHORT HALT. I NEED TIME TO CATCH MY SECOND WIND BEFORE FROGGY REACHES DOWN MY THROAT AND PULLS MY LUNGS OUT.

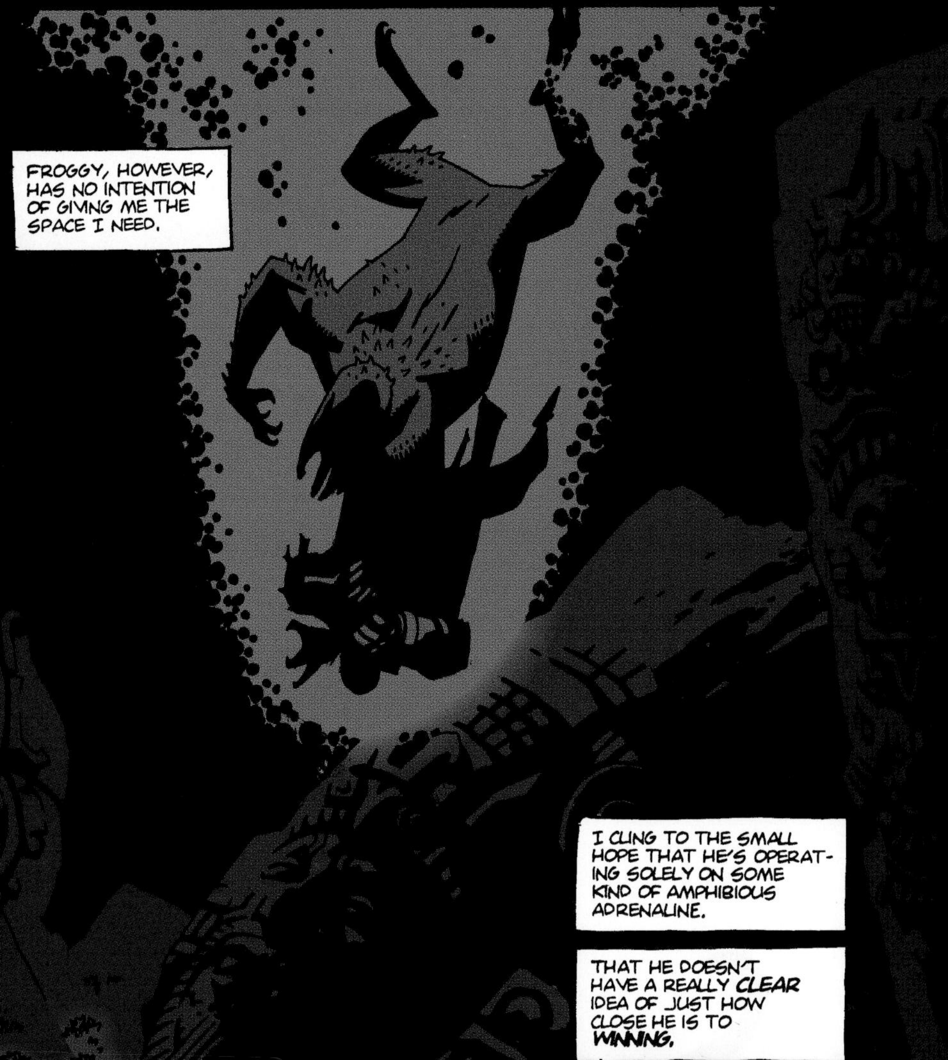
FROGGY, HOWEVER, HAS NO INTENTION OF GIVING ME THE SPACE I NEED.
I CLING TO THE SMALL HOPE THAT HE'S OPERATING SOLELY ON SOME KIND OF AMPHIBIOUS ADRENALINE.
THAT HE DOESN'T HAVE A REALLY CLEAR IDEA OF JUST HOW CLOSE HE IS TO WINNING.

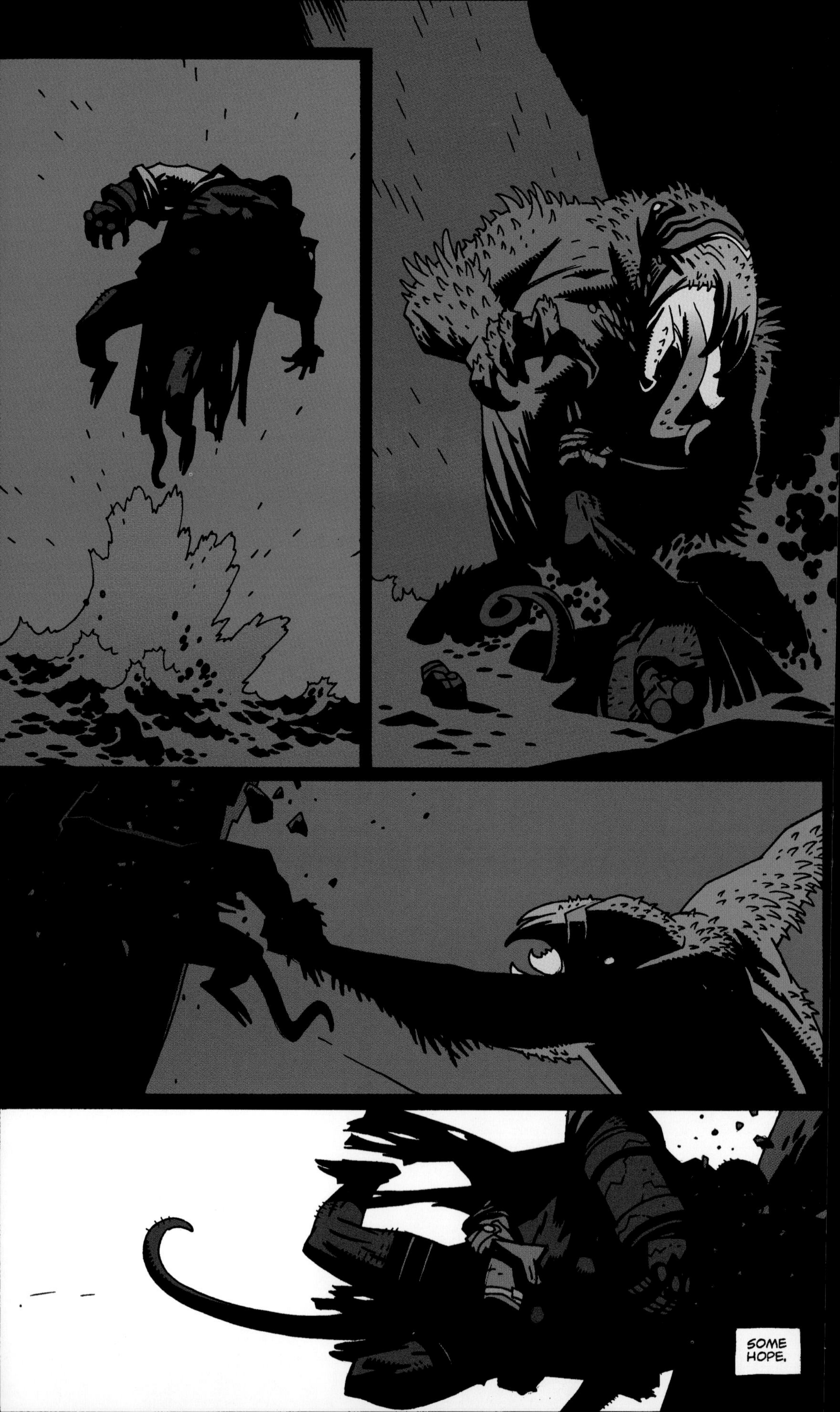
SOME HOPE.

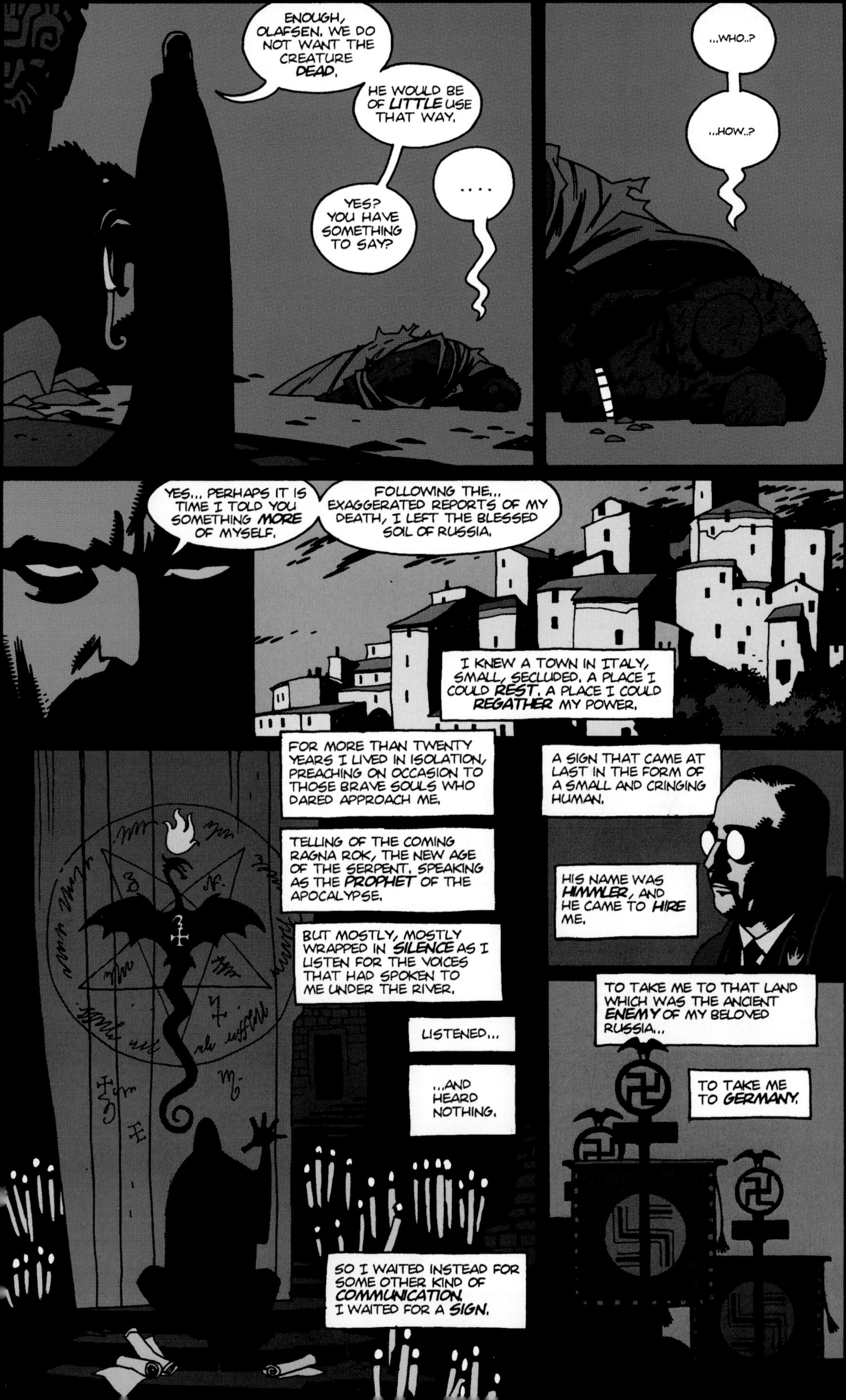
ENOUGH, OLAFSEN. WE DO NOT WANT THE CREATURE DEAD.
HE WOULD BE OF LITTLE USE THAT WAY.
YES? YOU HAVE SOMETHING TO SAY?
....
...WHO..?
...HOW..?
YES... PERHAPS IT IS TIME I TOLD YOU SOMETHING MORE OF MYSELF.
FOLLOWING THE... EXAGGERATED REPORTS OF MY DEATH, I LEFT THE BLESSED SOIL OF RUSSIA.
I KNEW A TOWN IN ITALY, SMALL, SECLUDED. A PLACE I COULD REST. A PLACE I COULD REGATHER MY POWER.
FOR MORE THAN TWENTY YEARS I LIVED IN ISOLATION, PREACHING ON OCCASION TO THOSE BRAVE SOULS WHO DARED APPROACH ME.
TELLING OF THE COMING RAGNA ROK, THE NEW AGE OF THE SERPENT, SPEAKING AS THE PROPHET OF THE APOCALYPSE.
BUT MOSTLY, MOSTLY WRAPPED IN SILENCE AS I LISTEN FOR THE VOICES THAT HAD SPOKEN TO ME UNDER THE RIVER.
LISTENED...
...AND HEARD NOTHING.
SO I WAITED INSTEAD FOR SOME OTHER KIND OF COMMUNICATION. I WAITED FOR A SIGN.
A SIGN THAT CAME AT LAST IN THE FORM OF A SMALL AND CRINGING HUMAN.
HIS NAME WAS HIMMLER, AND HE CAME TO HIRE ME.
TO TAKE ME TO THAT LAND WHICH WAS THE ANCIENT ENEMY OF MY BELOVED RUSSIA...
TO TAKE ME TO GERMANY.

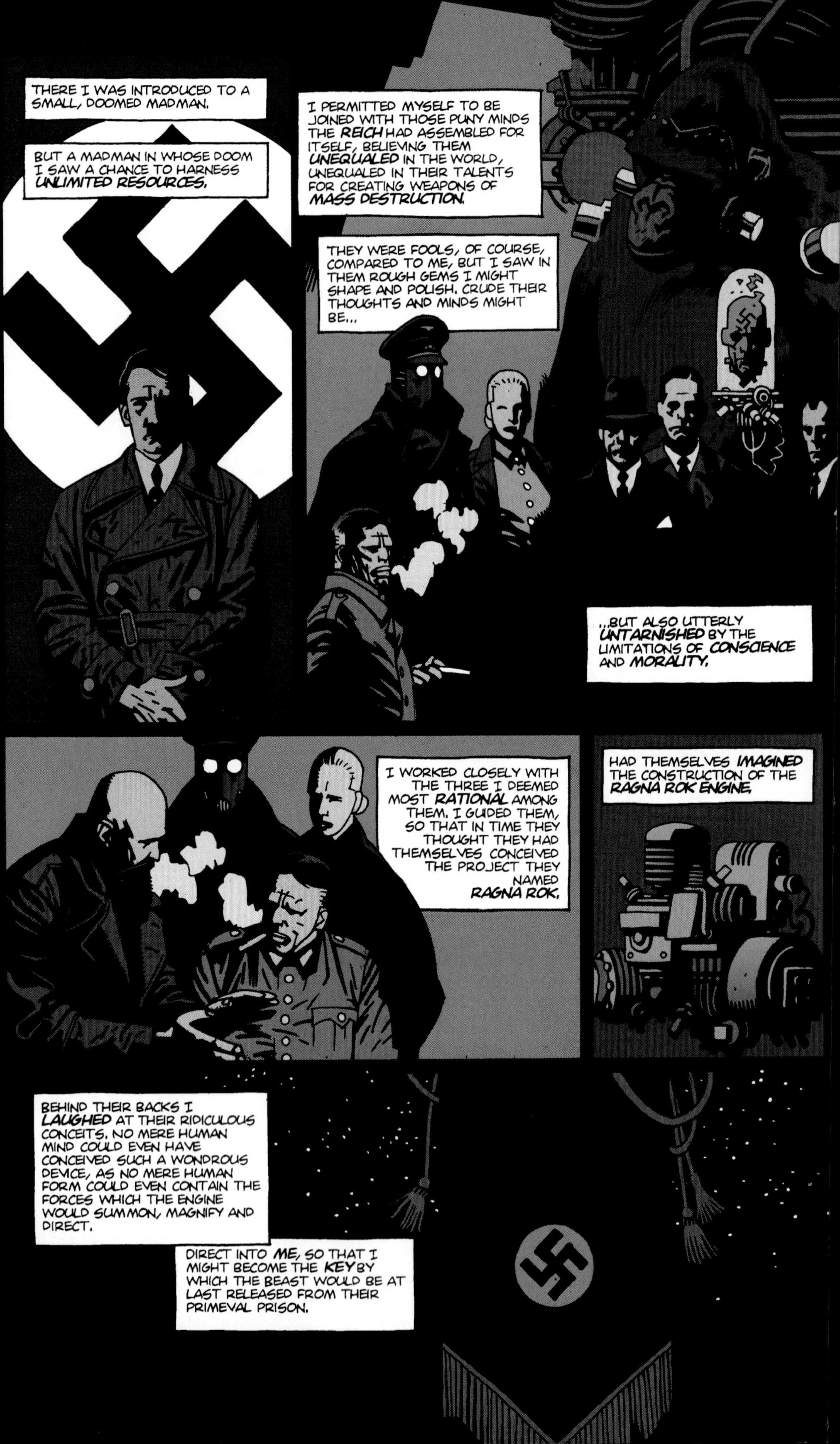

THERE I WAS INTRODUCED TO A SMALL, DOOMED MADMAN.
BUT A MADMAN IN WHOSE DOOM I SAW A CHANCE TO HARNESS UNLIMITED RESOURCES.
I PERMITTED MYSELF TO BE JOINED WITH THOSE PUNY MINDS THE REICH HAD ASSEMBLED FOR ITSELF, BELIEVING THEM UNEQUALED IN THE WORLD, UNEQUALED IN THEIR TALENTS FOR CREATING WEAPONS OF MASS DESTRUCTION.
THEY WERE FOOLS, OF COURSE, COMPARED TO ME, BUT I SAW IN THEM ROUGH GEMS I MIGHT SHAPE AND POLISH. CRUDE THEIR THOUGHTS AND MINDS MIGHT BE...
...BUT ALSO UTTERLY UNTARNISHED BY THE LIMITATIONS OF CONSCIENCE AND MORALITY.
I WORKED CLOSELY WITH THE THREE I DEEMED MOST RATIONAL AMONG THEM. I GUIDED THEM, SO THAT IN TIME THEY THOUGHT THEY HAD THEMSELVES CONCEIVED THE PROJECT THEY NAMED RAGNA ROK.
HAD THEMSELVES IMAGINED THE CONSTRUCTION OF THE RAGNA ROK ENGINE.
BEHIND THEIR BACKS I LAUGHED AT THEIR RIDICULOUS CONCEITS. NO MERE HUMAN MIND COULD EVEN HAVE CONCEIVED SUCH A WONDROUS DEVICE, AS NO MERE HUMAN FORM COULD EVEN CONTAIN THE FORCES WHICH THE ENGINE WOULD SUMMON, MAGNIFY AND DIRECT.
DIRECT INTO ME, SO THAT I MIGHT BECOME THE KEY BY WHICH THE BEAST WOULD BE AT LAST RELEASED FROM THEIR PRIMEVAL PRISON.

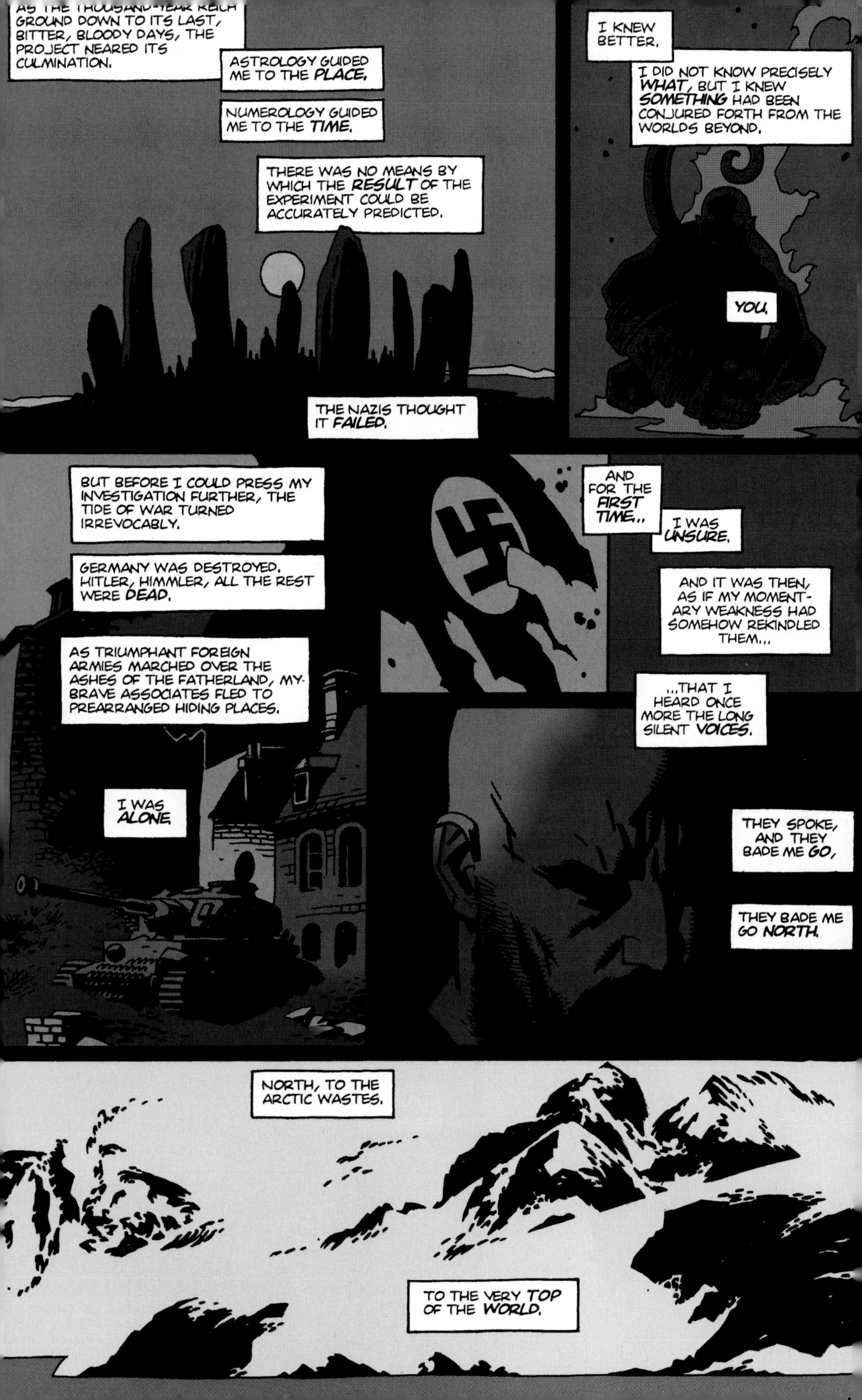
AS THE THOUSAND-YEAR REICH GROUND DOWN TO ITS LAST, BITTER, BLOODY DAYS, THE PROJECT NEARED ITS CULMINATION.
ASTROLOGY GUIDED ME TO THE PLACE.
NUMEROLOGY GUIDED ME TO THE TIME.
THERE WAS NO MEANS BY WHICH THE RESULT OF THE EXPERIMENT COULD BE ACCURATELY PREDICTED.
THE NAZIS THOUGHT IT FAILED.
I KNEW BETTER.
I DID NOT KNOW PRECISELY WHAT, BUT I KNEW SOMETHING HAD BEEN CONJURED FORTH FROM THE WORLDS BEYOND.
YOU.
BUT BEFORE I COULD PRESS MY INVESTIGATION FURTHER, THE TIDE OF WAR TURNED IRREVOCABLY.
GERMANY WAS DESTROYED. HITLER, HIMMLER, ALL THE REST WERE DEAD.
AS TRIUMPHANT FOREIGN ARMIES MARCHED OVER THE ASHES OF THE FATHERLAND, MY BRAVE ASSOCIATES FLED TO PREARRANGED HIDING PLACES.
I WAS ALONE.
AND FOR THE FIRST TIME...
I WAS UNSURE.
AND IT WAS THEN, AS IF MY MOMENTARY WEAKNESS HAD SOMEHOW REKINDLED THEM...
...THAT I HEARD ONCE MORE THE LONG SILENT VOICES.
THEY SPOKE, AND THEY BADE ME GO,
THEY BADE ME GO NORTH.
NORTH, TO THE ARCTIC WASTES.
TO THE VERY TOP OF THE WORLD.

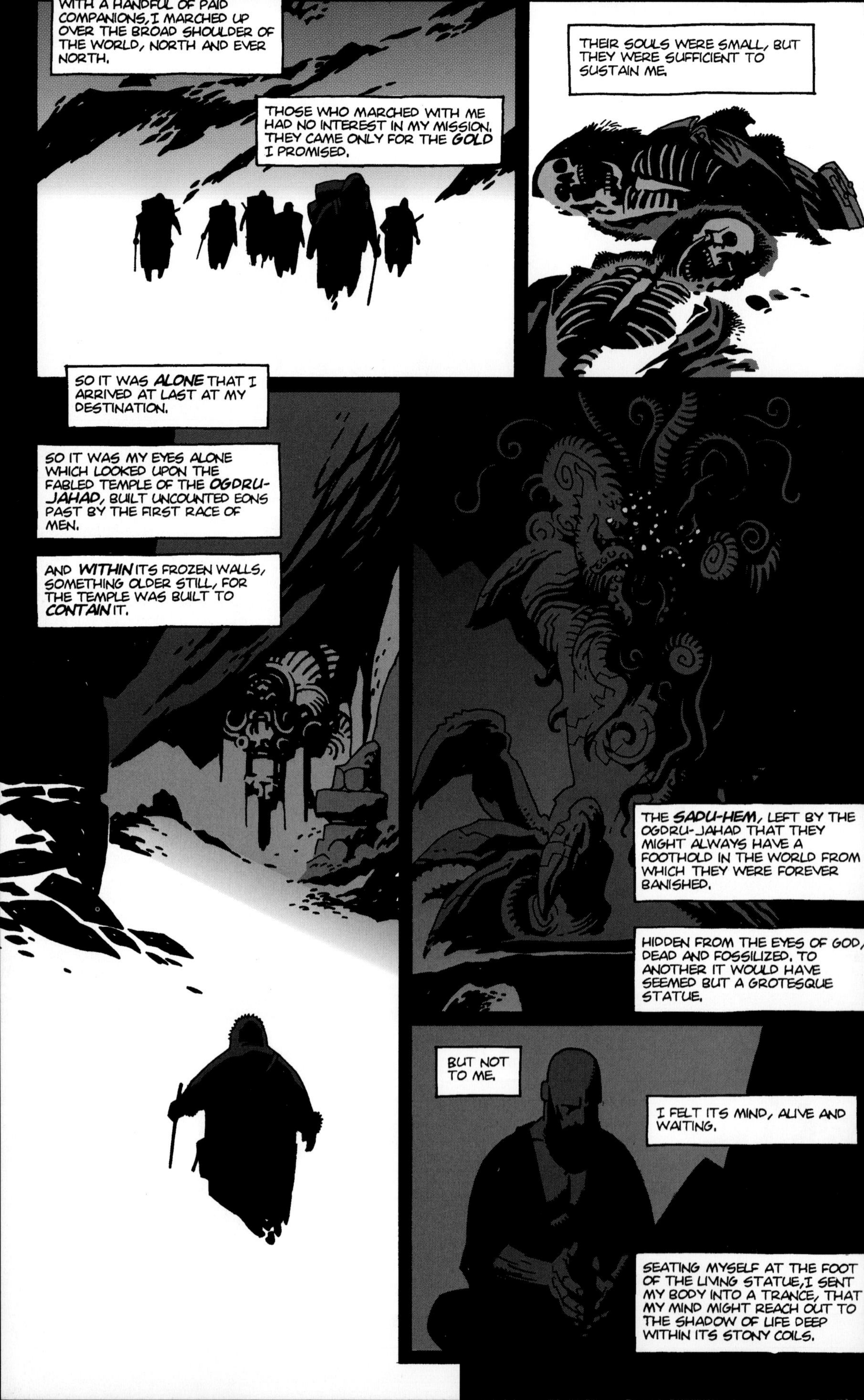

WITH A HANDFUL OF PAID COMPANIONS, I MARCHED UP OVER THE BROAD SHOULDER OF THE WORLD, NORTH AND EVER NORTH.
THOSE WHO MARCHED WITH ME HAD NO INTEREST IN MY MISSION. THEY CAME ONLY FOR THE GOLD I PROMISED.
THEIR SOULS WERE SMALL, BUT THEY WERE SUFFICIENT TO SUSTAIN ME.
SO IT WAS ALONE THAT I ARRIVED AT LAST AT MY DESTINATION.
SO IT WAS MY EYES ALONE WHICH LOOKED UPON THE FABLED TEMPLE OF THE OGDRU-JAHAD, BUILT UNCOUNTED EONS PAST BY THE FIRST RACE OF MEN.
AND WITHIN ITS FROZEN WALLS, SOMETHING OLDER STILL, FOR THE TEMPLE WAS BUILT TO CONTAIN IT.
THE SADU-HEM, LEFT BY THE OGDRU-JAHAD THAT THEY MIGHT ALWAYS HAVE A FOOTHOLD IN THE WORLD FROM WHICH THEY WERE FOREVER BANISHED.
HIDDEN FROM THE EYES OF GOD, DEAD AND FOSSILIZED. TO ANOTHER IT WOULD HAVE SEEMED BUT A GROTESQUE STATUE.
BUT NOT TO ME.
I FELT ITS MIND, ALIVE AND WAITING.
SEATING MYSELF AT THE FOOT OF THE LIVING STATUE, I SENT MY BODY INTO A TRANCE, THAT MY MIND MIGHT REACH OUT TO THE SHADOW OF LIFE DEEP WITHIN ITS STONY COILS.

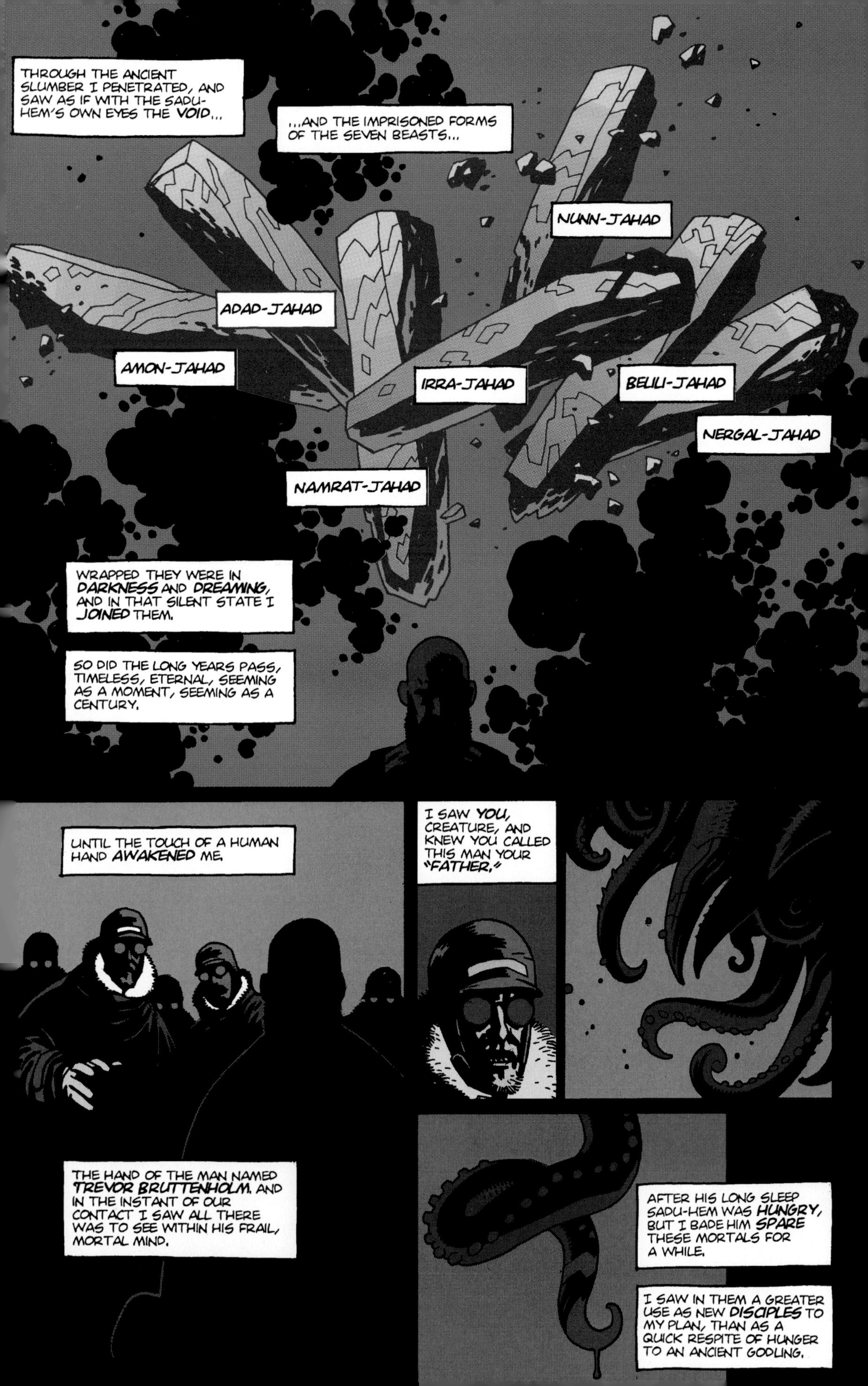
THROUGH THE ANCIENT SLUMBER I PENETRATED, AND SAW AS IF WITH THE SADU-HEM'S OWN EYES THE VOID...
...AND THE IMPRISONED FORMS OF THE SEVEN BEASTS...
NUNN-JAHAD
ADAD-JAHAD
AMON-JAHAD
IRRA-JAHAD
BELILI-JAHAD
NERGAL-JAHAD
NAMRAT-JAHAD
WRAPPED THEY WERE IN DARKNESS AND DREAMING, AND IN THAT SILENT STATE I JOINED THEM.
SO DID THE LONG YEARS PASS, TIMELESS, ETERNAL, SEEMING AS A MOMENT, SEEMING AS A CENTURY.
UNTIL THE TOUCH OF A HUMAN HAND AWAKENED ME.
I SAW YOU, CREATURE, AND KNEW YOU CALLED THIS MAN YOUR "FATHER."
THE HAND OF THE MAN NAMED TREVOR BRUTTENHOLM. AND IN THE INSTANT OF OUR CONTACT I SAW ALL THERE WAS TO SEE WITHIN HIS FRAIL, MORTAL MIND.
AFTER HIS LONG SLEEP SADU-HEM WAS HUNGRY, BUT I BADE HIM SPARE THESE MORTALS FOR A WHILE.
I SAW IN THEM A GREATER USE AS NEW DISCIPLES TO MY PLAN, THAN AS A QUICK RESPITE OF HUNGER TO AN ANCIENT GODLING.

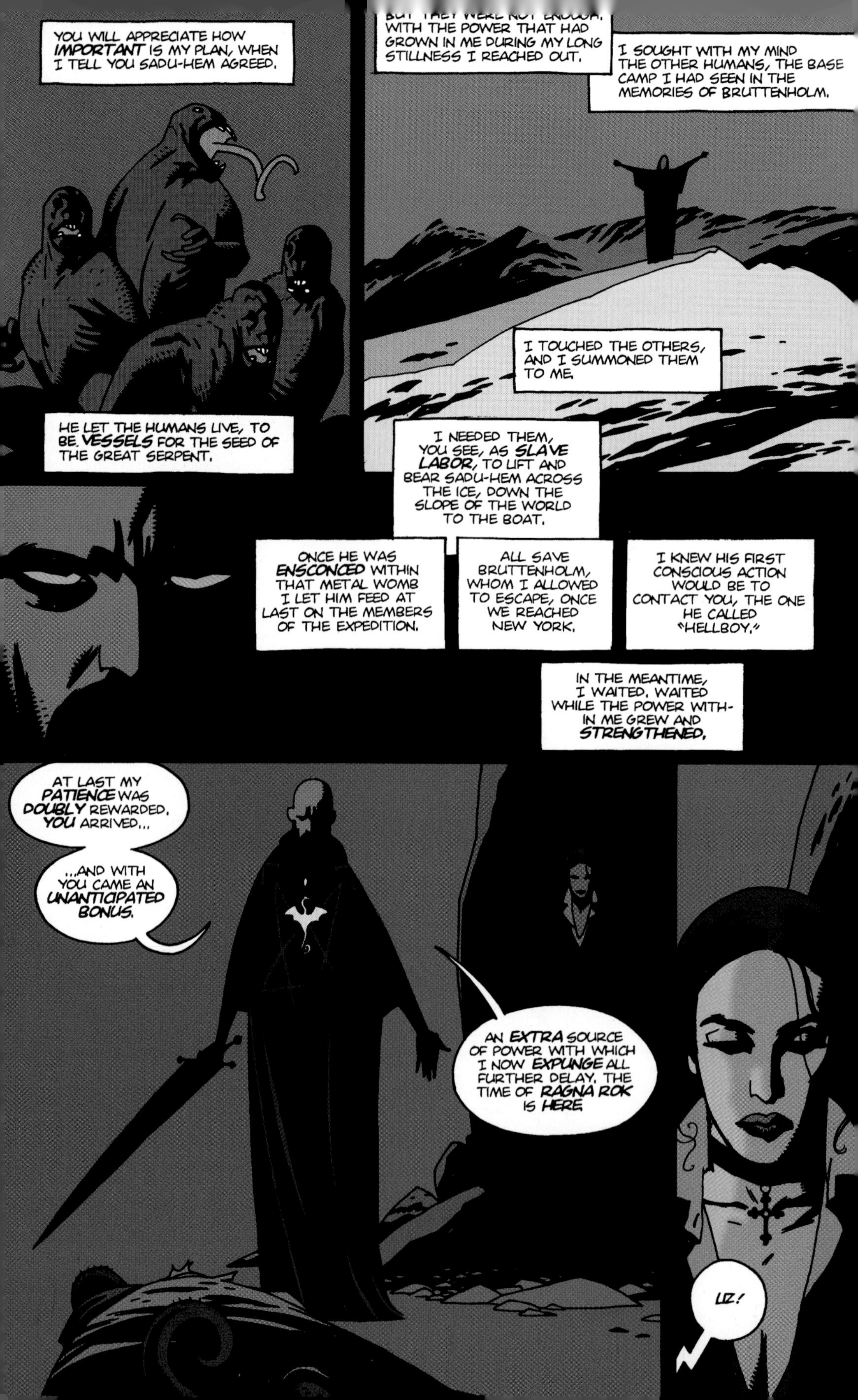
YOU WILL APPRECIATE HOW IMPORTANT IS MY PLAN, WHEN I TELL YOU SADU-HEM AGREED.
HE LET THE HUMANS LIVE, TO BE. VESSELS FOR THE SEED OF THE GREAT SERPENT.
WITH THE POWER THAT HAD GROWN IN ME DURING MY LONG STILLNESS I REACHED OUT.
I SOUGHT WITH MY MIND THE OTHER HUMANS, THE BASE CAMP I HAD SEEN IN THE MEMORIES OF BRUTTENHOLM.
I TOUCHED THE OTHERS, AND I SUMMONED THEM TO ME.
I NEEDED THEM, YOU SEE, AS SLAVE LABOR, TO LIFT AND BEAR SADU-HEM ACROSS THE ICE, DOWN THE SLOPE OF THE WORLD TO THE BOAT.
ONCE HE WAS ENSCONCED WITHIN THAT METAL WOMB I LET HIM FEED AT LAST ON THE MEMBERS OF THE EXPEDITION.
ALL SAVE BRUTTENHOLM, WHOM I ALLOWED TO ESCAPE, ONCE WE REACHED NEW YORK.
I KNEW HIS FIRST CONSCIOUS ACTION WOULD BE TO CONTACT YOU, THE ONE HE CALLED "HELLBOY."
IN THE MEANTIME, I WAITED. WAITED WHILE THE POWER WITH-IN ME GREW AND STRENGTHENED.
AT LAST MY PATIENCE WAS DOUBLY REWARDED. YOU ARRIVED...
...AND WITH YOU CAME AN UNANTICIPATED BONUS.
AN EXTRA SOURCE OF POWER WITH WHICH I NOW EXPUNGE ALL FURTHER DELAY. THE TIME OF RAGNA ROK IS HERE.
LIZ!

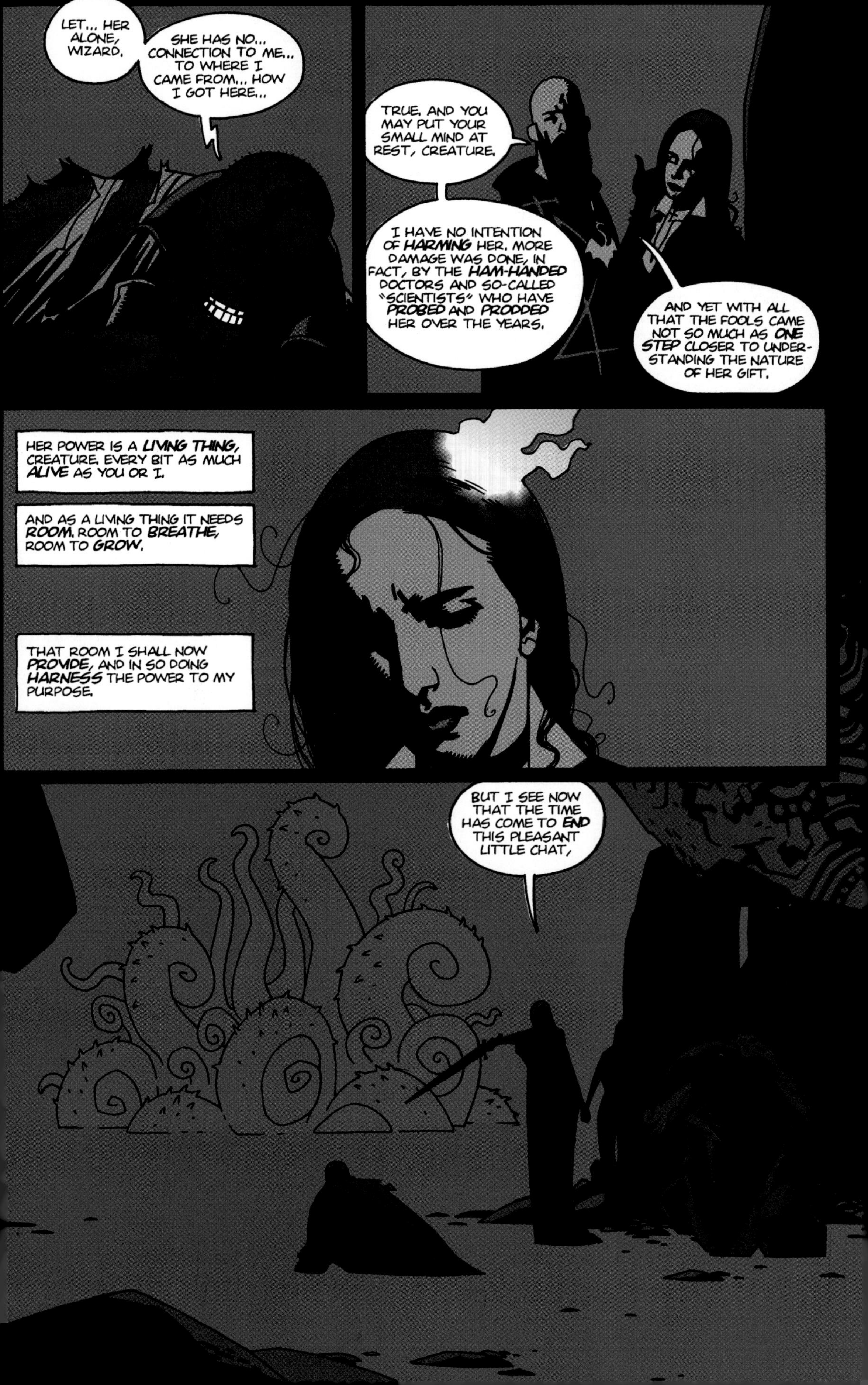
LET... HER ALONE, WIZARD.
SHE HAS NO... CONNECTION TO ME... TO WHERE I CAME FROM... HOW I GOT HERE...
TRUE, AND YOU MAY PUT YOUR SMALL MIND AT REST, CREATURE.
I HAVE NO INTENTION OF HARMING HER. MORE DAMAGE WAS DONE, IN FACT, BY THE HAM-HANDED DOCTORS AND SO-CALLED "SCIENTISTS" WHO HAVE PROBED AND PRODDED HER OVER THE YEARS.
AND YET WITH ALL THAT THE FOOLS CAME NOT SO MUCH AS ONE STEP CLOSER TO UNDER-STANDING THE NATURE OF HER GIFT.
HER POWER IS A LIVING THING, CREATURE. EVERY BIT AS MUCH ALIVE AS YOU OR I.
AND AS A LIVING THING IT NEEDS ROOM. ROOM TO BREATHE, ROOM TO GROW.
THAT ROOM I SHALL NOW PROVIDE, AND IN SO DOING HARNESS THE POWER TO MY PURPOSE.
BUT I SEE NOW THAT THE TIME HAS COME TO END THIS PLEASANT LITTLE CHAT,

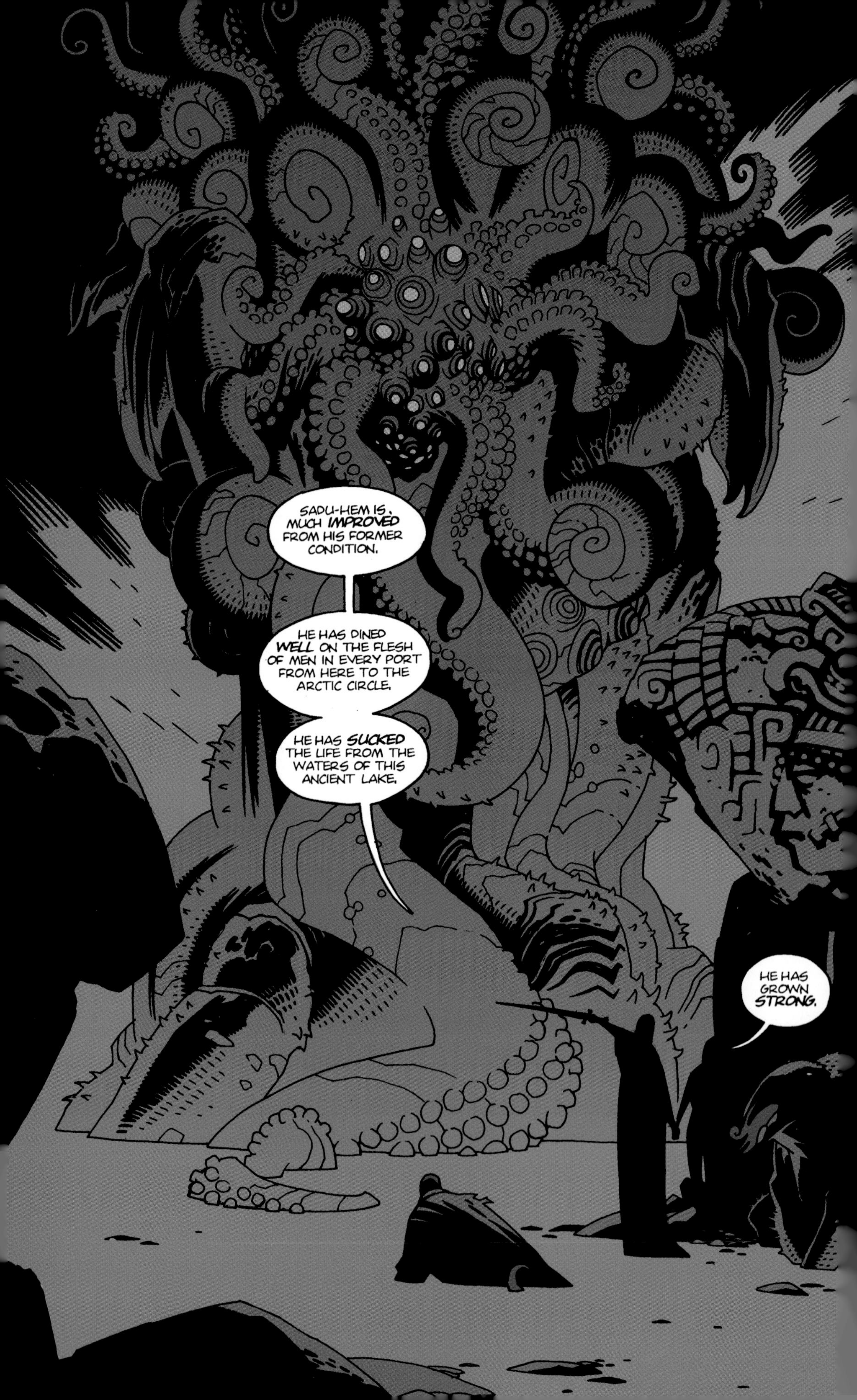

SADU-HEM IS MUCH IMPROVED FROM HIS FORMER CONDITION.
HE HAS DINED WELL ON THE FLESH OF MEN IN EVERY PORT FROM HERE TO THE ARCTIC CIRCLE.
HE HAS SUCKED THE LIFE FROM THE WATERS OF THIS ANCIENT LAKE.
HE HAS GROWN STRONG.

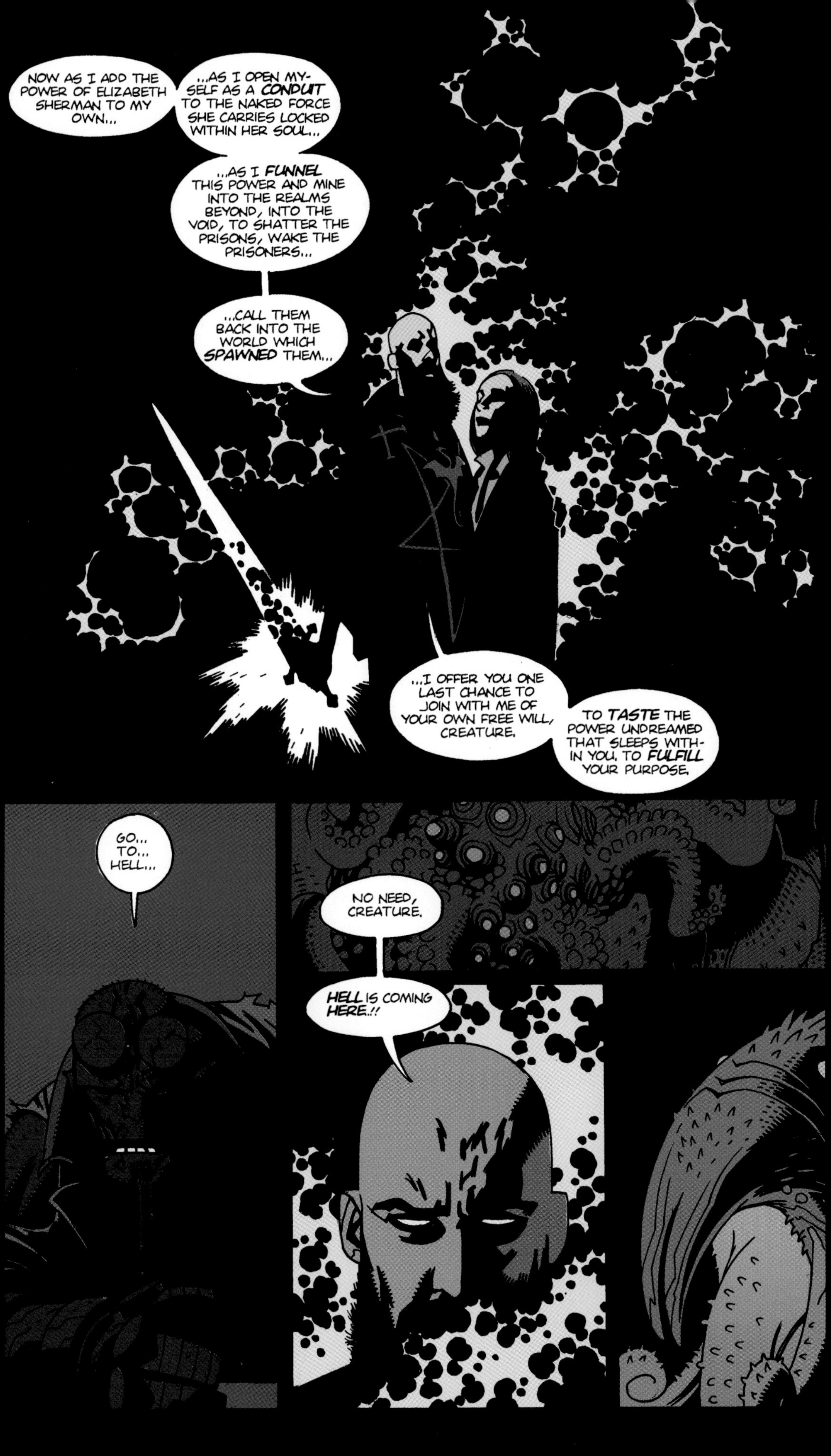
NOW AS I ADD THE POWER OF ELIZABETH SHERMAN TO MY OWN...
...AS I OPEN MYSELF AS A CONDUIT TO THE NAKED FORCE SHE CARRIES LOCKED WITHIN HER SOUL...
...AS I FUNNEL THIS POWER AND MINE INTO THE REALMS BEYOND, INTO THE VOID, TO SHATTER THE PRISONS, WAKE THE PRISONERS...
...CALL THEM BACK INTO THE WORLD WHICH SPAWNED THEM...
...I OFFER YOU ONE LAST CHANCE TO JOIN WITH ME OF YOUR OWN FREE WILL, CREATURE.
TO TASTE THE POWER UNDREAMED THAT SLEEPS WITHIN YOU. TO FULFILL YOUR PURPOSE.
GO... TO... HELL...
NO NEED, CREATURE.
HELL IS COMING HERE.!!

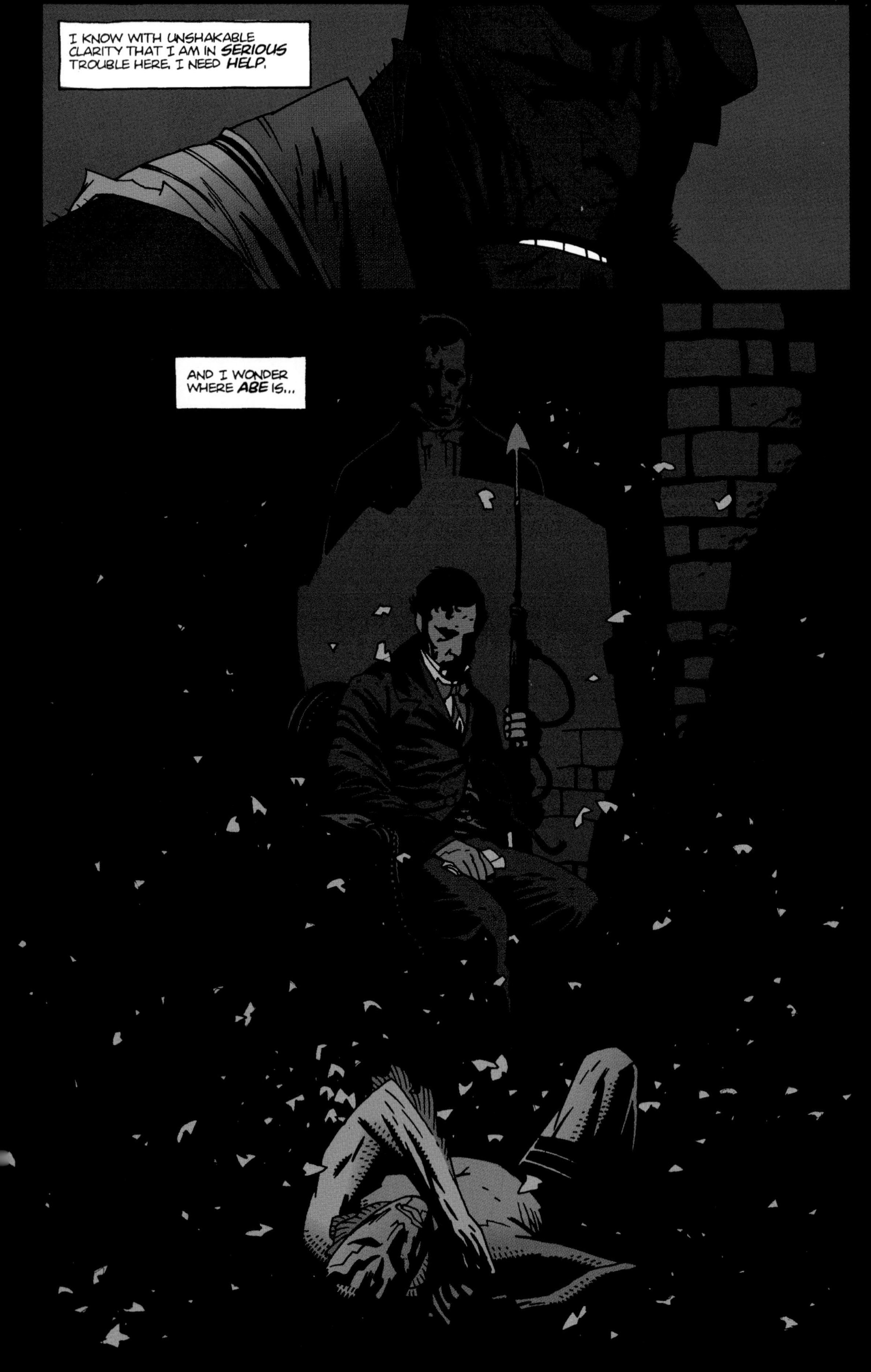
I KNOW WITH UNSHAKABLE CLARITY THAT I AM IN SERIOUS TROUBLE HERE. I NEED HELP.
AND I WONDER WHERE ABE IS...

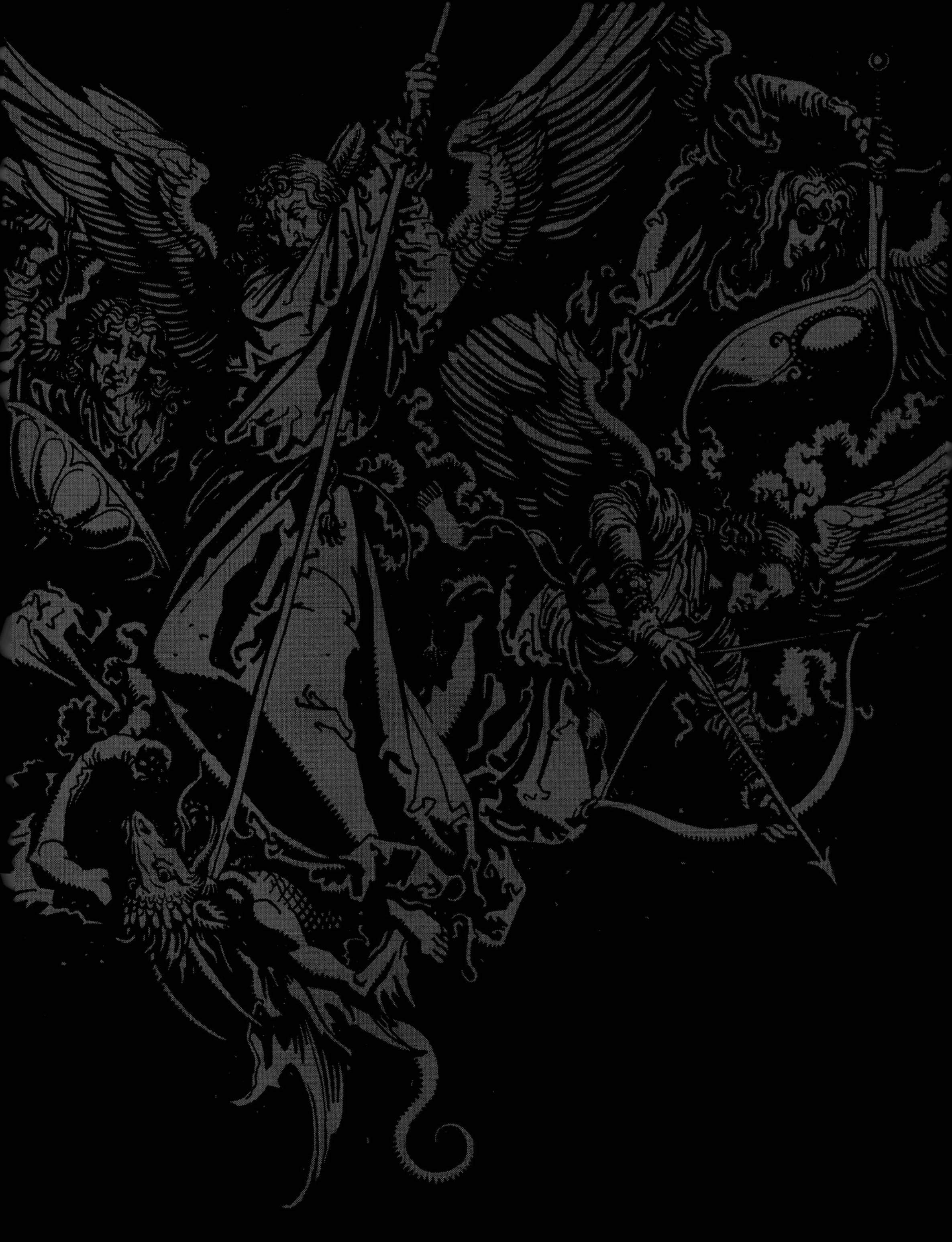

CHAPTER FOUR

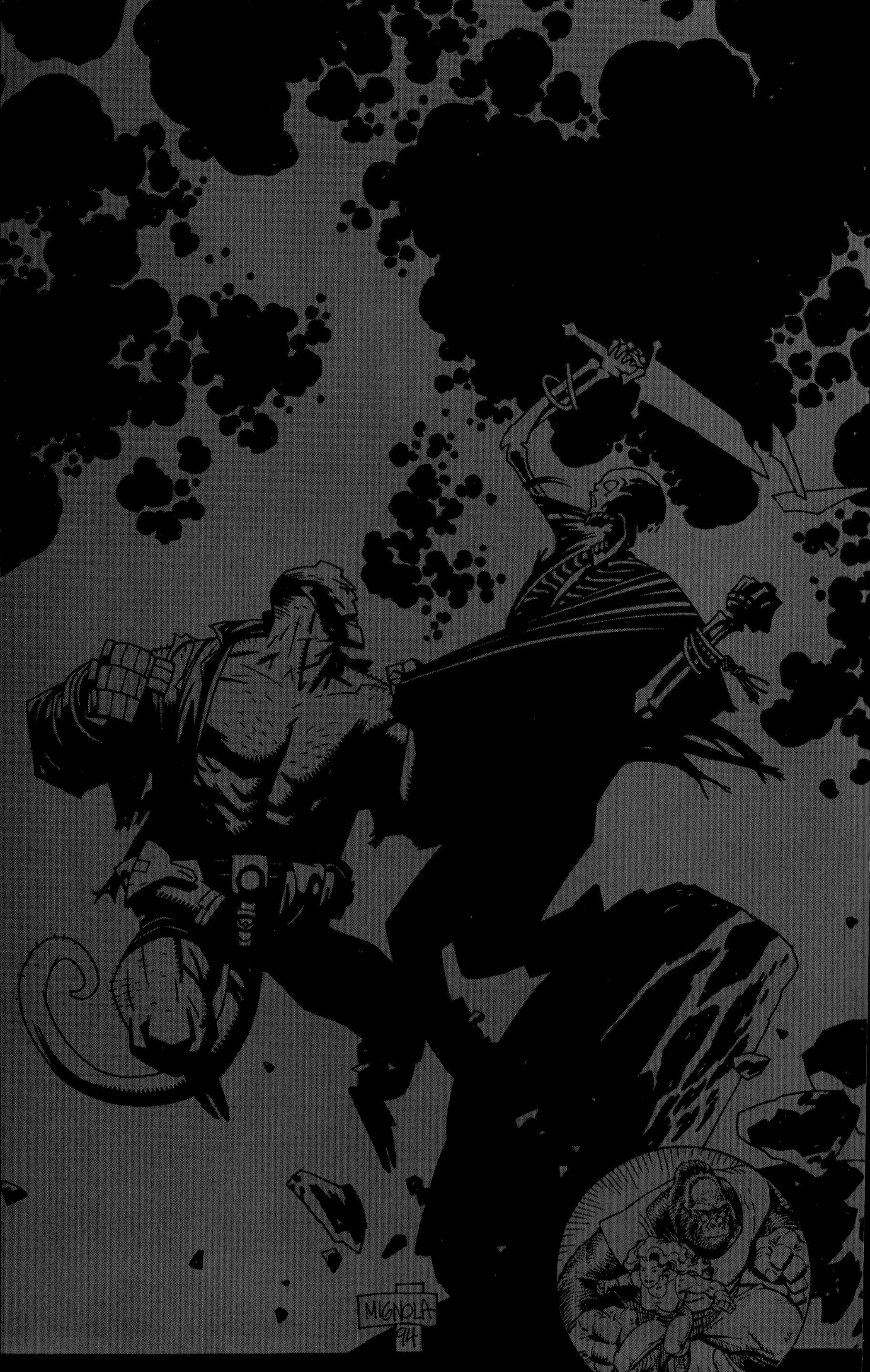
MIGNOLA
94

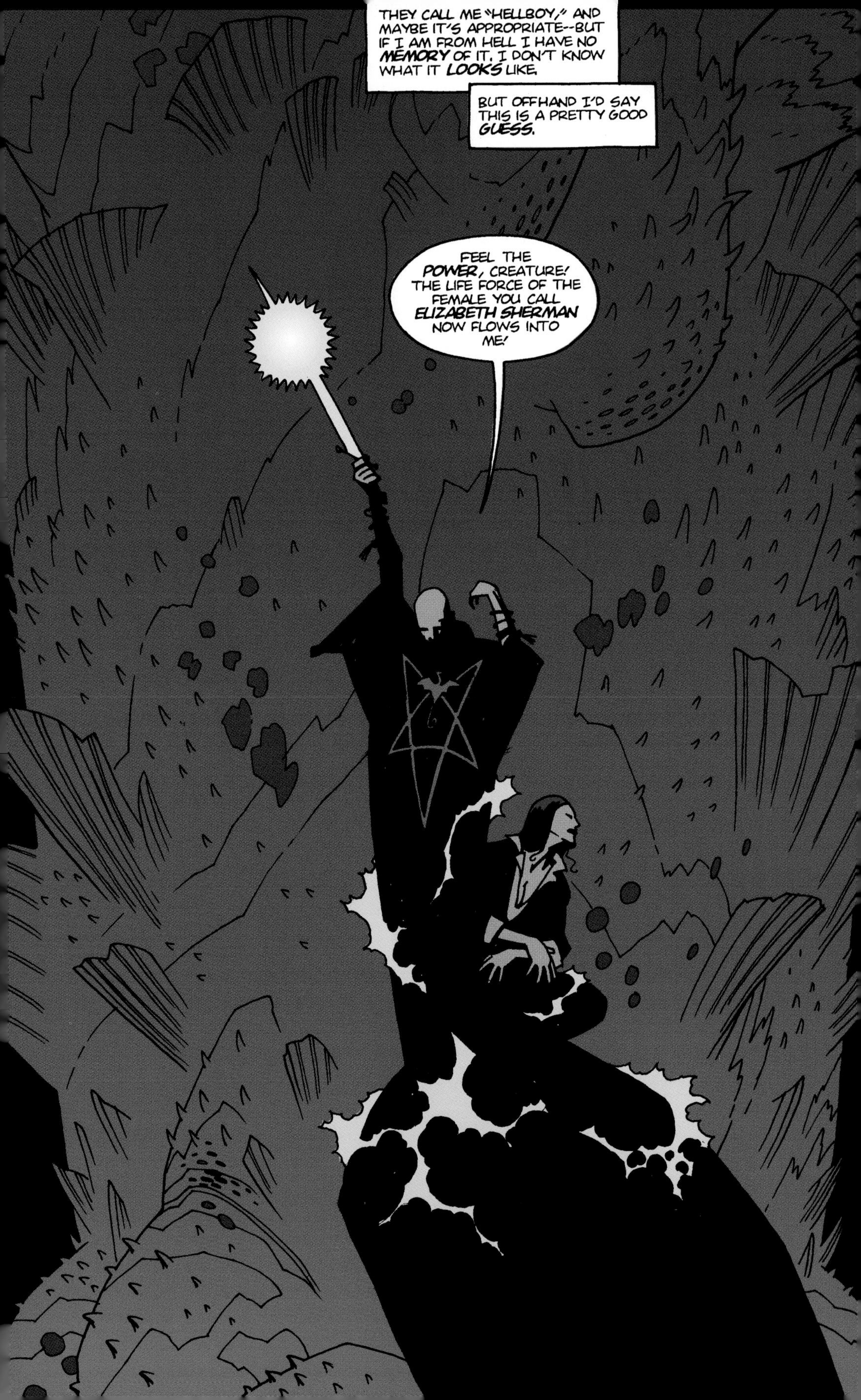
THEY CALL ME "HELLBOY," AND MAYBE IT'S APPROPRIATE--BUT IF I AM FROM HELL I HAVE NO **MEMORY** OF IT. I DON'T KNOW WHAT IT **LOOKS** LIKE.
BUT OFFHAND I'D SAY THIS IS A PRETTY GOOD **GUESS**.
FEEL THE **POWER**, CREATURE! THE LIFE FORCE OF THE FEMALE YOU CALL **ELIZABETH SHERMAN** NOW FLOWS INTO ME!

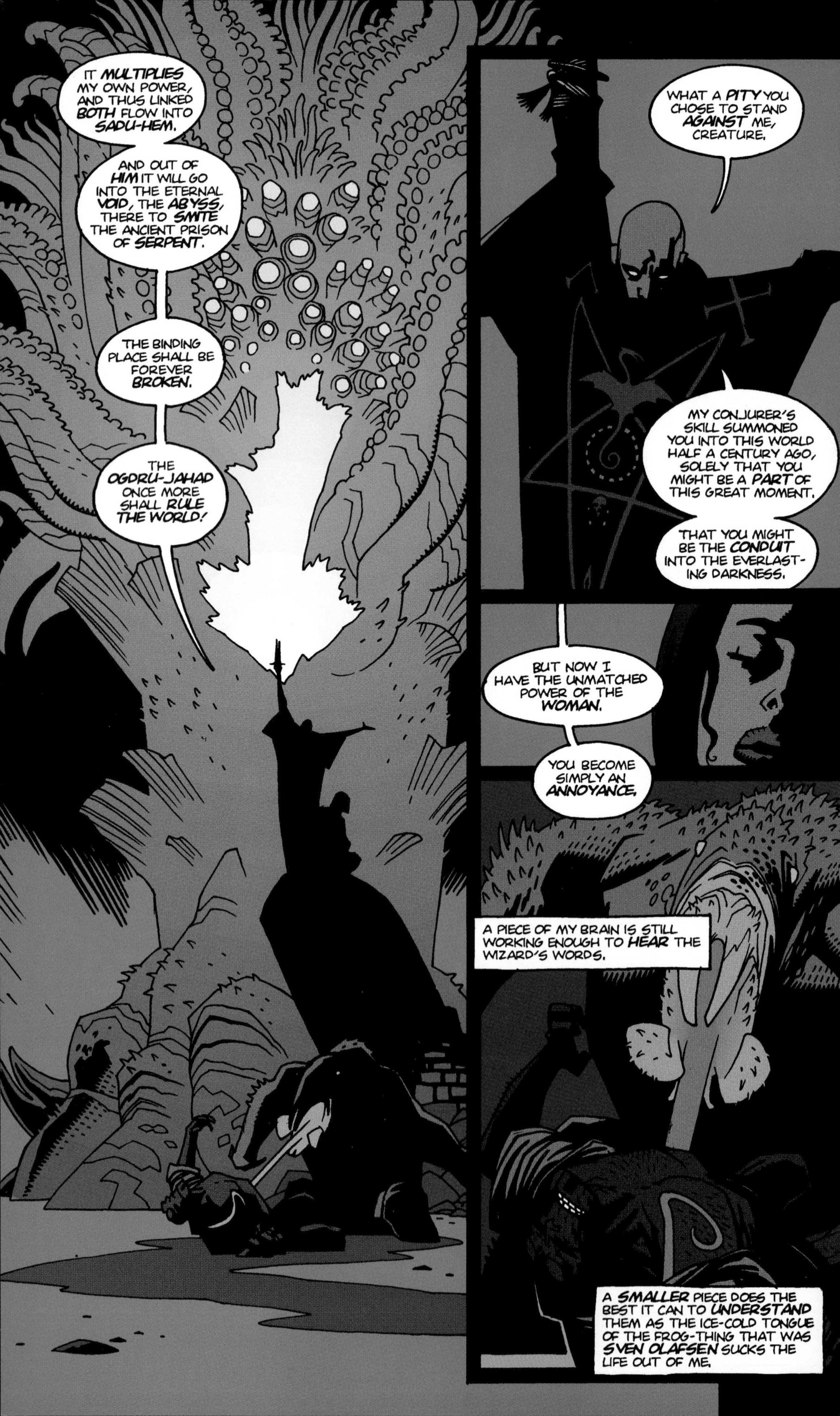
IT MULTIPLIES MY OWN POWER, AND THUS LINKED BOTH FLOW INTO SADU-HEM.
AND OUT OF HIM IT WILL GO INTO THE ETERNAL VOID, THE ABYSS, THERE TO SMITE THE ANCIENT PRISON OF SERPENT.
THE BINDING PLACE SHALL BE FOREVER BROKEN.
THE OGDRU-JAHAD ONCE MORE SHALL RULE THE WORLD!
WHAT A PITY YOU CHOSE TO STAND AGAINST ME, CREATURE.
MY CONJURER'S SKILL SUMMONED YOU INTO THIS WORLD HALF A CENTURY AGO, SOLELY THAT YOU MIGHT BE A PART OF THIS GREAT MOMENT.
THAT YOU MIGHT BE THE CONDUIT INTO THE EVERLASTING DARKNESS.
BUT NOW I HAVE THE UNMATCHED POWER OF THE WOMAN.
YOU BECOME SIMPLY AN ANNOYANCE.
A PIECE OF MY BRAIN IS STILL WORKING ENOUGH TO HEAR THE WIZARD'S WORDS.
A SMALLER PIECE DOES THE BEST IT CAN TO UNDERSTAND THEM AS THE ICE-COLD TONGUE OF THE FROG-THING THAT WAS SVEN OLAFSEN SUCKS THE LIFE OUT OF ME.

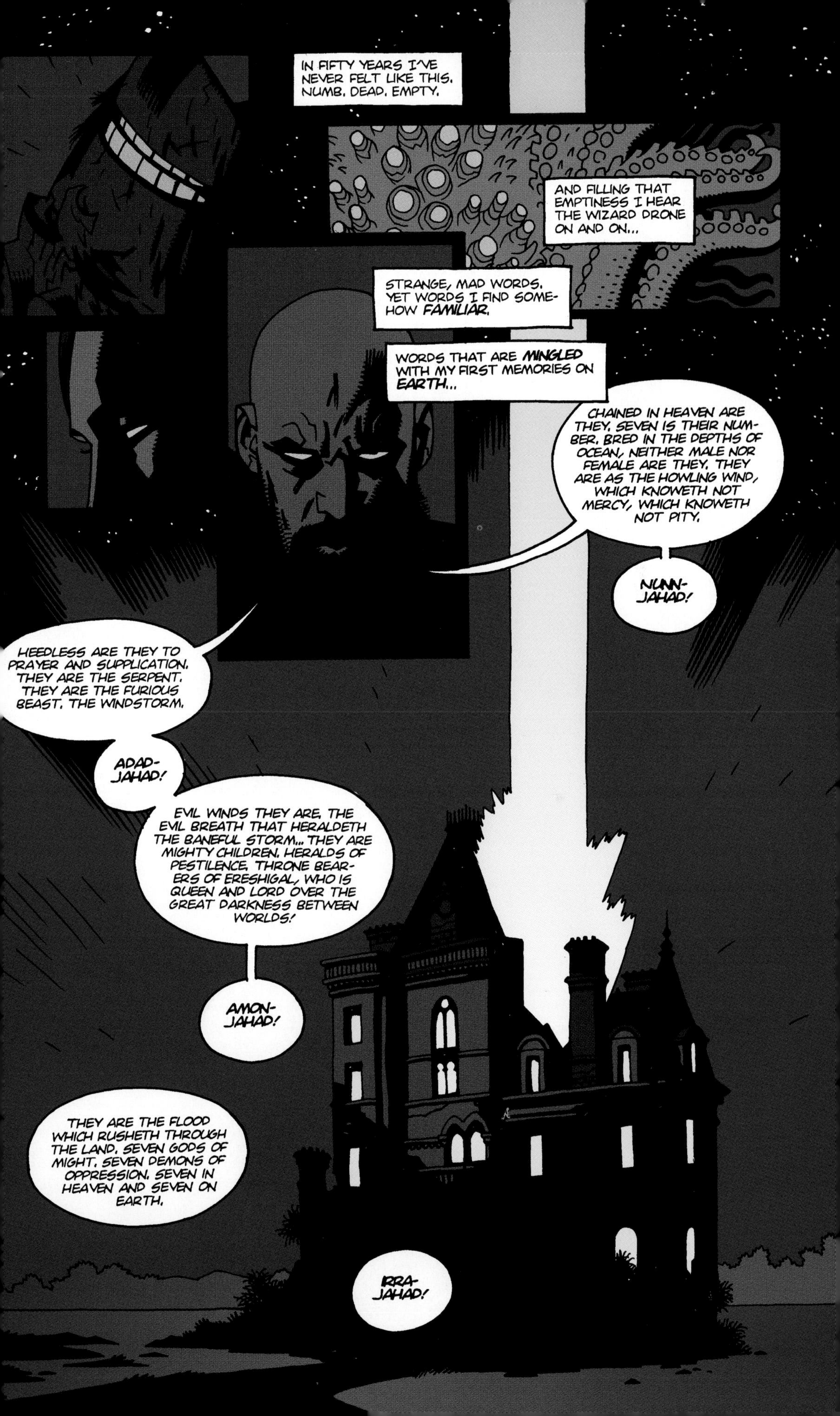

IN FIFTY YEARS I'VE NEVER FELT LIKE THIS. NUMB. DEAD. EMPTY.
AND FILLING THAT EMPTINESS I HEAR THE WIZARD DRONE ON AND ON...
STRANGE, MAD WORDS. YET WORDS I FIND SOMEHOW FAMILIAR.
WORDS THAT ARE MINGLED WITH MY FIRST MEMORIES ON EARTH...
CHAINED IN HEAVEN ARE THEY. SEVEN IS THEIR NUMBER. BRED IN THE DEPTHS OF OCEAN, NEITHER MALE NOR FEMALE ARE THEY. THEY ARE AS THE HOWLING WIND, WHICH KNOWETH NOT MERCY, WHICH KNOWETH NOT PITY.
NUNN-JAHAD!
HEEDLESS ARE THEY TO PRAYER AND SUPPLICATION. THEY ARE THE SERPENT. THEY ARE THE FURIOUS BEAST. THE WINDSTORM.
ADAD-JAHAD!
EVIL WINDS THEY ARE, THE EVIL BREATH THAT HERALDETH THE BANEFUL STORM... THEY ARE MIGHTY CHILDREN. HERALDS OF PESTILENCE. THRONE BEARERS OF ERESHIGAL, WHO IS QUEEN AND LORD OVER THE GREAT DARKNESS BETWEEN WORLDS!
AMON-JAHAD!
THEY ARE THE FLOOD WHICH RUSHETH THROUGH THE LAND. SEVEN GODS OF MIGHT. SEVEN DEMONS OF OPPRESSION. SEVEN IN HEAVEN AND SEVEN ON EARTH.
IRRA-JAHAD!

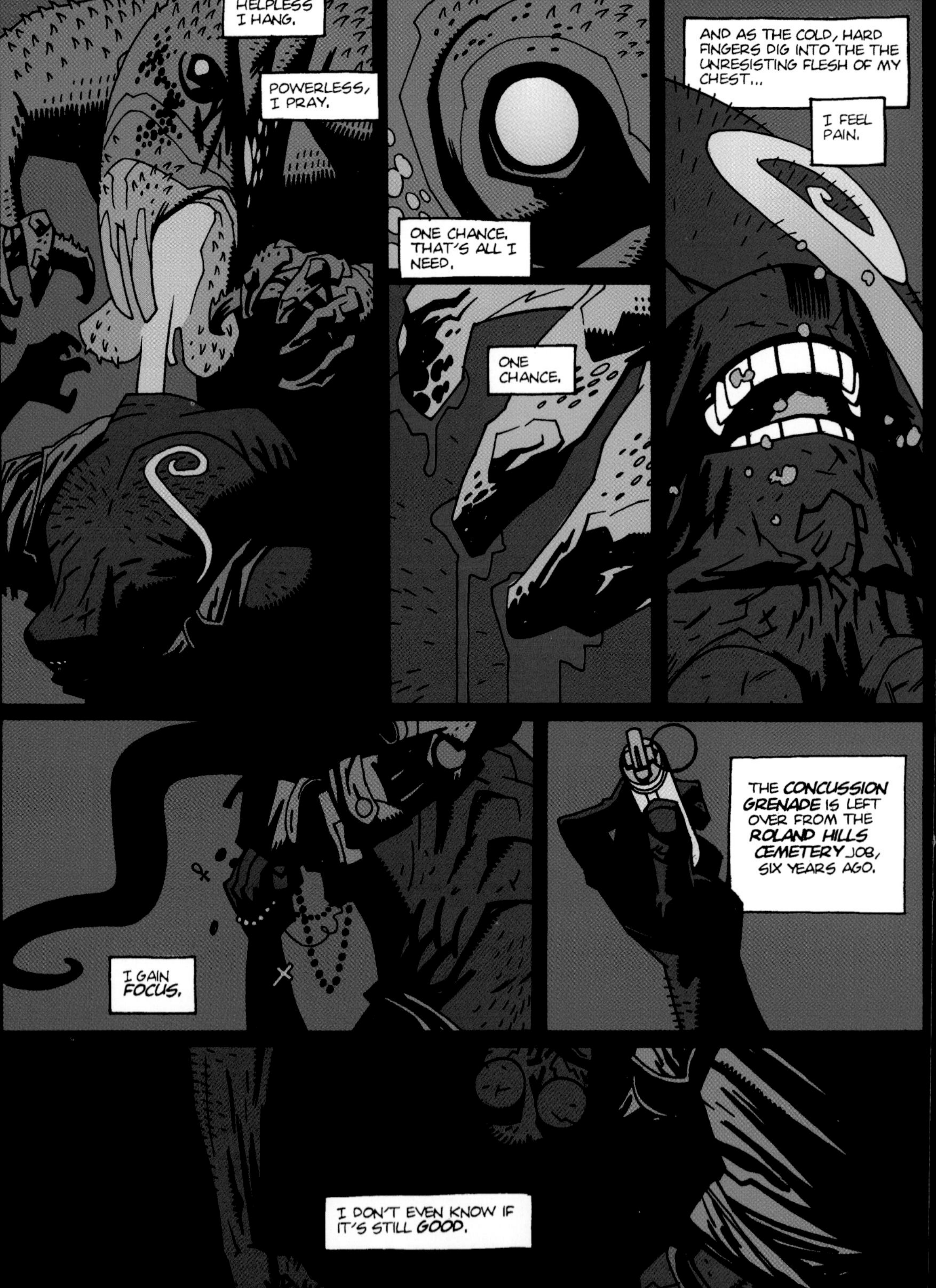
HELPLESS I HANG.
POWERLESS, I PRAY.
ONE CHANCE. THAT'S ALL I NEED.
ONE CHANCE.
AND AS THE COLD, HARD FINGERS DIG INTO THE THE UNRESISTING FLESH OF MY CHEST...
I FEEL PAIN.
I GAIN FOCUS.
THE CONCUSSION GRENADE IS LEFT OVER FROM THE ROLAND HILLS CEMETERY JOB, SIX YEARS AGO.
I DON'T EVEN KNOW IF IT'S STILL GOOD.

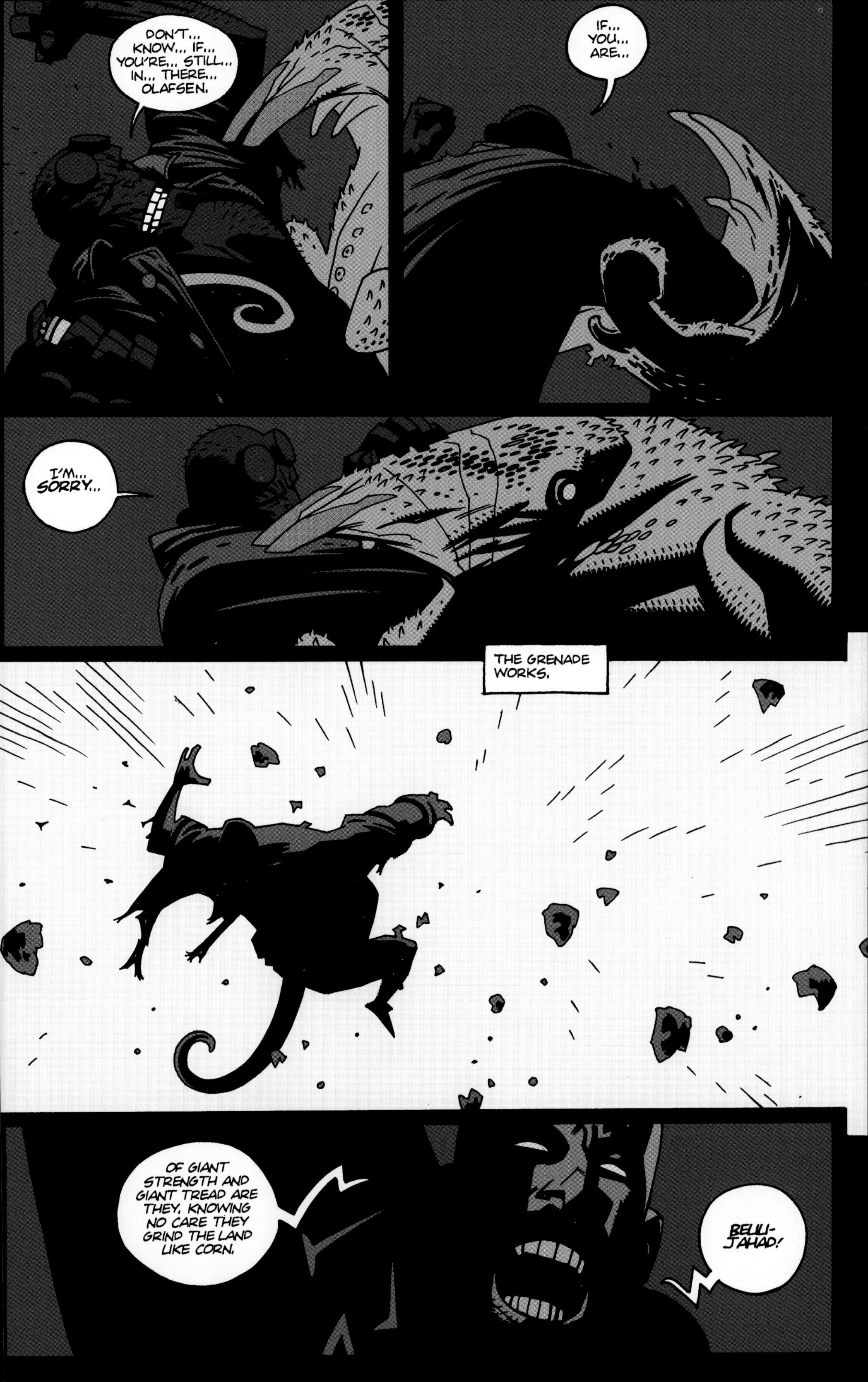
DON'T... KNOW... IF... YOU'RE... STILL... IN... THERE... OLAFSEN.
IF... YOU... ARE...
I'M... SORRY...
THE GRENADE WORKS.
OF GIANT STRENGTH AND GIANT TREAD ARE THEY, KNOWING NO CARE THEY GRIND THE LAND LIKE CORN.
BELILI-JAHAD!

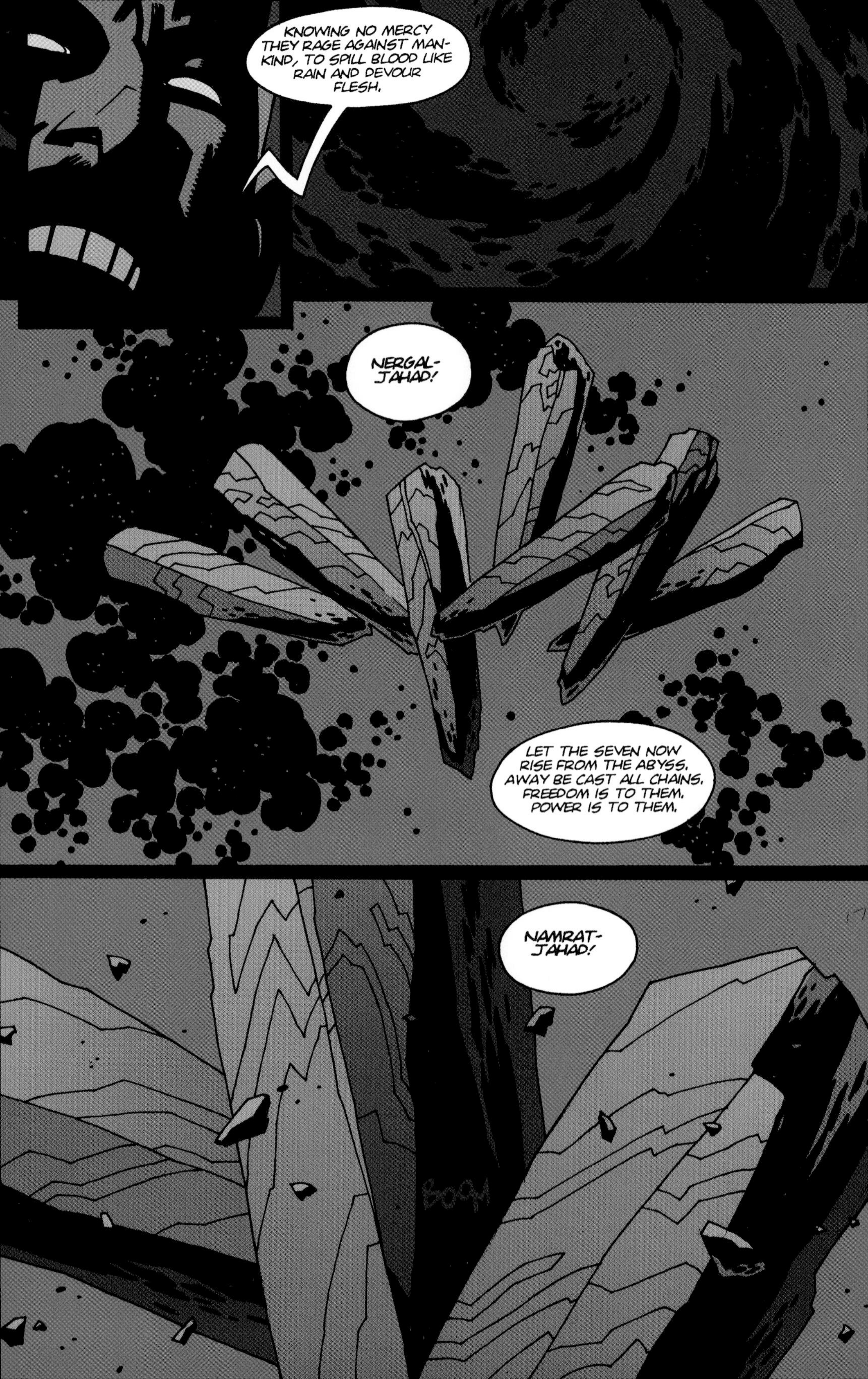
KNOWING NO MERCY THEY RAGE AGAINST MAN-KIND, TO SPILL BLOOD LIKE RAIN AND DEVOUR FLESH.
NERGAL-JAHAD!
LET THE SEVEN NOW RISE FROM THE ABYSS. AWAY BE CAST ALL CHAINS. FREEDOM IS TO THEM. POWER IS TO THEM.
NAMRAT-JAHAD!
BOOM

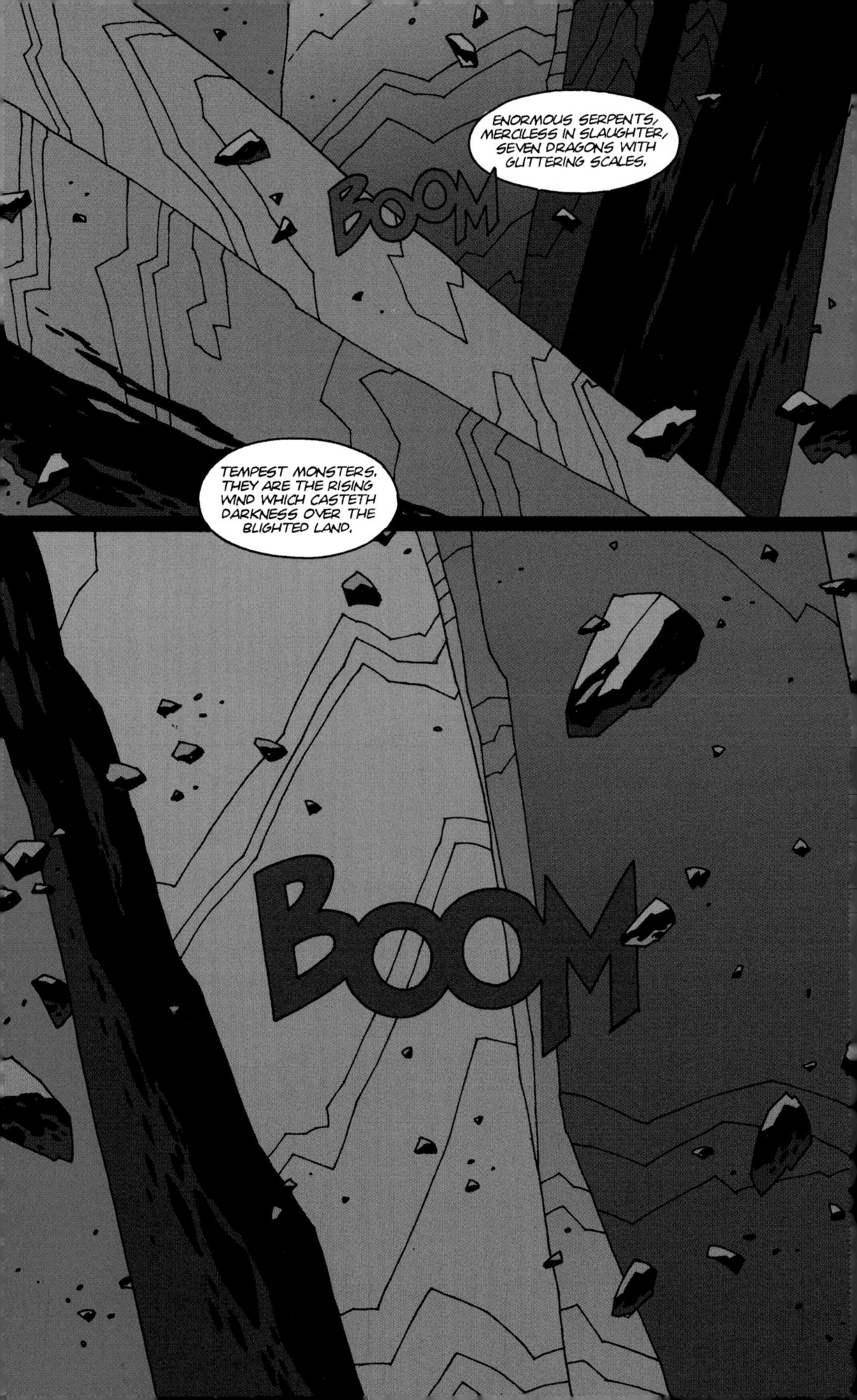
ENORMOUS SERPENTS, MERCILESS IN SLAUGHTER, SEVEN DRAGONS WITH GLITTERING SCALES.
BOOM
TEMPEST MONSTERS. THEY ARE THE RISING WIND WHICH CASTETH DARKNESS OVER THE BLIGHTED LAND.
BOOM

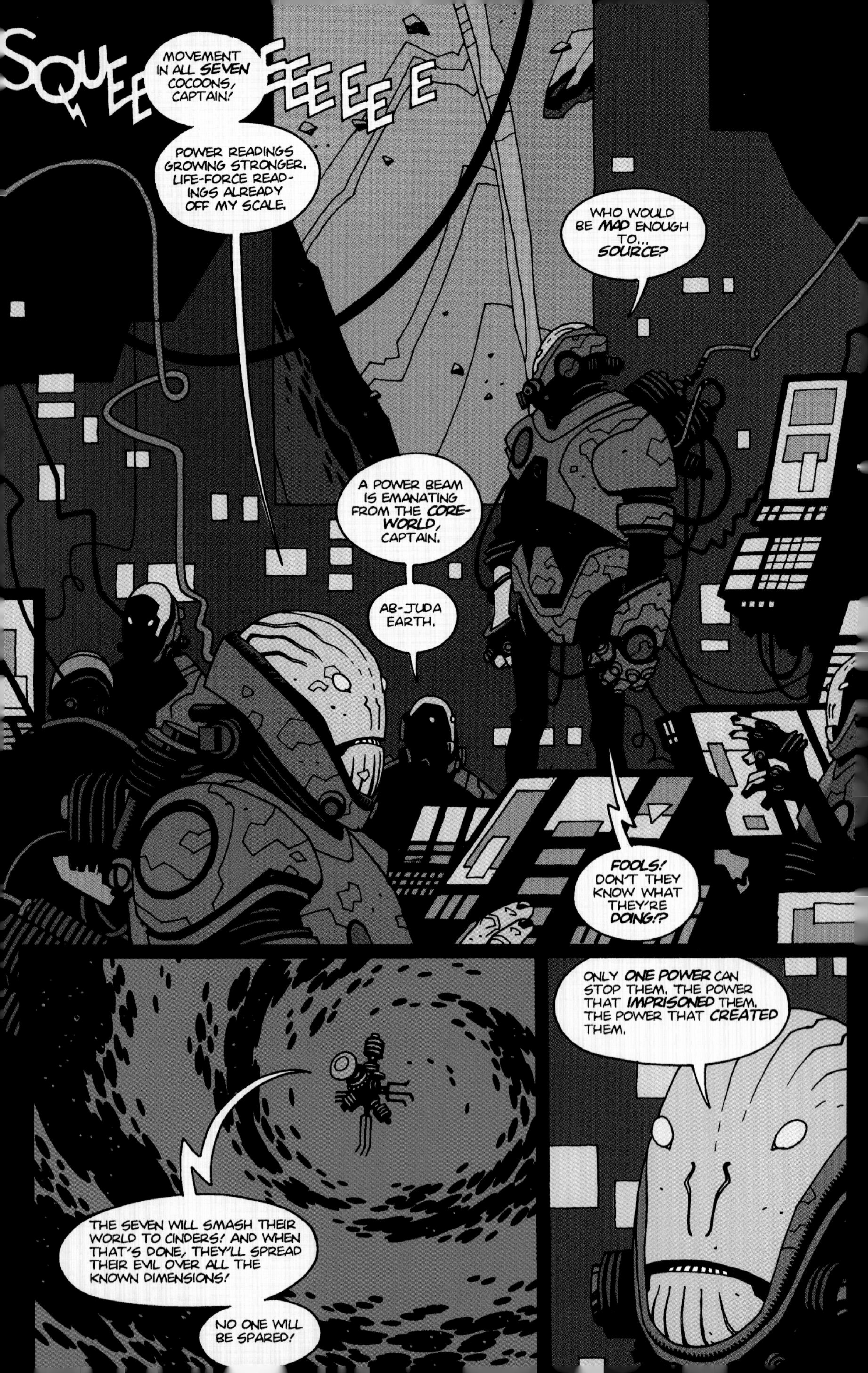
SQUEEEEEEEEEE
MOVEMENT IN ALL SEVEN COCOONS, CAPTAIN!
POWER READINGS GROWING STRONGER. LIFE-FORCE READ-INGS ALREADY OFF MY SCALE.
WHO WOULD BE MAD ENOUGH TO... SOURCE?
A POWER BEAM IS EMANATING FROM THE CORE-WORLD, CAPTAIN.
AB-JUDA EARTH.
FOOLS! DON'T THEY KNOW WHAT THEY'RE DOING!?
THE SEVEN WILL SMASH THEIR WORLD TO CINDERS! AND WHEN THAT'S DONE, THEY'LL SPREAD THEIR EVIL OVER ALL THE KNOWN DIMENSIONS!
NO ONE WILL BE SPARED!
ONLY ONE POWER CAN STOP THEM. THE POWER THAT IMPRISONED THEM. THE POWER THAT CREATED THEM.

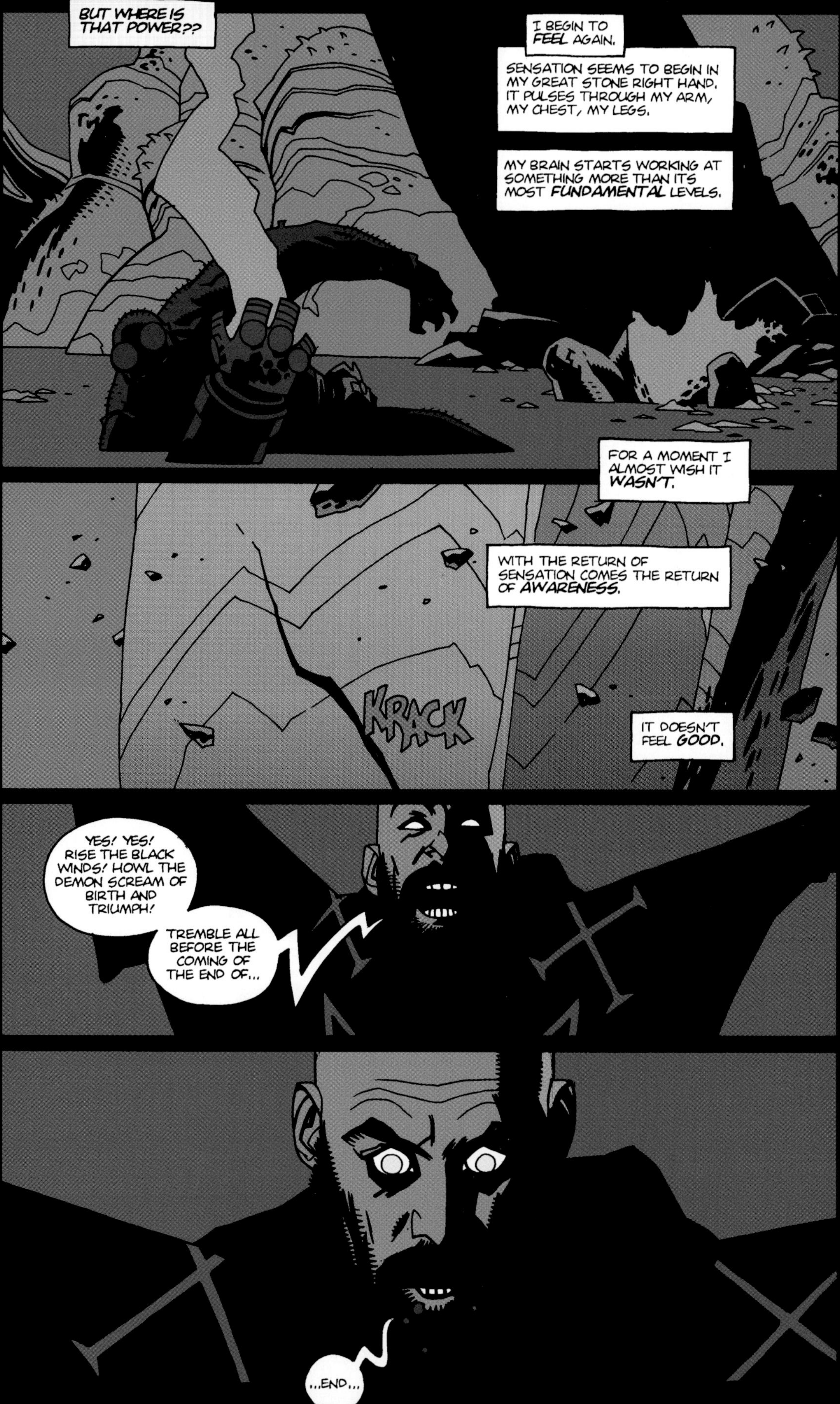
BUT WHERE IS THAT POWER??
I BEGIN TO FEEL AGAIN.
SENSATION SEEMS TO BEGIN IN MY GREAT STONE RIGHT HAND. IT PULSES THROUGH MY ARM, MY CHEST, MY LEGS.
MY BRAIN STARTS WORKING AT SOMETHING MORE THAN ITS MOST FUNDAMENTAL LEVELS.
FOR A MOMENT I ALMOST WISH IT WASN'T.
WITH THE RETURN OF SENSATION COMES THE RETURN OF AWARENESS.
KRACK
IT DOESN'T FEEL GOOD.
YES! YES! RISE THE BLACK WINDS! HOWL THE DEMON SCREAM OF BIRTH AND TRIUMPH!
TREMBLE ALL BEFORE THE COMING OF THE END OF...
...END...

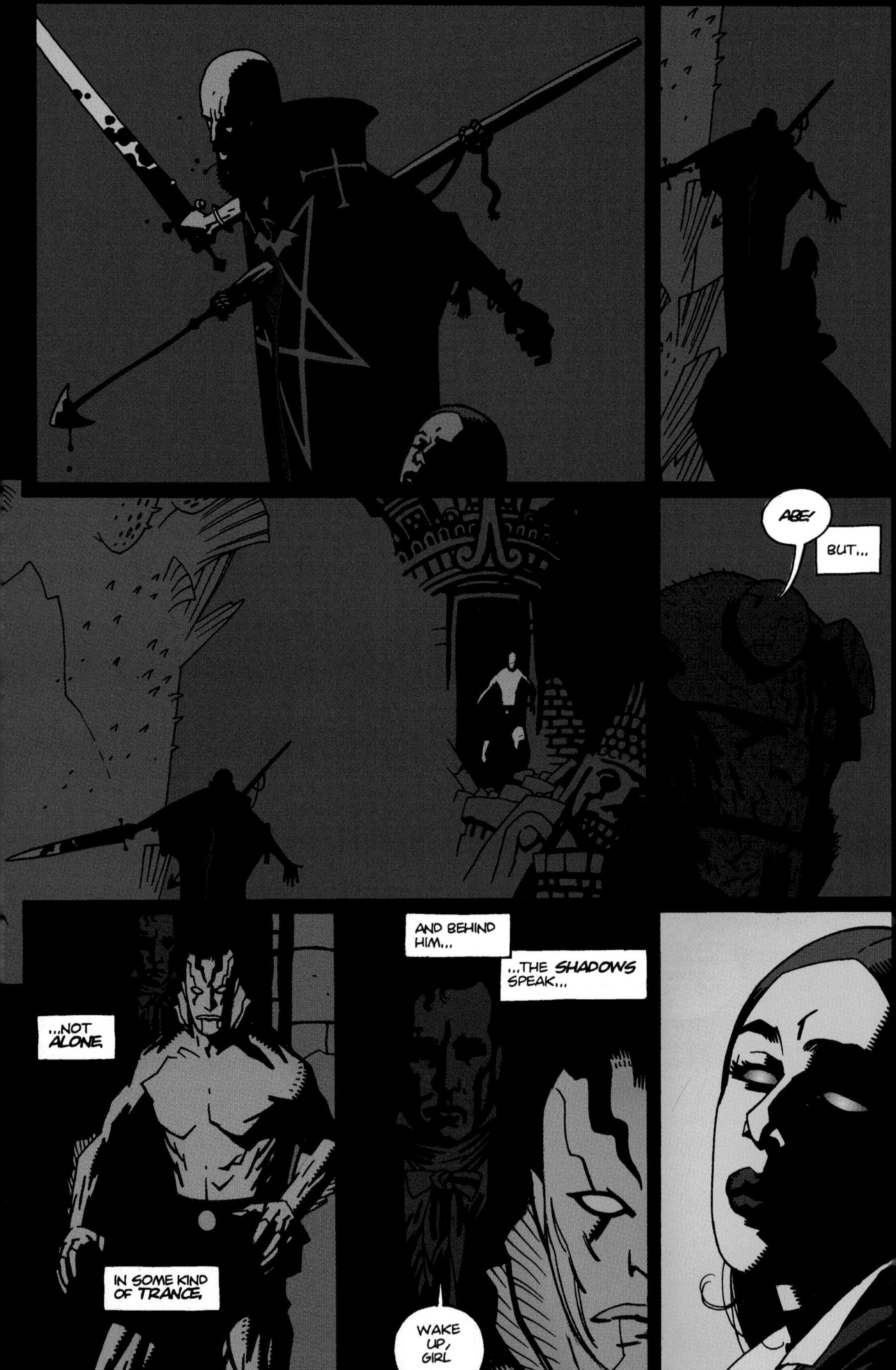
ABE!
BUT...
...NOT ALONE.
IN SOME KIND OF TRANCE.
AND BEHIND HIM...
...THE SHADOWS SPEAK...
WAKE UP, GIRL

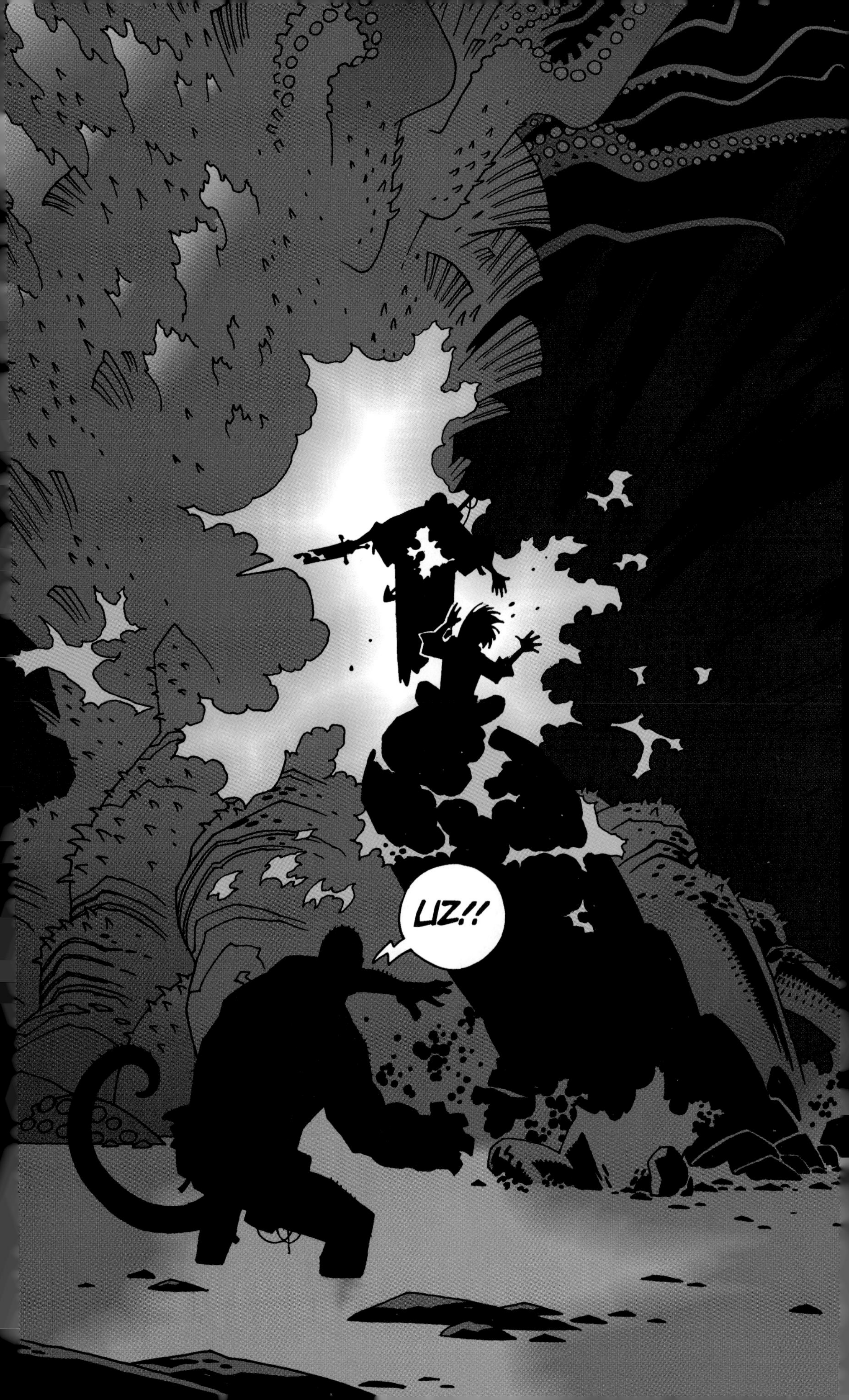
LIZ!!

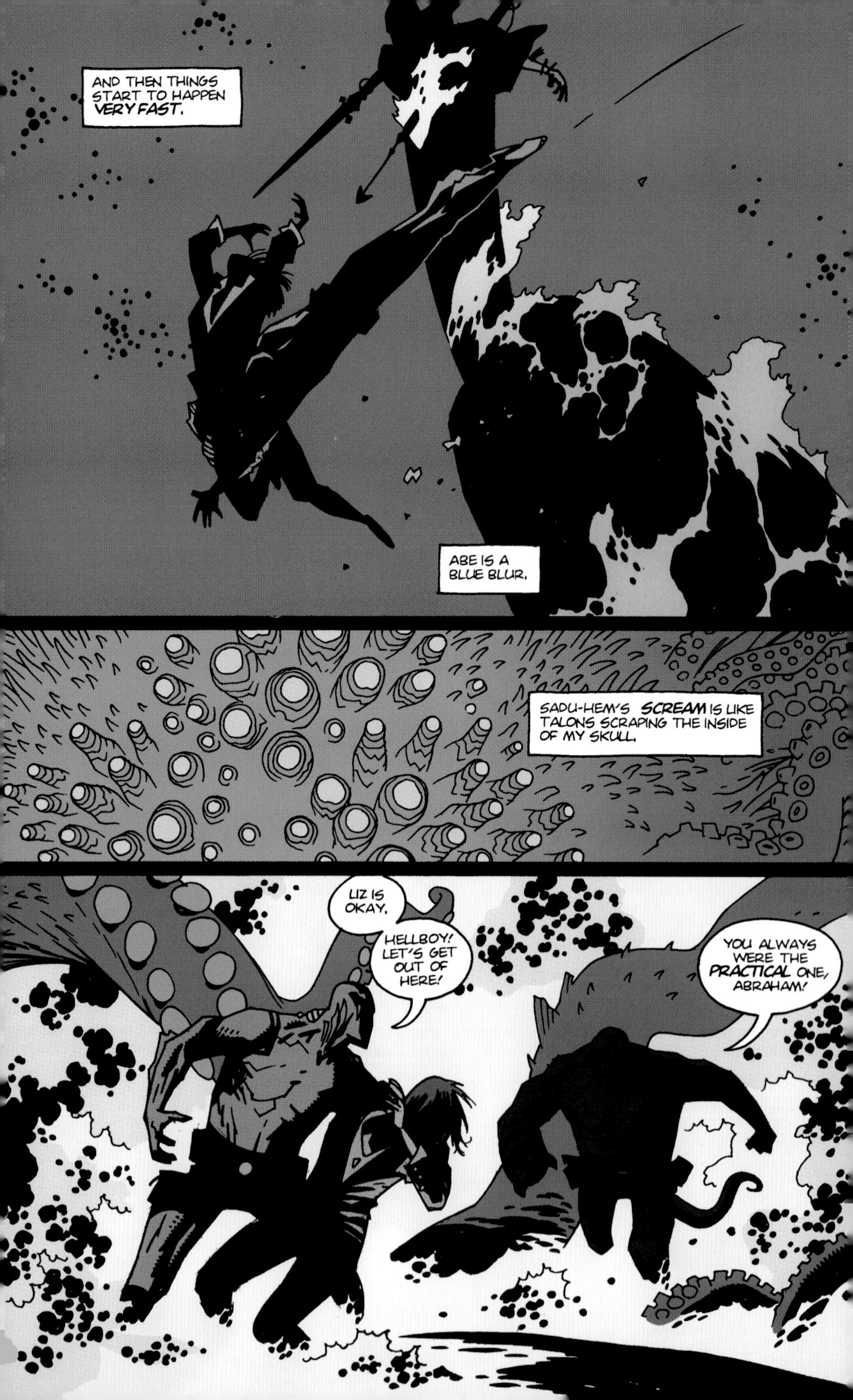
AND THEN THINGS START TO HAPPEN VERY FAST.
ABE IS A BLUE BLUR.
SADU-HEM'S SCREAM IS LIKE TALONS SCRAPING THE INSIDE OF MY SKULL.
LIZ IS OKAY.
HELLBOY! LET'S GET OUT OF HERE!
YOU ALWAYS WERE THE PRACTICAL ONE, ABRAHAM!

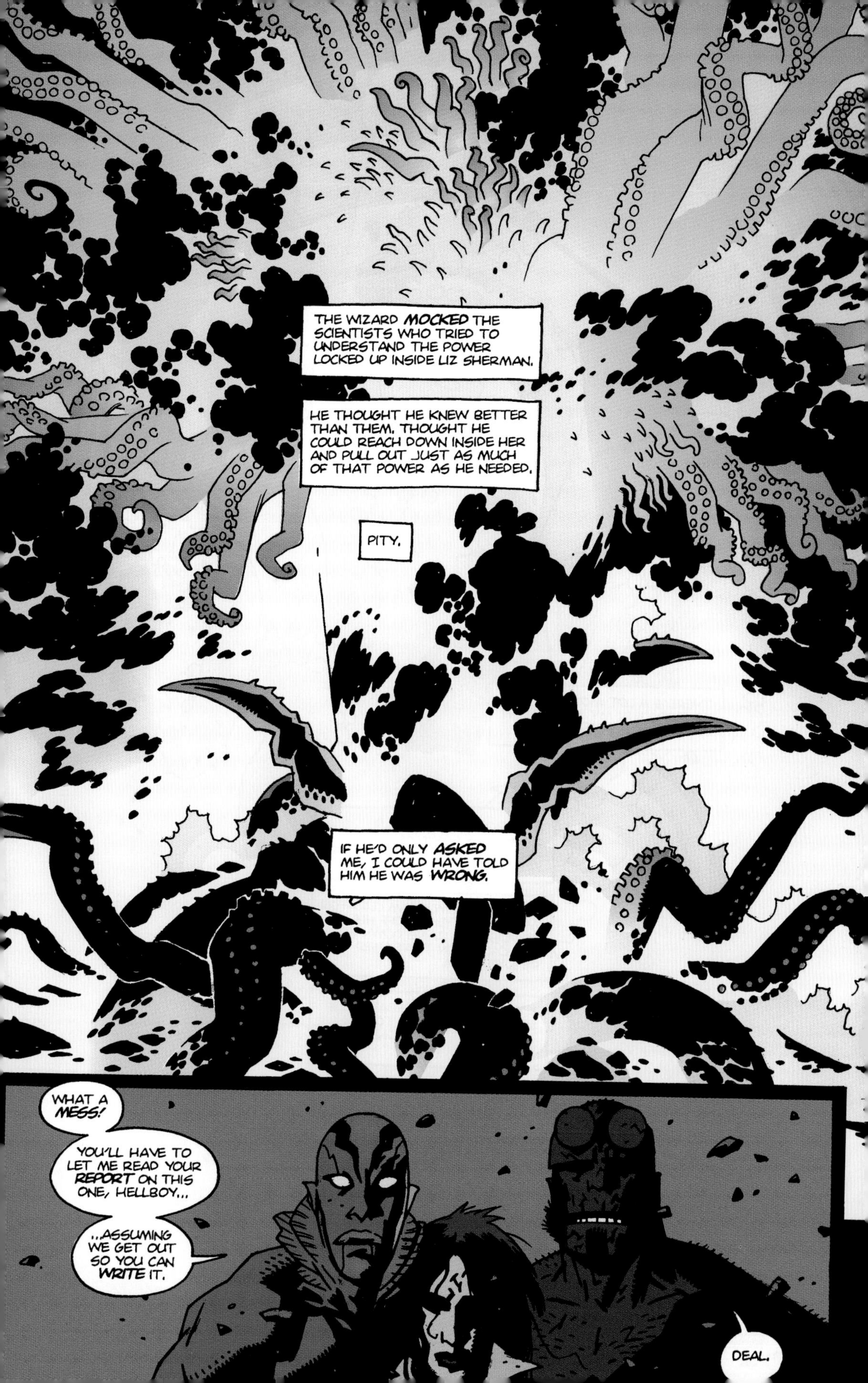
THE WIZARD MOCKED THE SCIENTISTS WHO TRIED TO UNDERSTAND THE POWER LOCKED UP INSIDE LIZ SHERMAN.
HE THOUGHT HE KNEW BETTER THAN THEM. THOUGHT HE COULD REACH DOWN INSIDE HER AND PULL OUT JUST AS MUCH OF THAT POWER AS HE NEEDED.
PITY.
IF HE'D ONLY ASKED ME, I COULD HAVE TOLD HIM HE WAS WRONG.
WHAT A MESS!
YOU'LL HAVE TO LET ME READ YOUR REPORT ON THIS ONE, HELLBOY...
...ASSUMING WE GET OUT SO YOU CAN WRITE IT.
DEAL.

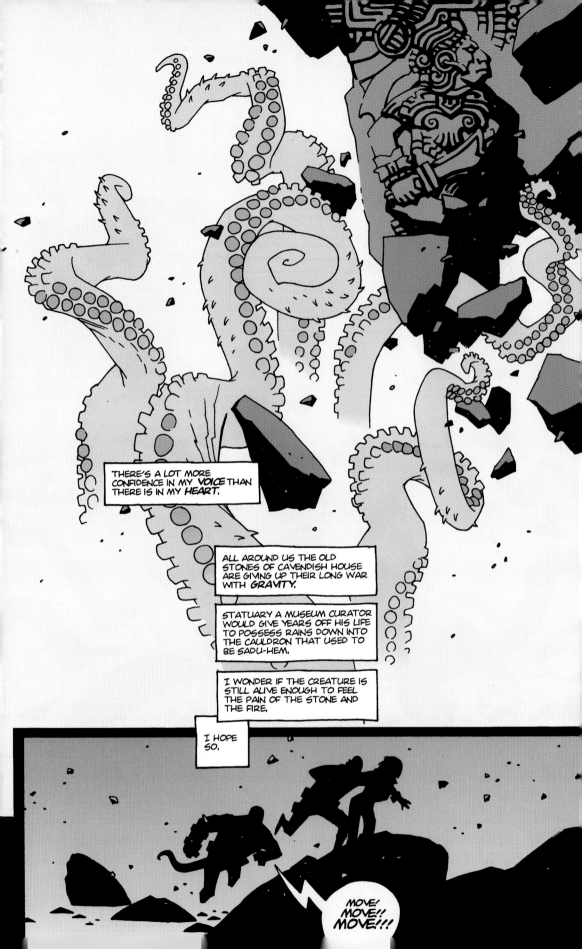

THERE'S A LOT MORE CONFIDENCE IN MY **VOICE** THAN THERE IS IN MY **HEART.**

ALL AROUND US THE OLD STONES OF CAVENDISH HOUSE ARE GIVING UP THEIR LONG WAR WITH **GRAVITY.**

STATUARY A MUSEUM CURATOR WOULD GIVE YEARS OFF HIS LIFE TO POSSESS RAINS DOWN INTO THE CAULDRON THAT USED TO BE SADU-HEM.

I WONDER IF THE CREATURE IS STILL ALIVE ENOUGH TO FEEL THE PAIN OF THE STONE AND THE FIRE.

I HOPE SO.

MOVE! MOVE!! MOVE!!!

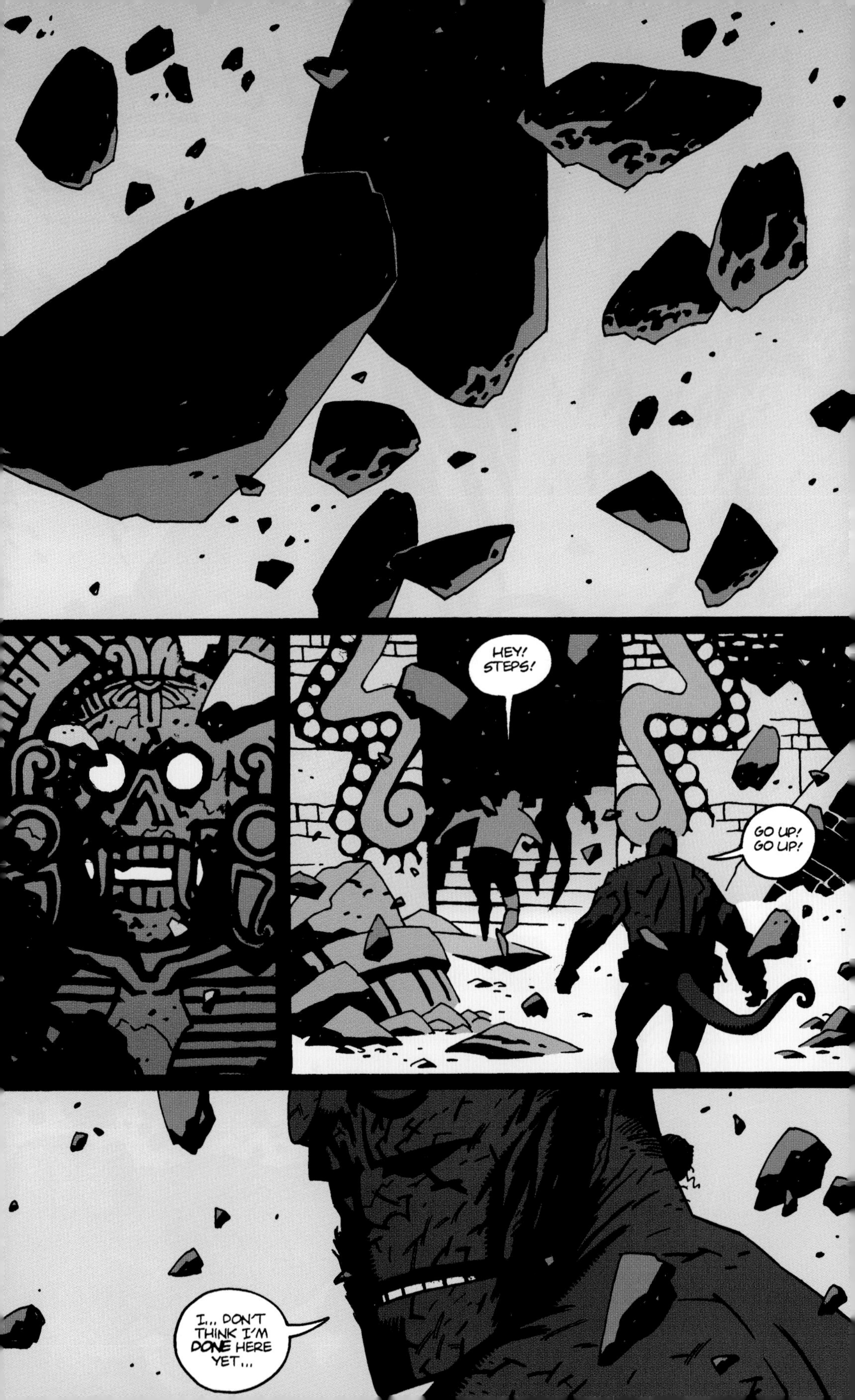
HEY! STEPS!
GO UP! GO UP!
I... DON'T THINK I'M **DONE** HERE YET...

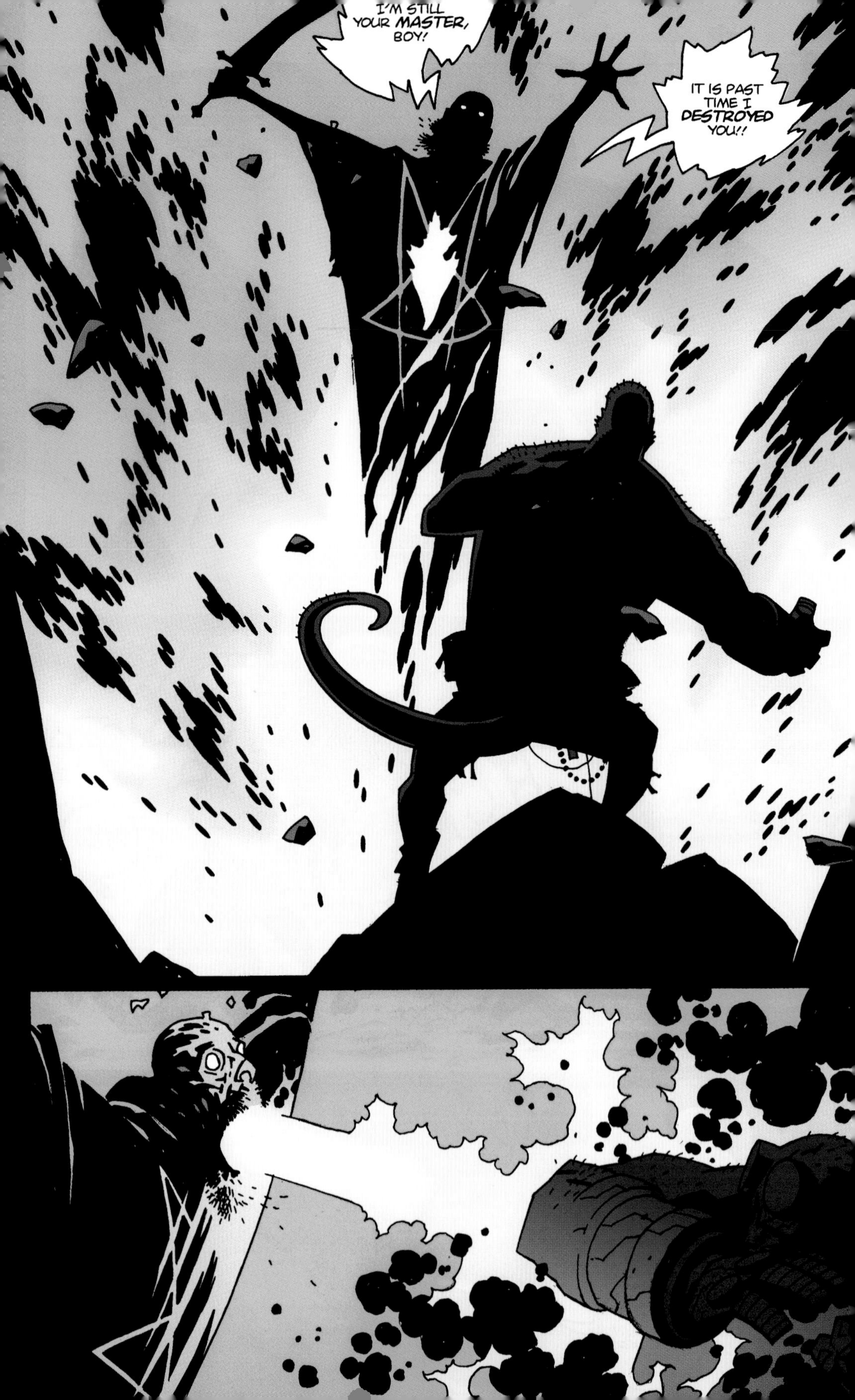
I'M STILL YOUR MASTER, BOY!
IT IS PAST TIME I DESTROYED YOU!!

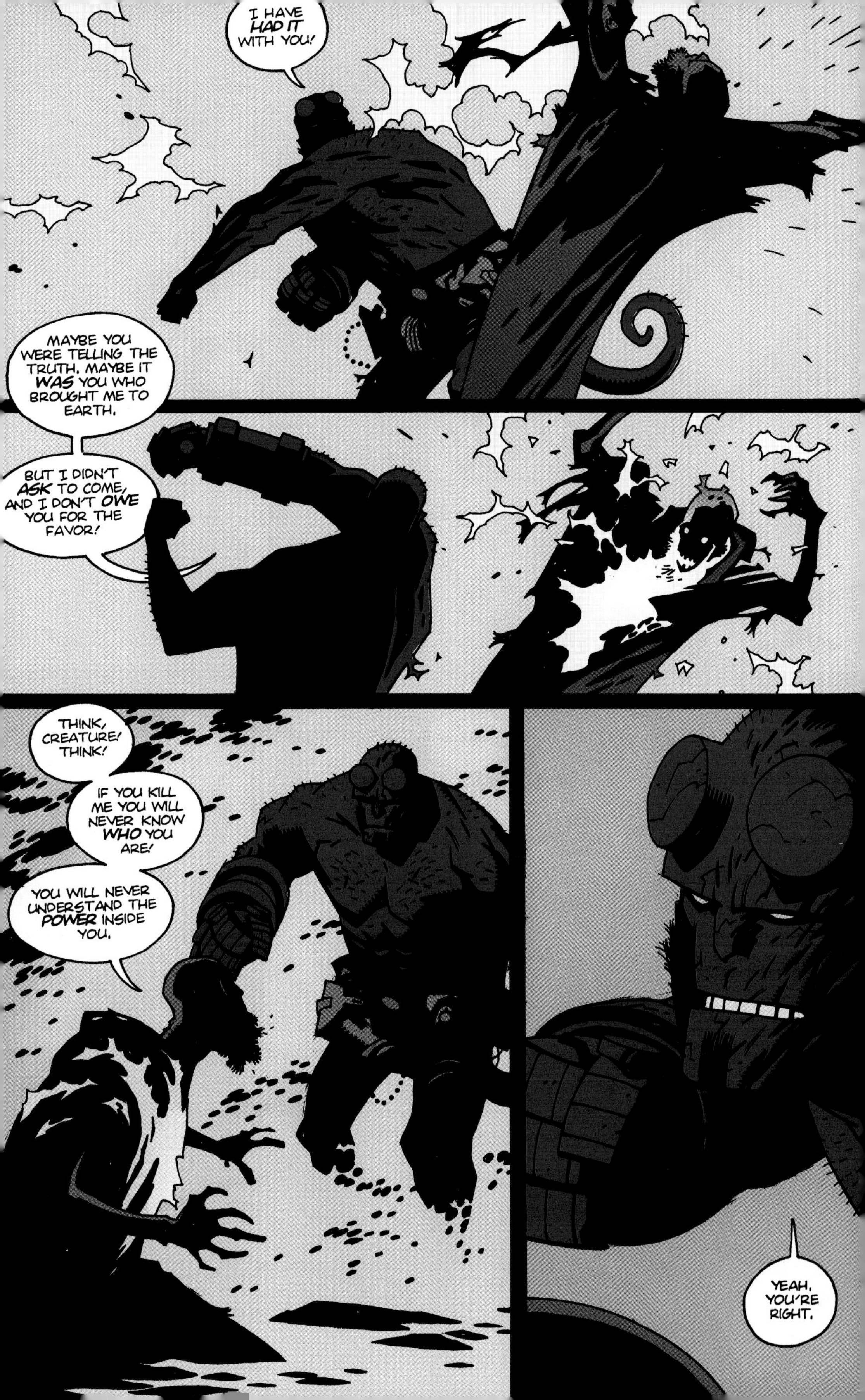
I HAVE HAD IT WITH YOU!
MAYBE YOU WERE TELLING THE TRUTH. MAYBE IT WAS YOU WHO BROUGHT ME TO EARTH.
BUT I DIDN'T ASK TO COME, AND I DON'T OWE YOU FOR THE FAVOR!
THINK, CREATURE! THINK!
IF YOU KILL ME YOU WILL NEVER KNOW WHO YOU ARE!
YOU WILL NEVER UNDERSTAND THE POWER INSIDE YOU.
YEAH, YOU'RE RIGHT.

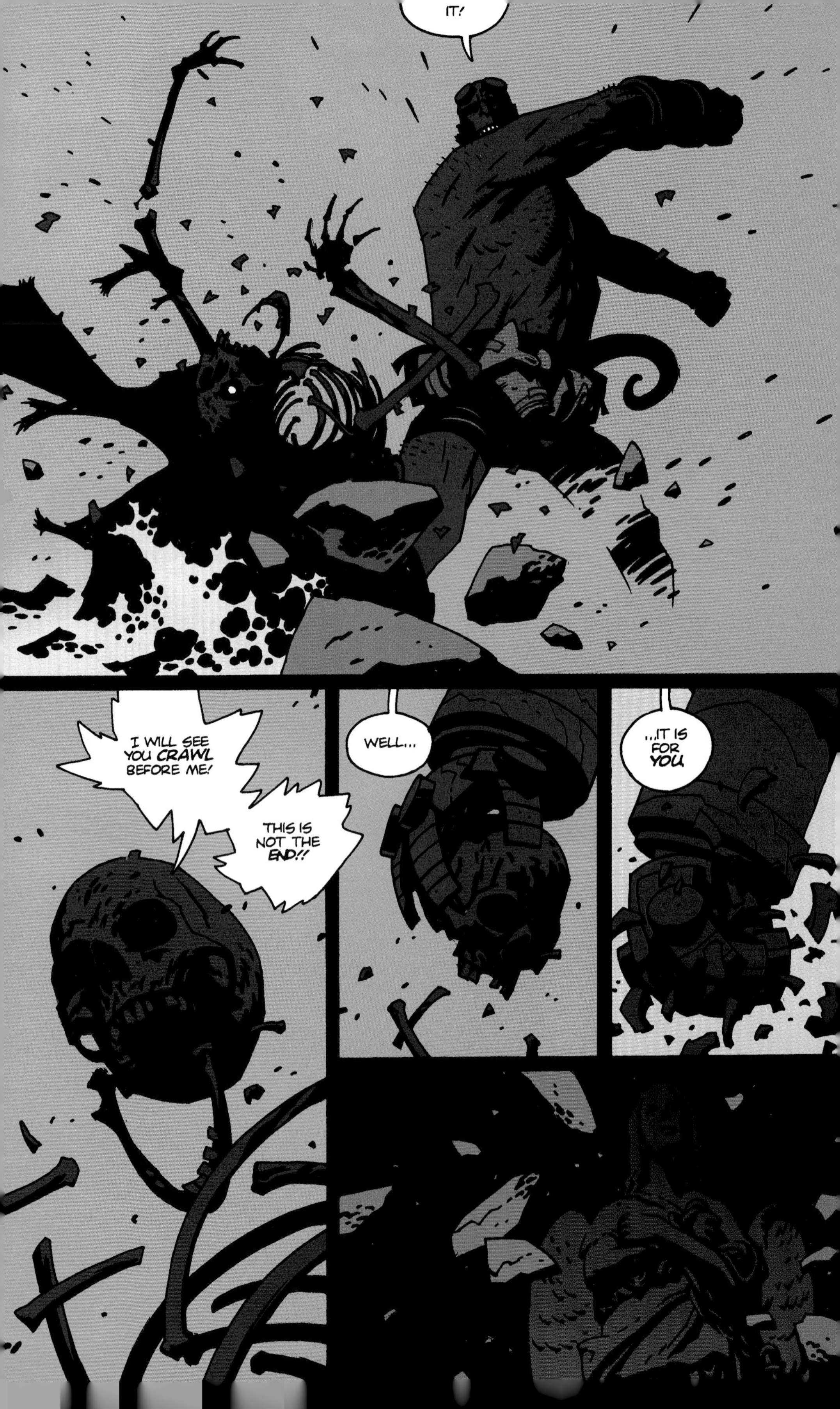
IT!
I WILL SEE YOU CRAWL BEFORE ME!
THIS IS NOT THE END!!
WELL...
...IT IS FOR YOU

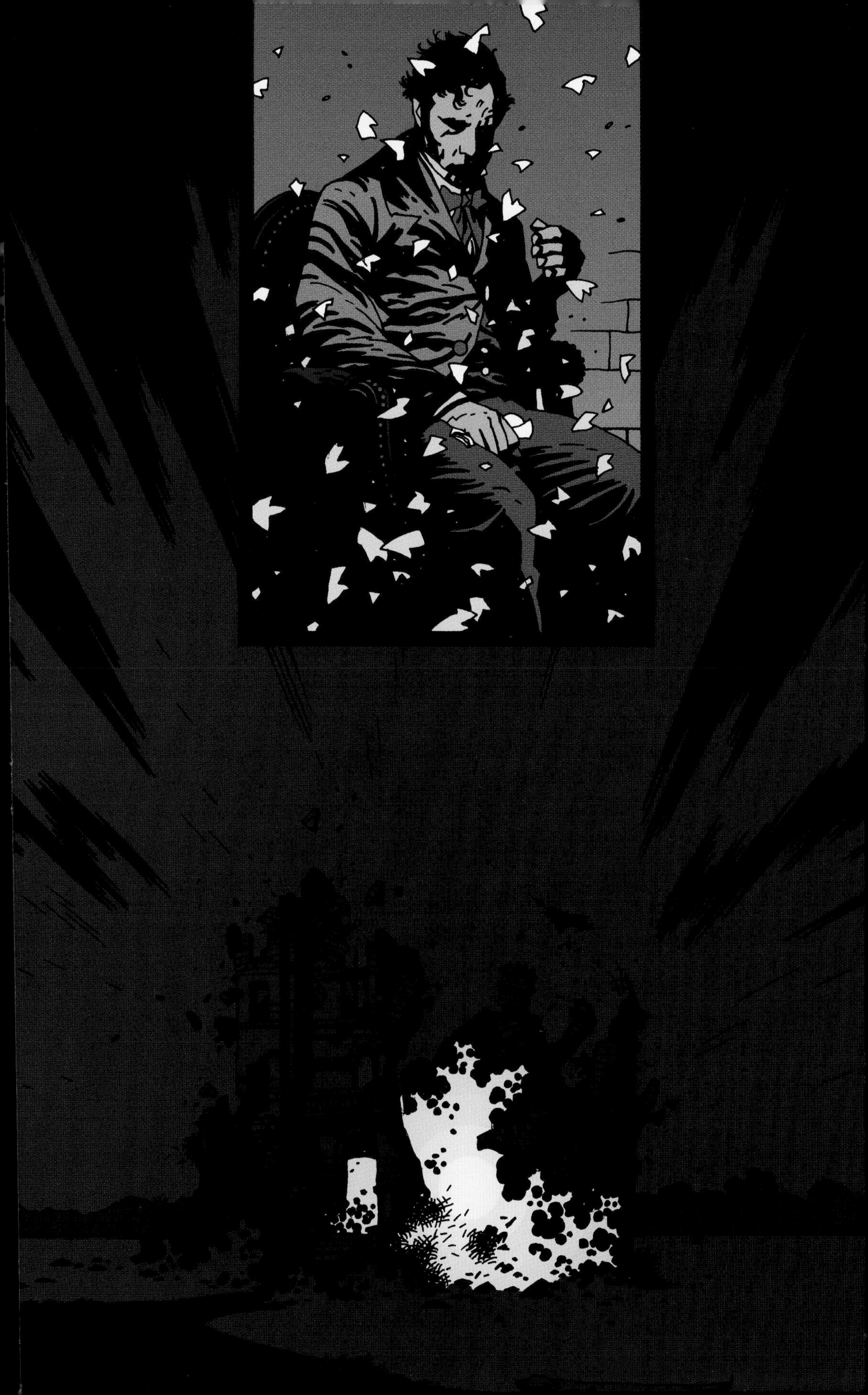

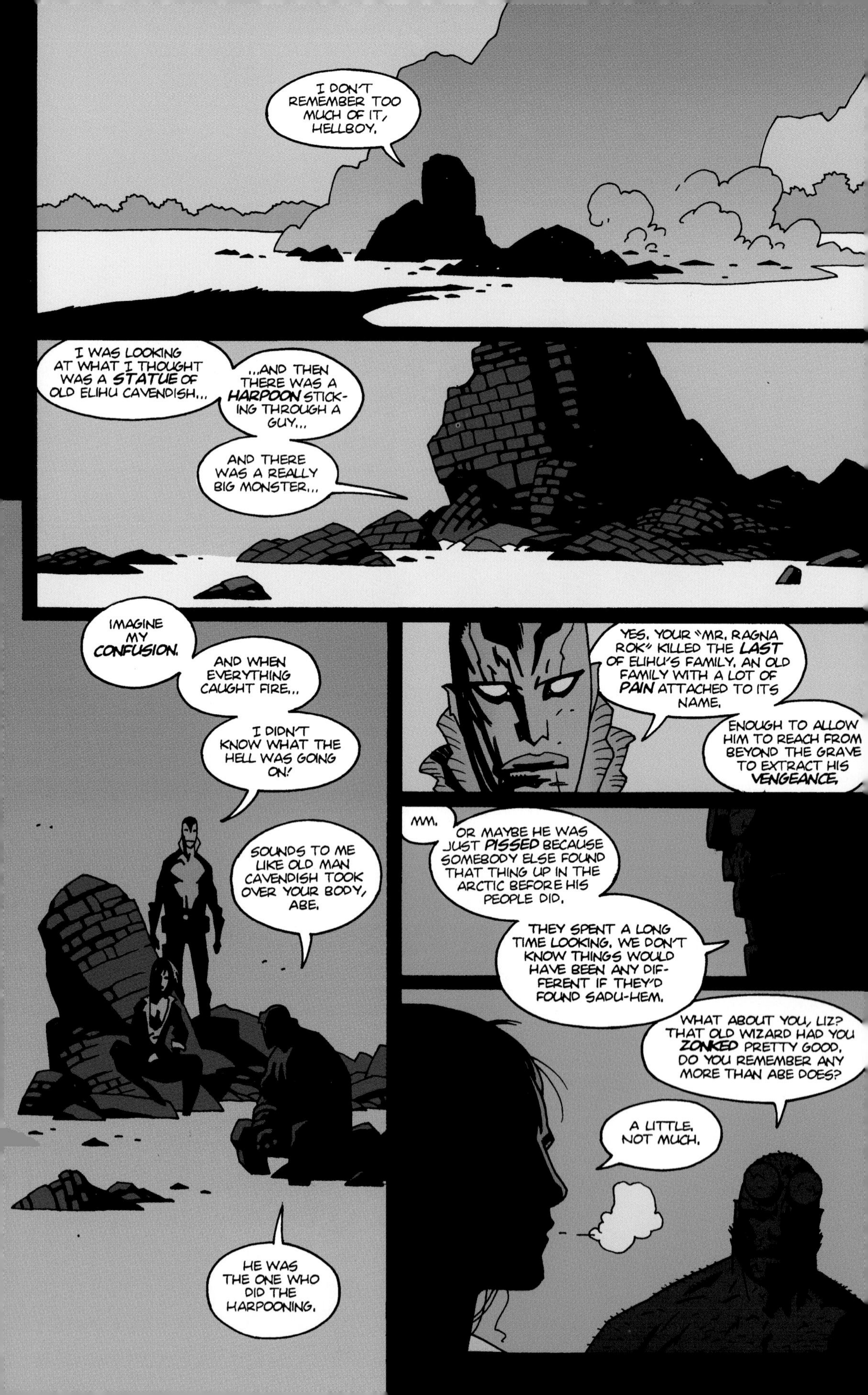

I DON'T REMEMBER TOO MUCH OF IT, HELLBOY.
I WAS LOOKING AT WHAT I THOUGHT WAS A STATUE OF OLD ELIHU CAVENDISH...
...AND THEN THERE WAS A HARPOON STICKING THROUGH A GUY...
AND THERE WAS A REALLY BIG MONSTER...
IMAGINE MY CONFUSION.
AND WHEN EVERYTHING CAUGHT FIRE...
I DIDN'T KNOW WHAT THE HELL WAS GOING ON!
SOUNDS TO ME LIKE OLD MAN CAVENDISH TOOK OVER YOUR BODY, ABE.
HE WAS THE ONE WHO DID THE HARPOONING.
YES. YOUR "MR. RAGNA ROK" KILLED THE LAST OF ELIHU'S FAMILY. AN OLD FAMILY WITH A LOT OF PAIN ATTACHED TO ITS NAME.
ENOUGH TO ALLOW HIM TO REACH FROM BEYOND THE GRAVE TO EXTRACT HIS VENGEANCE.
MM.
OR MAYBE HE WAS JUST PISSED BECAUSE SOMEBODY ELSE FOUND THAT THING UP IN THE ARCTIC BEFORE HIS PEOPLE DID.
THEY SPENT A LONG TIME LOOKING. WE DON'T KNOW THINGS WOULD HAVE BEEN ANY DIFFERENT IF THEY'D FOUND SADU-HEM.
WHAT ABOUT YOU, LIZ? THAT OLD WIZARD HAD YOU ZONKED PRETTY GOOD. DO YOU REMEMBER ANY MORE THAN ABE DOES?
A LITTLE. NOT MUCH.

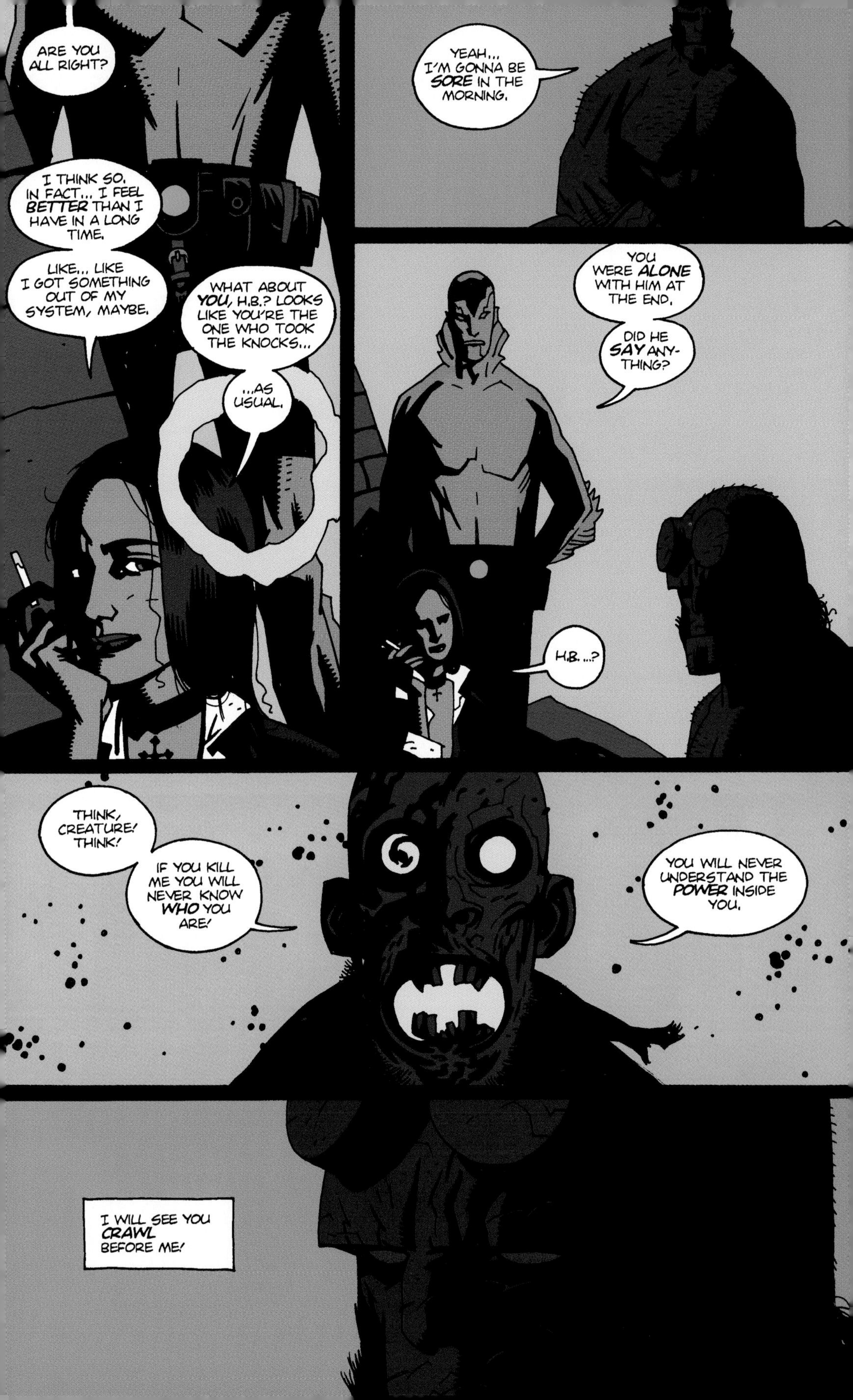
ARE YOU ALL RIGHT?
YEAH... I'M GONNA BE SORE IN THE MORNING.
I THINK SO. IN FACT... I FEEL BETTER THAN I HAVE IN A LONG TIME.
LIKE... LIKE I GOT SOMETHING OUT OF MY SYSTEM, MAYBE.
WHAT ABOUT YOU, H.B.? LOOKS LIKE YOU'RE THE ONE WHO TOOK THE KNOCKS...
...AS USUAL.
YOU WERE ALONE WITH HIM AT THE END.
DID HE SAY ANYTHING?
H.B. ...?
THINK, CREATURE! THINK!
IF YOU KILL ME YOU WILL NEVER KNOW WHO YOU ARE!
YOU WILL NEVER UNDERSTAND THE POWER INSIDE YOU.
I WILL SEE YOU CRAWL BEFORE ME!

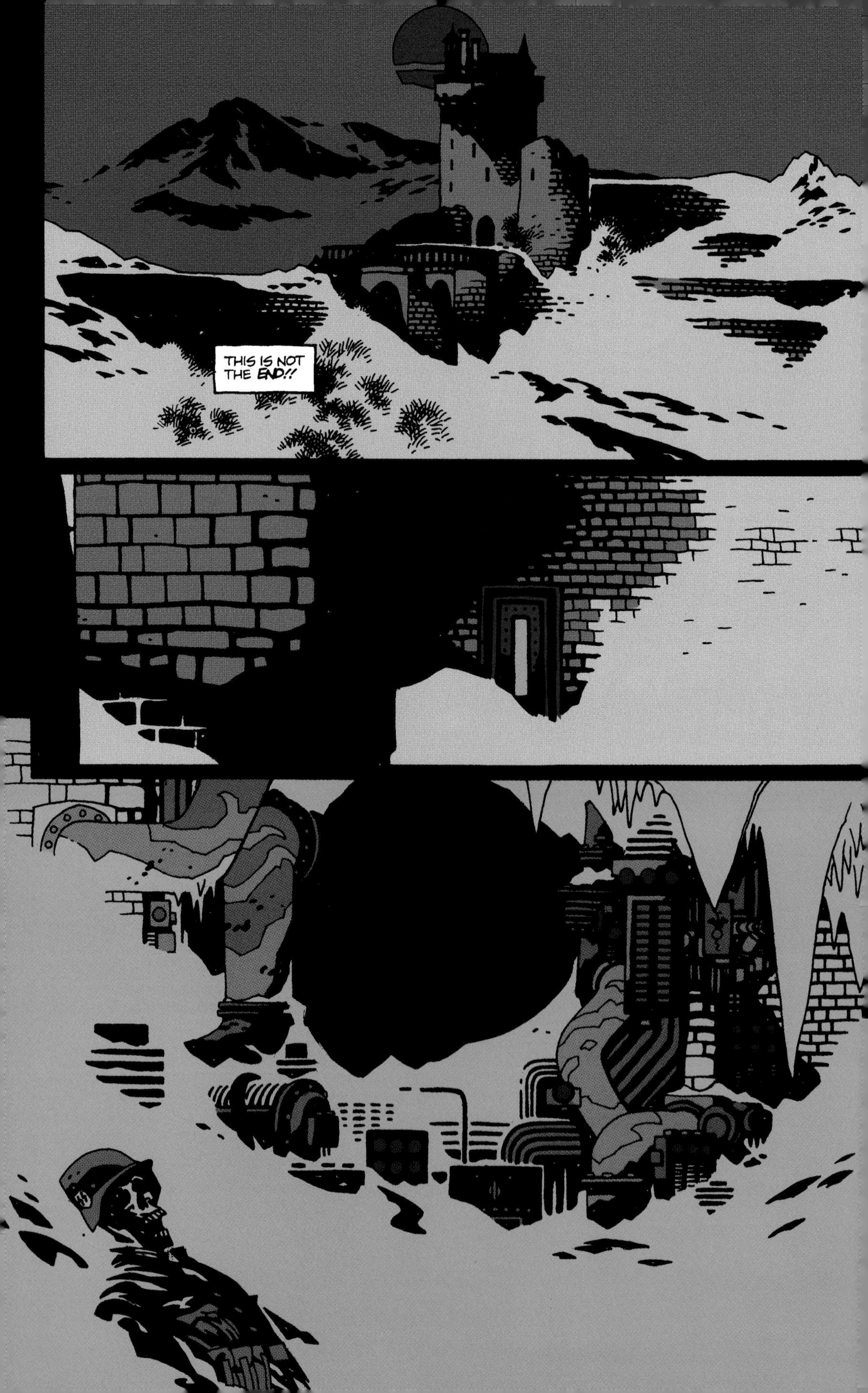
THIS IS NOT THE END!!

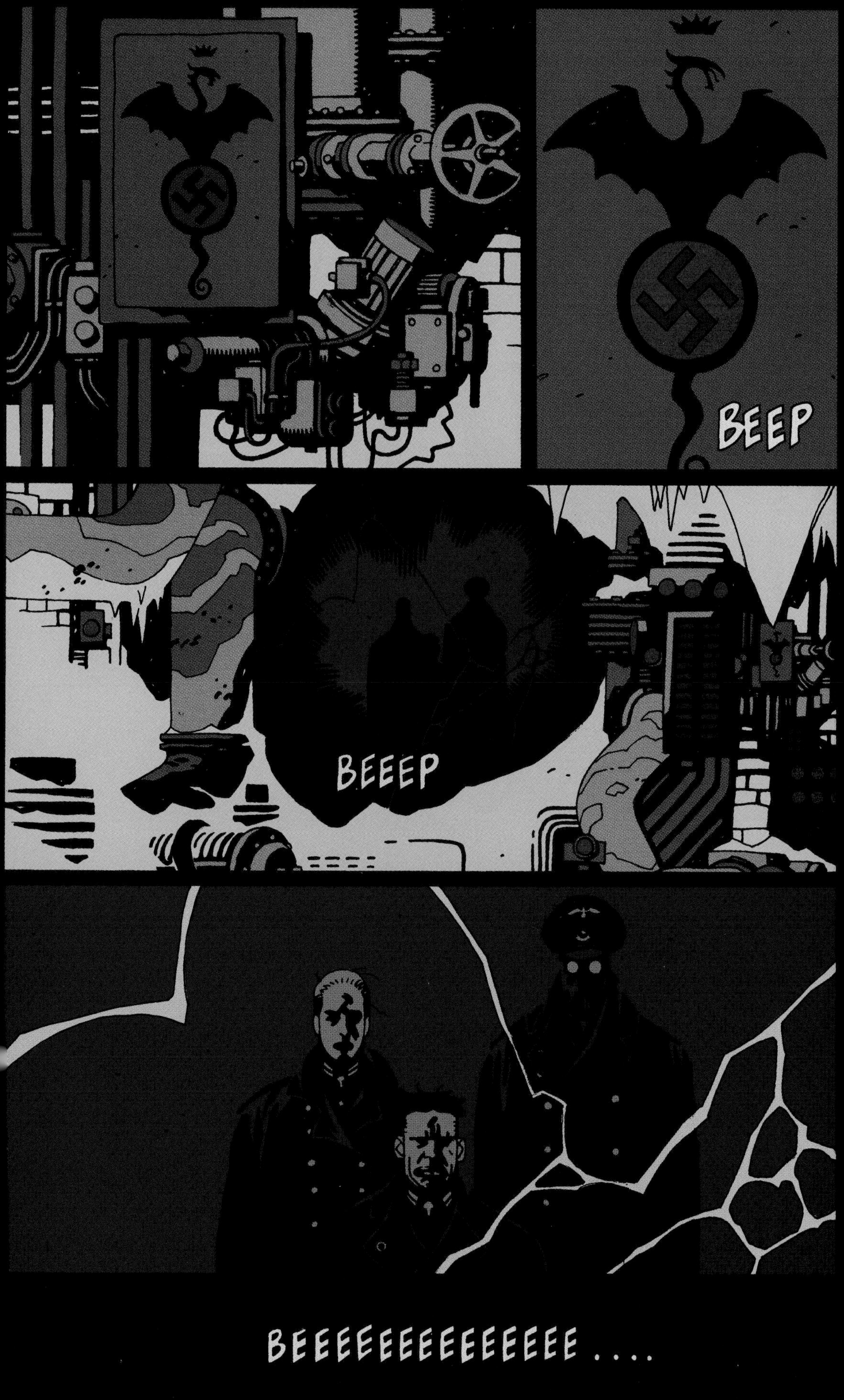
BEEP
BEEEP
BEEEEEEEEEEEEEE ....

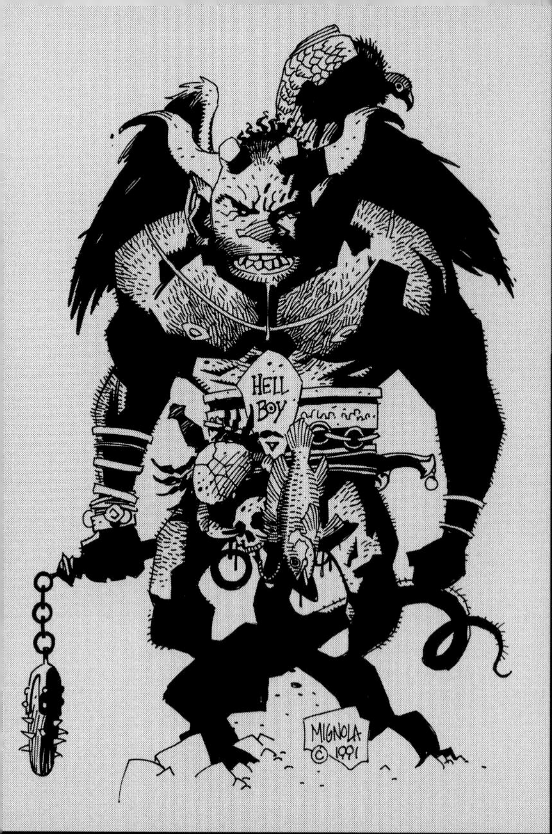
HELL BOY
MIGNOLA © 1991

WHERE THE HELL DID HE COME FROM?

Personal reminiscences by Mike Mignola.

LEFT: This is a drawing done for a convention program book — I added the name Hellboy at the last minute and it made me laugh. The name stuck and the character started to take shape in my head.

BELOW: I first envisioned *Hellboy* as a team book, but I couldn't come up with a name for any of the other characters or the team. Hellboy's in the process of mutating from that first drawing into the guy we know and love today — look at the size of his neck!

RIGHT: Hellboy in his final form. I originally intended this piece to be a promotional poster for the first *Hellboy* miniseries but I wasn't happy with Hellboy's right hand.

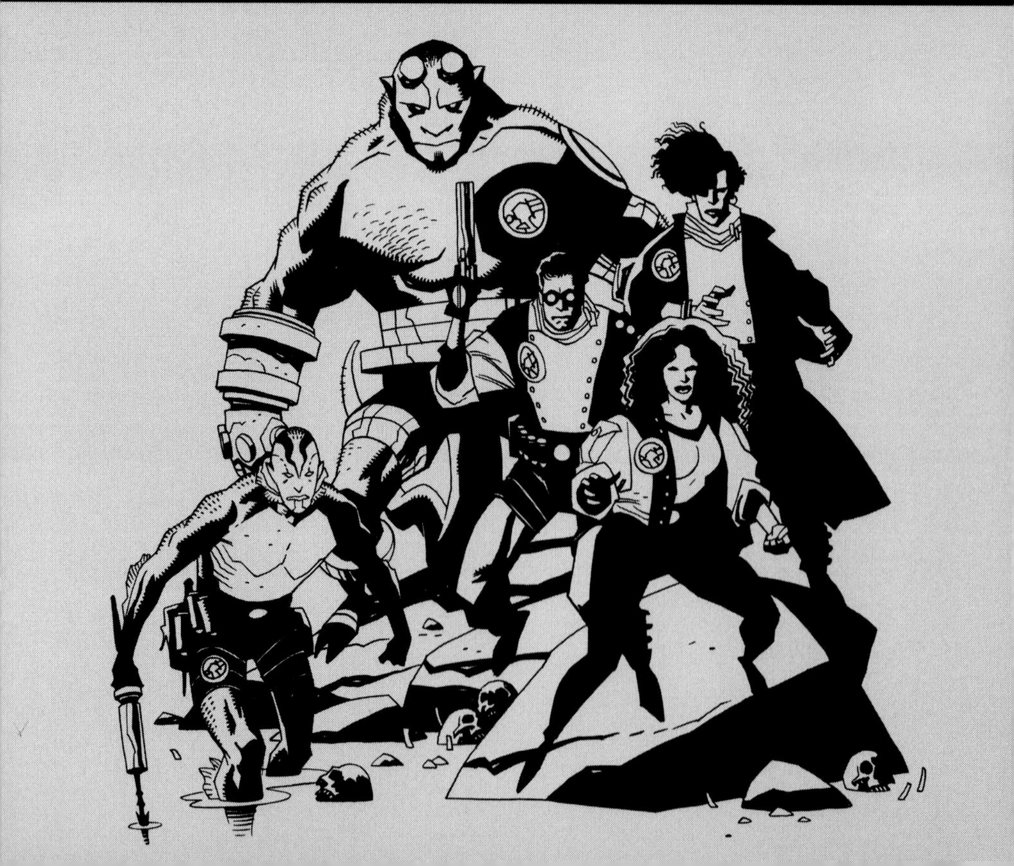

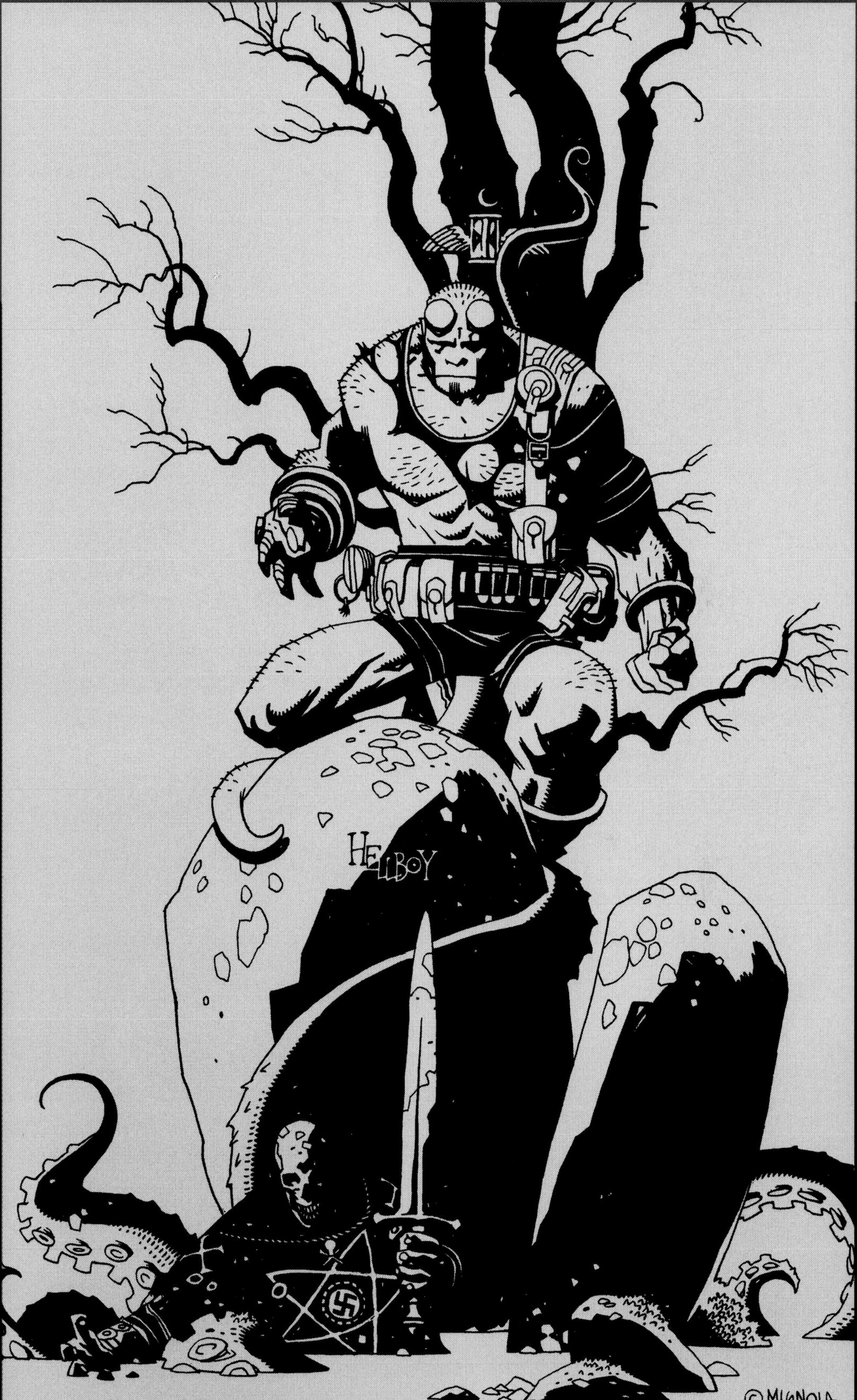
©MIGNOLA
93

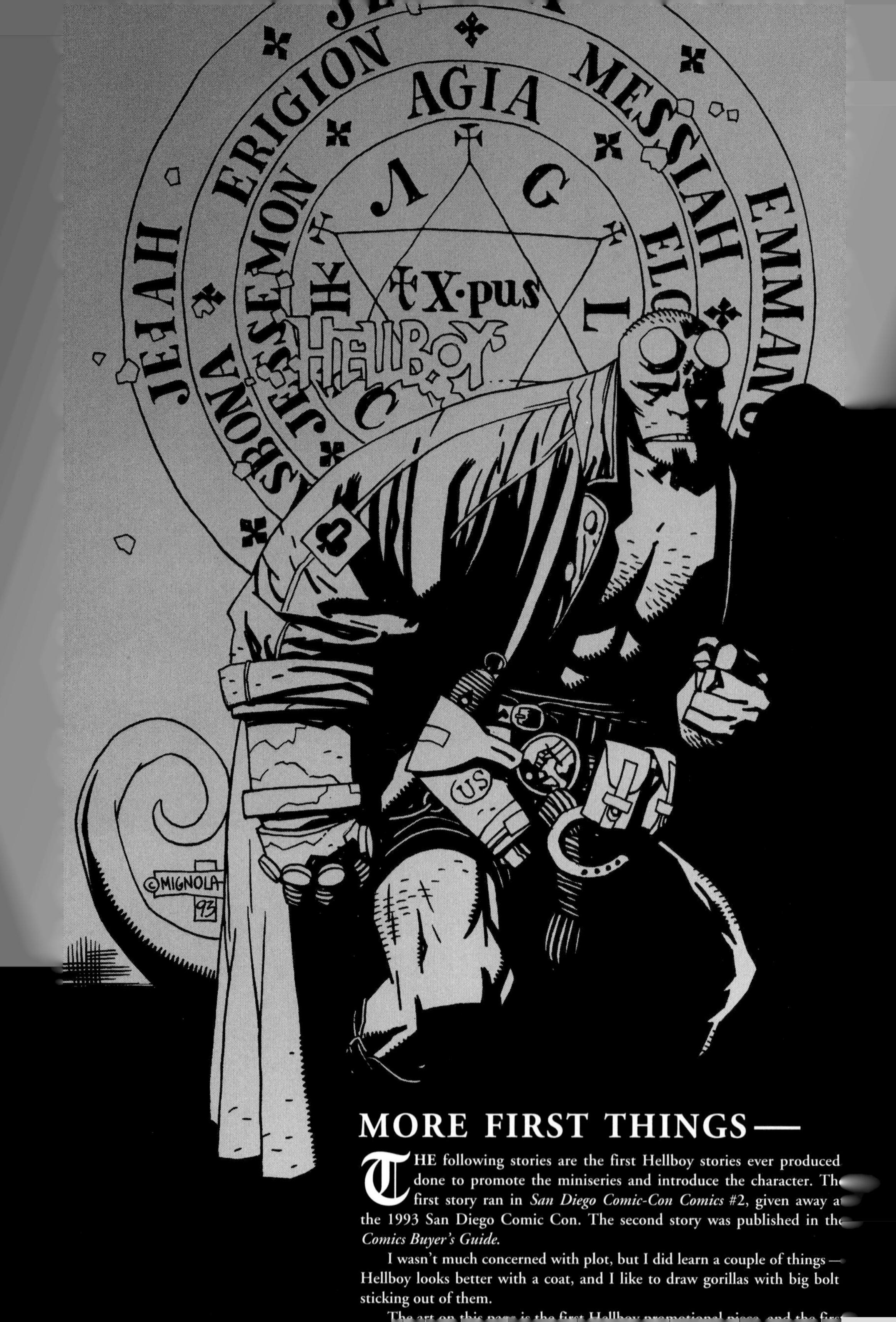

JEHAH
ERIGION
AGIA
MESSIAH
EMMAN
SBONA
JESSEMON
X·pus
HELLBOY
©MIGNOLA 93

MORE FIRST THINGS—

THE following stories are the first Hellboy stories ever produced done to promote the miniseries and introduce the character. The first story ran in *San Diego Comic-Con Comics* #2, given away at the 1993 San Diego Comic Con. The second story was published in the *Comics Buyer's Guide.*

I wasn't much concerned with plot, but I did learn a couple of things—Hellboy looks better with a coat, and I like to draw gorillas with big bolt sticking out of them.

The art on this page is the first Hellboy promotional piece, and the fir

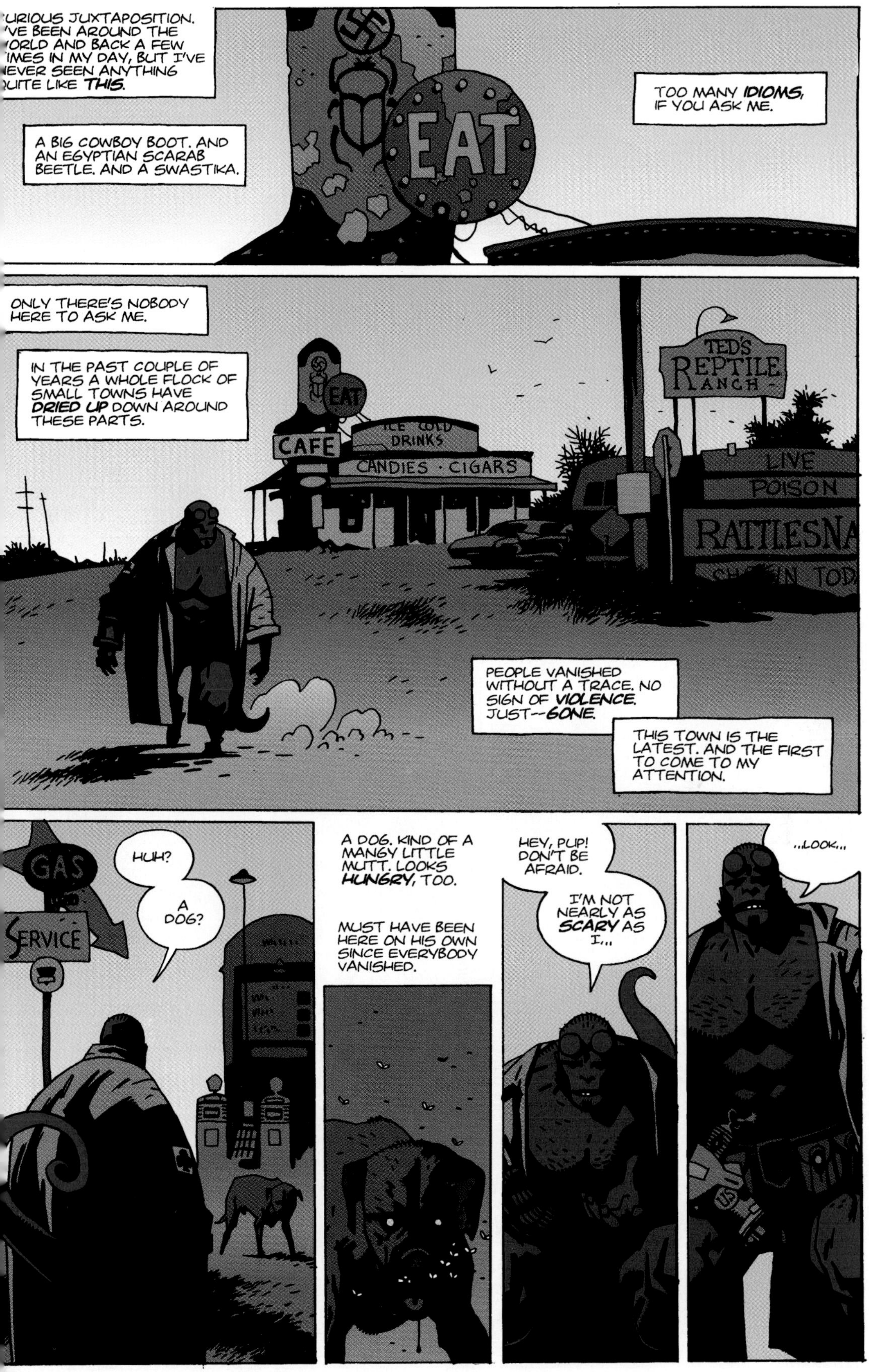

URIOUS JUXTAPOSITION. VE BEEN AROUND THE ORLD AND BACK A FEW IMES IN MY DAY, BUT I'VE IEVER SEEN ANYTHING UITE LIKE THIS.
A BIG COWBOY BOOT. AND AN EGYPTIAN SCARAB BEETLE. AND A SWASTIKA.
EAT
TOO MANY IDIOMS, IF YOU ASK ME.
ONLY THERE'S NOBODY HERE TO ASK ME.
IN THE PAST COUPLE OF YEARS A WHOLE FLOCK OF SMALL TOWNS HAVE DRIED UP DOWN AROUND THESE PARTS.
EAT
CAFE
ICE COLD DRINKS
CANDIES · CIGARS
TED'S REPTILE ANCH
LIVE
POISON
RATTLESNA
PEOPLE VANISHED WITHOUT A TRACE. NO SIGN OF VIOLENCE. JUST--GONE.
THIS TOWN IS THE LATEST. AND THE FIRST TO COME TO MY ATTENTION.
GAS
SERVICE
HUH?
A DOG?
A DOG. KIND OF A MANGY LITTLE MUTT. LOOKS HUNGRY, TOO.
MUST HAVE BEEN HERE ON HIS OWN SINCE EVERYBODY VANISHED.
HEY, PUP! DON'T BE AFRAID.
I'M NOT NEARLY AS SCARY AS I...
...LOOK...

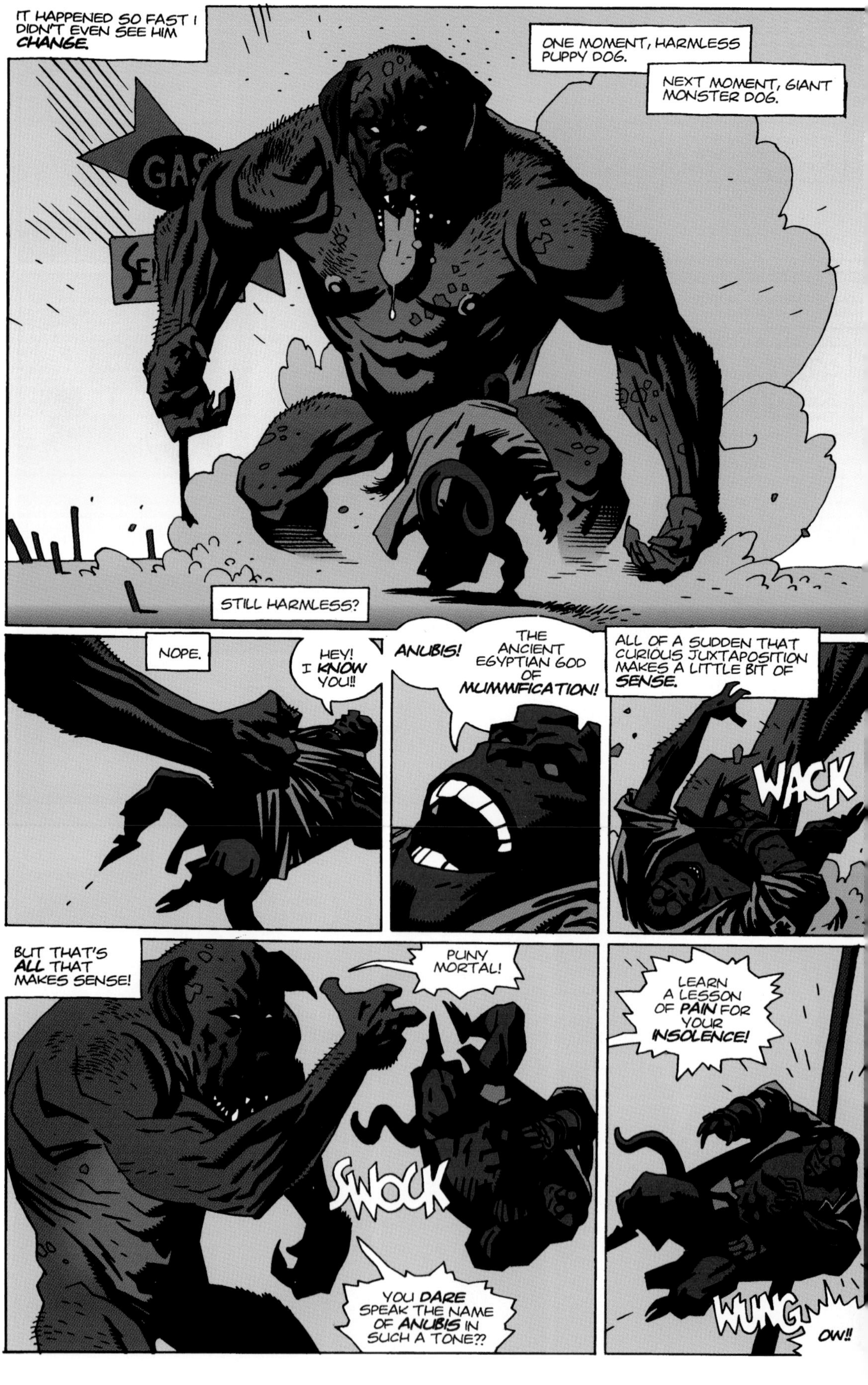

IT HAPPENED SO FAST I DIDN'T EVEN SEE HIM CHANGE.
ONE MOMENT, HARMLESS PUPPY DOG.
NEXT MOMENT, GIANT MONSTER DOG.
GAS
STILL HARMLESS?
NOPE.
HEY! I KNOW YOU!!
ANUBIS!
THE ANCIENT EGYPTIAN GOD OF MUMMIFICATION!
ALL OF A SUDDEN THAT CURIOUS JUXTAPOSITION MAKES A LITTLE BIT OF SENSE.
WACK
BUT THAT'S ALL THAT MAKES SENSE!
PUNY MORTAL!
SWOCK
YOU DARE SPEAK THE NAME OF ANUBIS IN SUCH A TONE??
LEARN A LESSON OF PAIN FOR YOUR INSOLENCE!
WUNG
OW!!

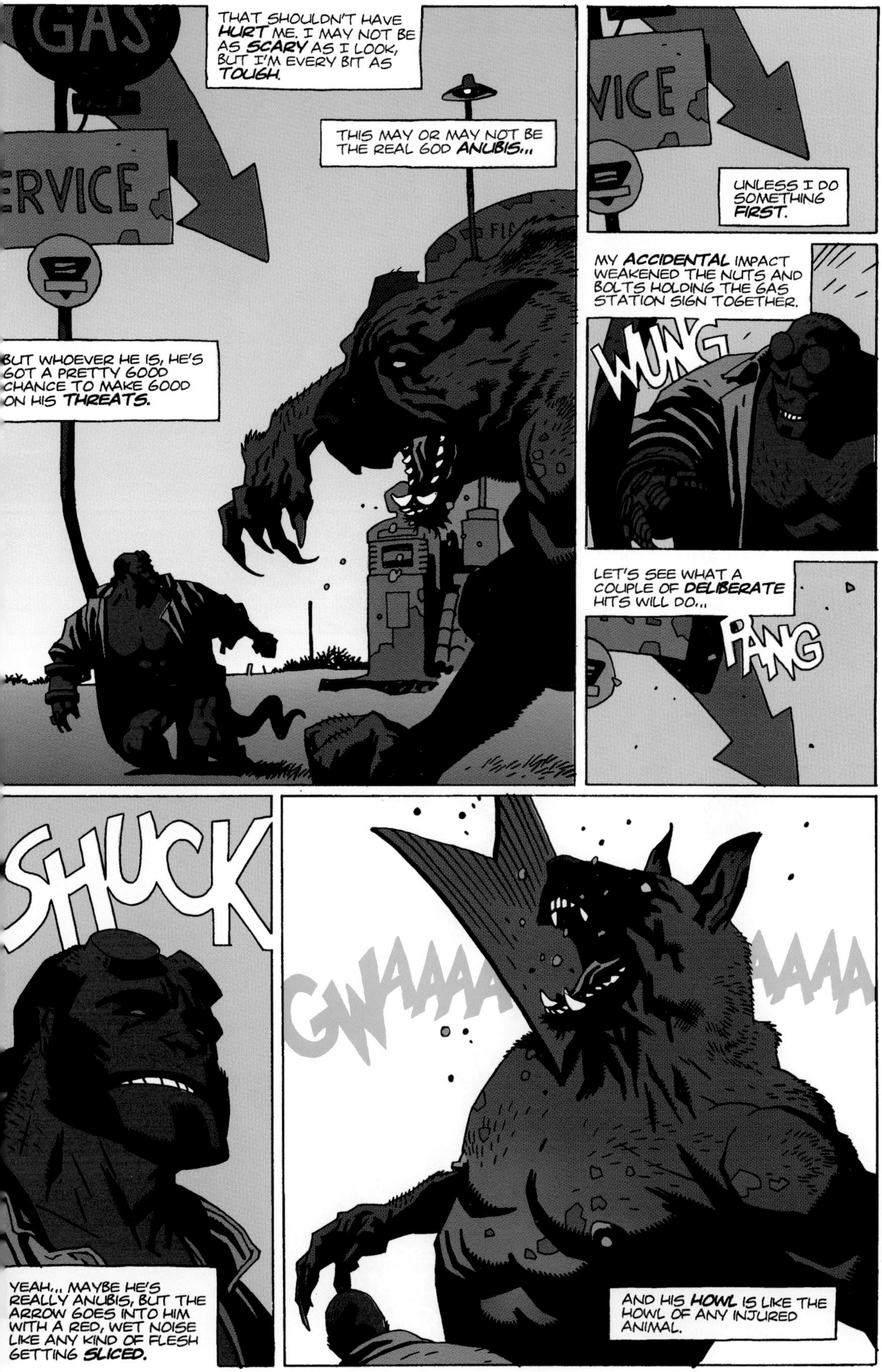
GAS
SERVICE
THAT SHOULDN'T HAVE HURT ME. I MAY NOT BE AS SCARY AS I LOOK, BUT I'M EVERY BIT AS TOUGH.
THIS MAY OR MAY NOT BE THE REAL GOD ANUBIS...
BUT WHOEVER HE IS, HE'S GOT A PRETTY GOOD CHANCE TO MAKE GOOD ON HIS THREATS.
VICE
UNLESS I DO SOMETHING FIRST.
MY ACCIDENTAL IMPACT WEAKENED THE NUTS AND BOLTS HOLDING THE GAS STATION SIGN TOGETHER.
WUNG
LET'S SEE WHAT A COUPLE OF DELIBERATE HITS WILL DO...
PANG
SHUCK
YEAH... MAYBE HE'S REALLY ANUBIS, BUT THE ARROW GOES INTO HIM WITH A RED, WET NOISE LIKE ANY KIND OF FLESH GETTING SLICED.
GWAAAA AAAAA
AND HIS HOWL IS LIKE THE HOWL OF ANY INJURED ANIMAL.

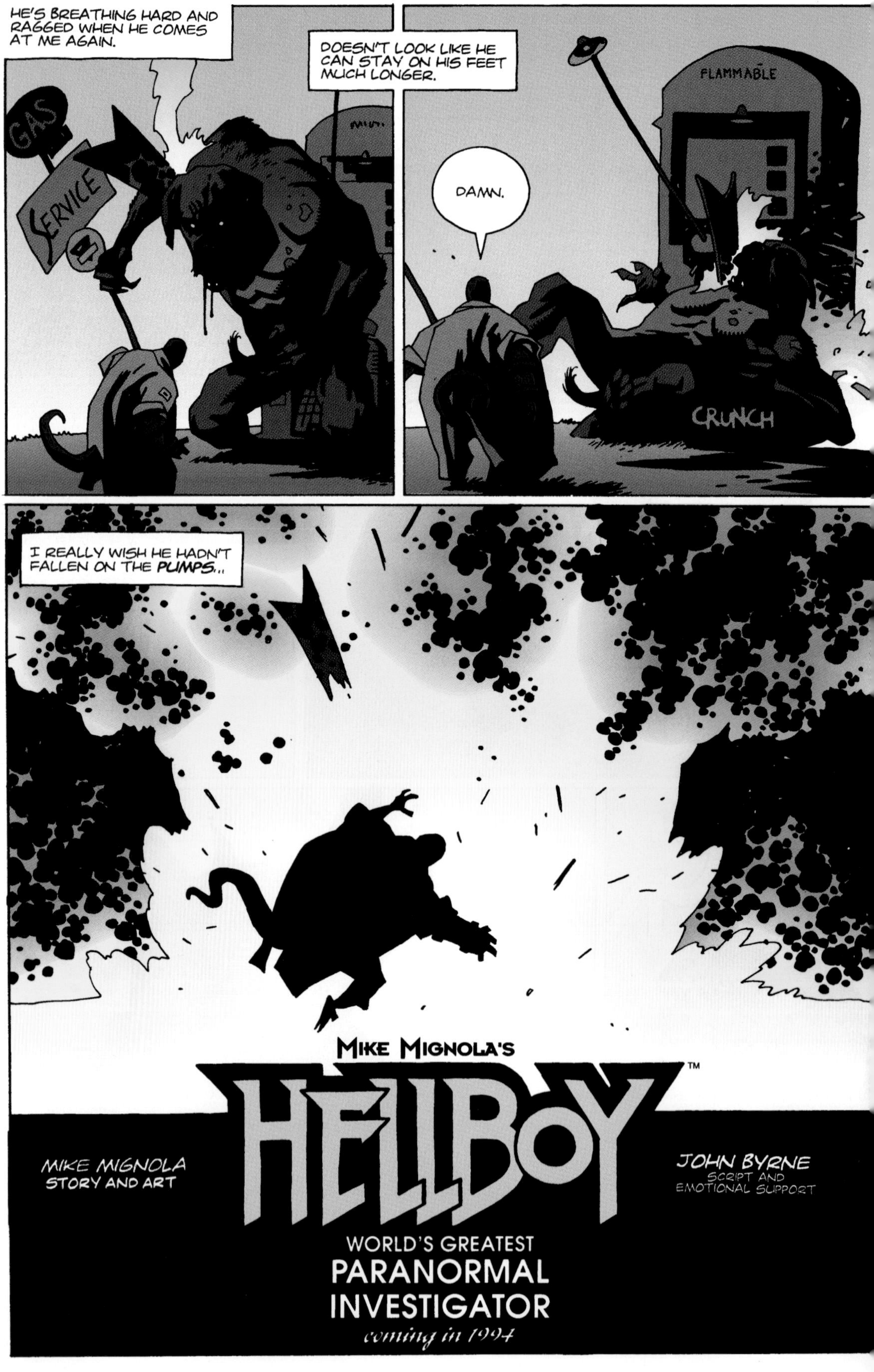
HE'S BREATHING HARD AND RAGGED WHEN HE COMES AT ME AGAIN.
GAS
SERVICE
DOESN'T LOOK LIKE HE CAN STAY ON HIS FEET MUCH LONGER.
FLAMMABLE
DAMN.
CRUNCH
I REALLY WISH HE HADN'T FALLEN ON THE PUMPS...
MIKE MIGNOLA'S
HELLBOY™
MIKE MIGNOLA
STORY AND ART
JOHN BYRNE
SCRIPT AND
EMOTIONAL SUPPORT
WORLD'S GREATEST
PARANORMAL
INVESTIGATOR
coming in 1994

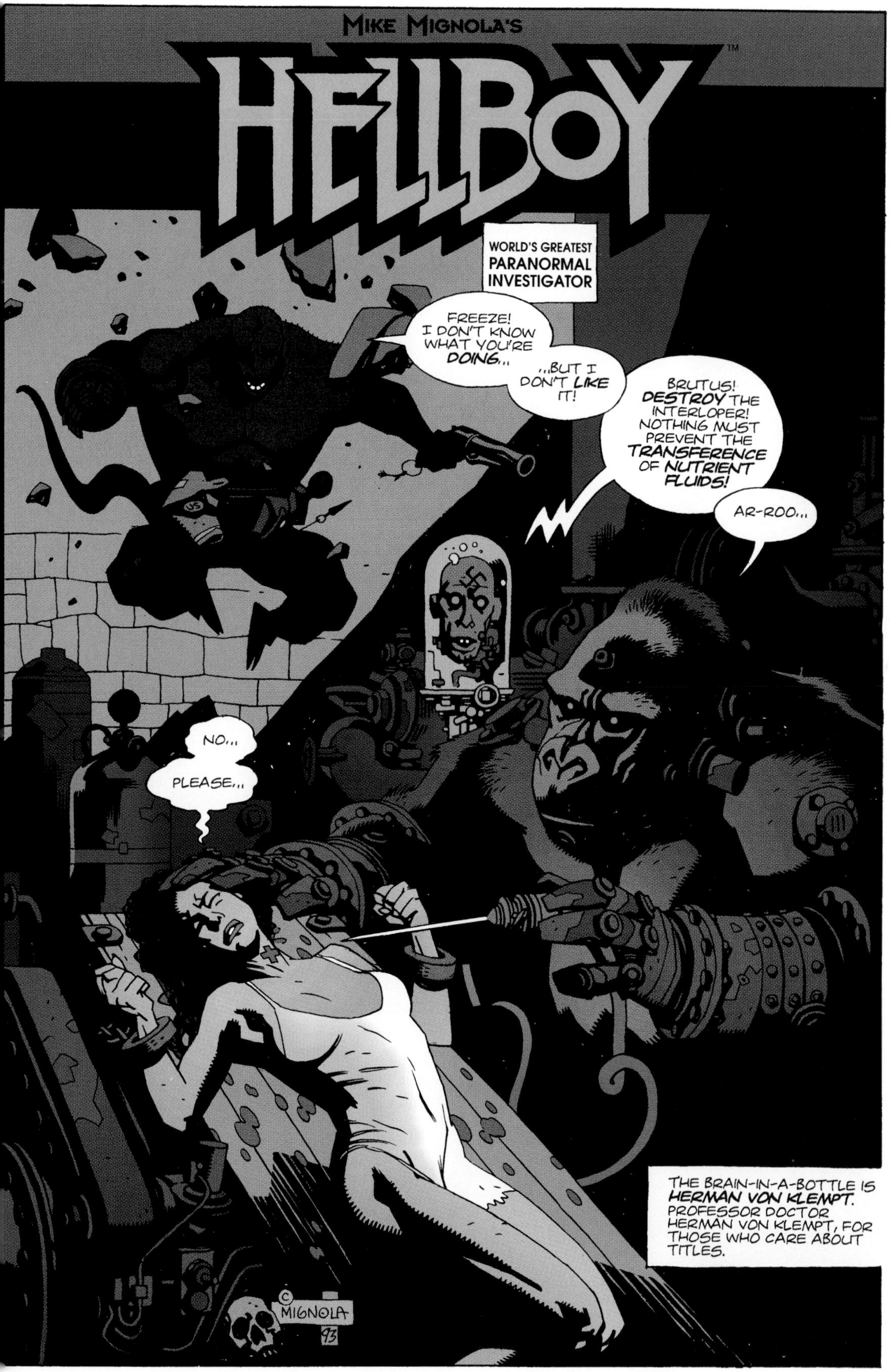
MIKE MIGNOLA'S
HELLBOY™
WORLD'S GREATEST PARANORMAL INVESTIGATOR
FREEZE! I DON'T KNOW WHAT YOU'RE DOING...
...BUT I DON'T LIKE IT!
BRUTUS! DESTROY THE INTERLOPER! NOTHING MUST PREVENT THE TRANSFERENCE OF NUTRIENT FLUIDS!
AR-ROO...
NO...
PLEASE...
THE BRAIN-IN-A-BOTTLE IS HERMAN VON KLEMPT. PROFESSOR DOCTOR HERMAN VON KLEMPT, FOR THOSE WHO CARE ABOUT TITLES.
© MIGNOLA 93

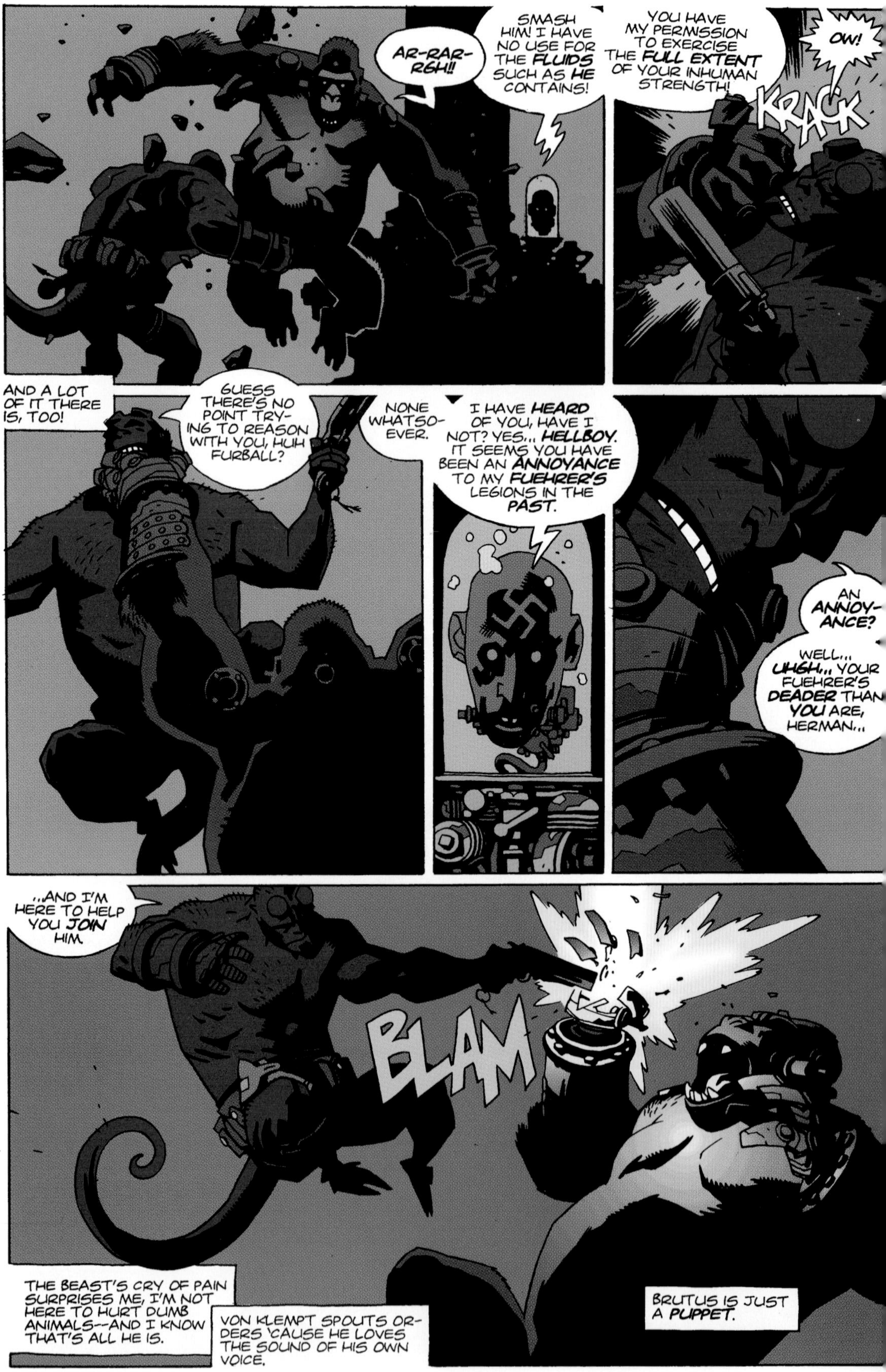
AR-RAR-RGH!!
SMASH HIM! I HAVE NO USE FOR THE FLUIDS SUCH AS HE CONTAINS!
YOU HAVE MY PERMISSION TO EXERCISE THE FULL EXTENT OF YOUR INHUMAN STRENGTH!
OW!
KRACK
AND A LOT OF IT THERE IS, TOO!
GUESS THERE'S NO POINT TRYING TO REASON WITH YOU, HUH FURBALL?
NONE WHATSOEVER.
I HAVE HEARD OF YOU, HAVE I NOT? YES... HELLBOY. IT SEEMS YOU HAVE BEEN AN ANNOYANCE TO MY FUEHRER'S LEGIONS IN THE PAST.
AN ANNOYANCE?
WELL... UHGH... YOUR FUEHRER'S DEADER THAN YOU ARE, HERMAN...
...AND I'M HERE TO HELP YOU JOIN HIM.
BLAM
THE BEAST'S CRY OF PAIN SURPRISES ME, I'M NOT HERE TO HURT DUMB ANIMALS--AND I KNOW THAT'S ALL HE IS.
VON KLEMPT SPOUTS ORDERS 'CAUSE HE LOVES THE SOUND OF HIS OWN VOICE.
BRUTUS IS JUST A PUPPET.

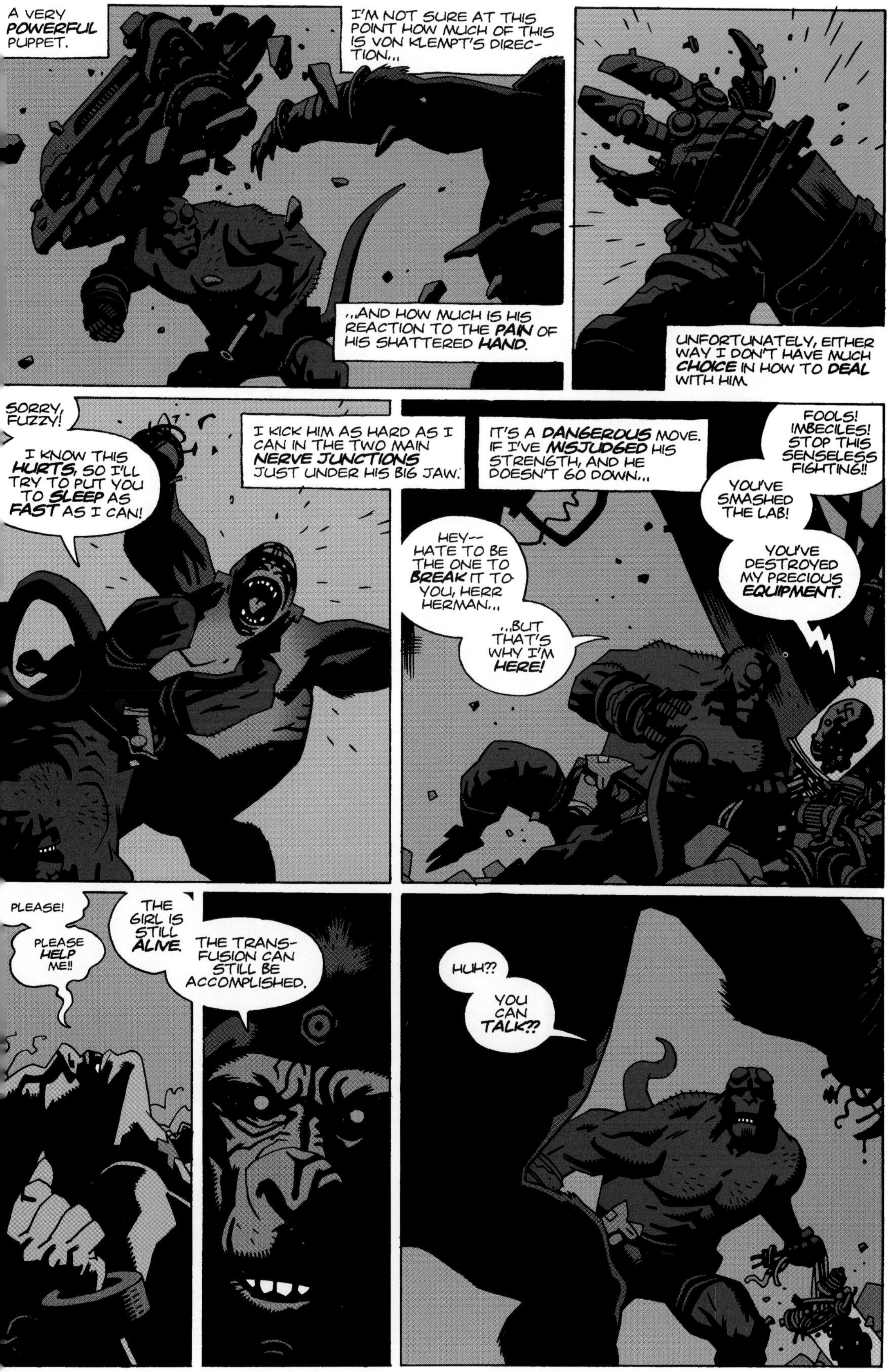

A VERY POWERFUL PUPPET.
I'M NOT SURE AT THIS POINT HOW MUCH OF THIS IS VON KLEMPT'S DIRECTION...
...AND HOW MUCH IS HIS REACTION TO THE PAIN OF HIS SHATTERED HAND.
UNFORTUNATELY, EITHER WAY I DON'T HAVE MUCH CHOICE IN HOW TO DEAL WITH HIM.
SORRY, FUZZY!
I KNOW THIS HURTS, SO I'LL TRY TO PUT YOU TO SLEEP AS FAST AS I CAN!
I KICK HIM AS HARD AS I CAN IN THE TWO MAIN NERVE JUNCTIONS JUST UNDER HIS BIG JAW.
IT'S A DANGEROUS MOVE. IF I'VE MISJUDGED HIS STRENGTH, AND HE DOESN'T GO DOWN...
FOOLS! IMBECILES! STOP THIS SENSELESS FIGHTING!!
YOU'VE SMASHED THE LAB!
YOU'VE DESTROYED MY PRECIOUS EQUIPMENT.
HEY-- HATE TO BE THE ONE TO BREAK IT TO YOU, HERR HERMAN...
...BUT THAT'S WHY I'M HERE!
PLEASE!
PLEASE HELP ME!!
THE GIRL IS STILL ALIVE.
THE TRANSFUSION CAN STILL BE ACCOMPLISHED.
HUH??
YOU CAN TALK??

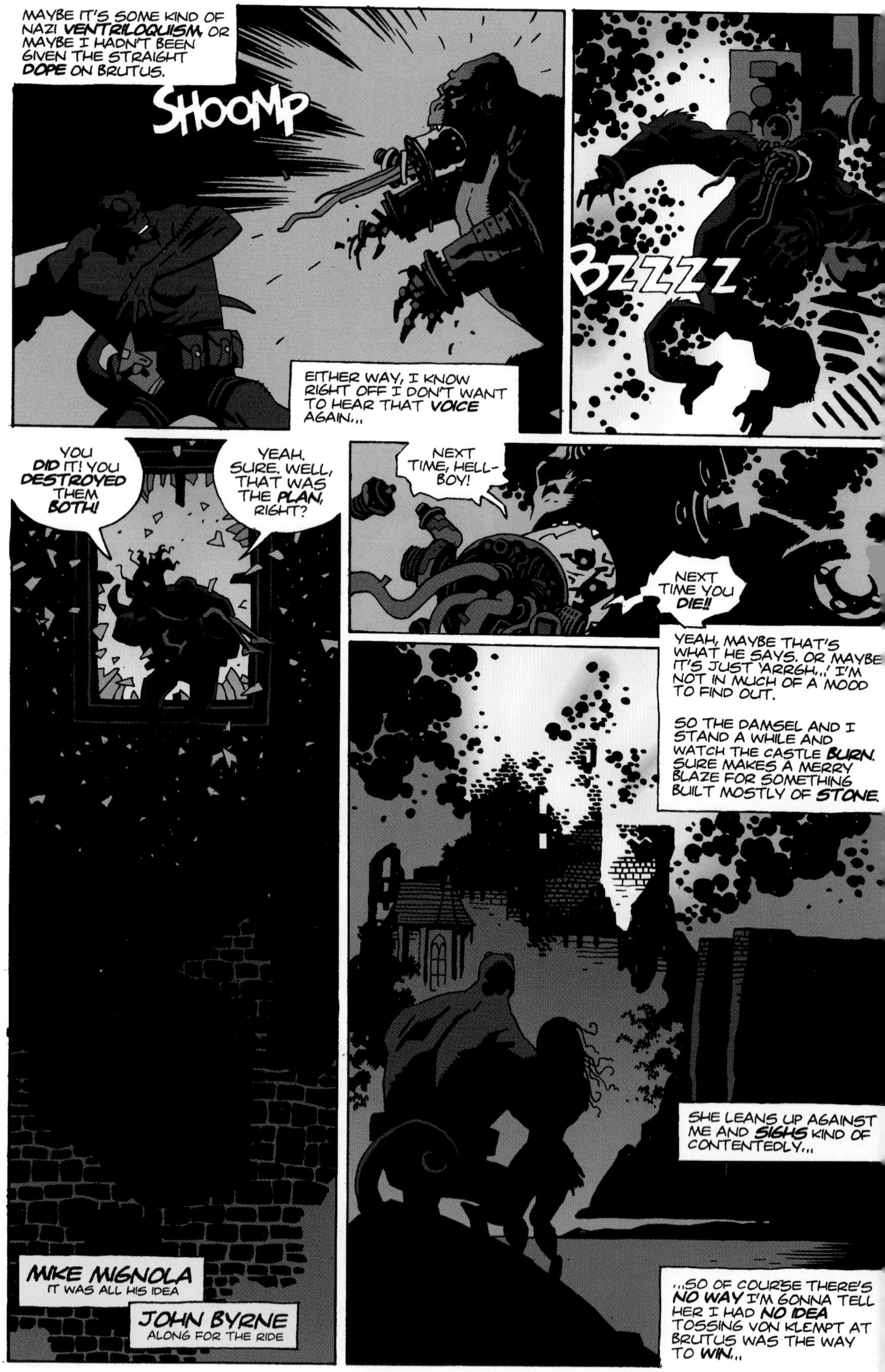
MAYBE IT'S SOME KIND OF NAZI VENTRILOQUISM, OR MAYBE I HADN'T BEEN GIVEN THE STRAIGHT DOPE ON BRUTUS.
SHOOMP
EITHER WAY, I KNOW RIGHT OFF I DON'T WANT TO HEAR THAT VOICE AGAIN...
BZZZZ
YOU DID IT! YOU DESTROYED THEM BOTH!
YEAH. SURE. WELL, THAT WAS THE PLAN, RIGHT?
NEXT TIME, HELL-BOY!
NEXT TIME YOU DIE!!
YEAH, MAYBE THAT'S WHAT HE SAYS. OR MAYBE IT'S JUST 'ARRGH...' I'M NOT IN MUCH OF A MOOD TO FIND OUT.
SO THE DAMSEL AND I STAND A WHILE AND WATCH THE CASTLE BURN. SURE MAKES A MERRY BLAZE FOR SOMETHING BUILT MOSTLY OF STONE.
SHE LEANS UP AGAINST ME AND SIGHS KIND OF CONTENTEDLY...
...SO OF COURSE THERE'S NO WAY I'M GONNA TELL HER I HAD NO IDEA TOSSING VON KLEMPT AT BRUTUS WAS THE WAY TO WIN...
MIKE MIGNOLA
IT WAS ALL HIS IDEA
JOHN BYRNE
ALONG FOR THE RIDE

HELLBOY™

G A L L E R Y

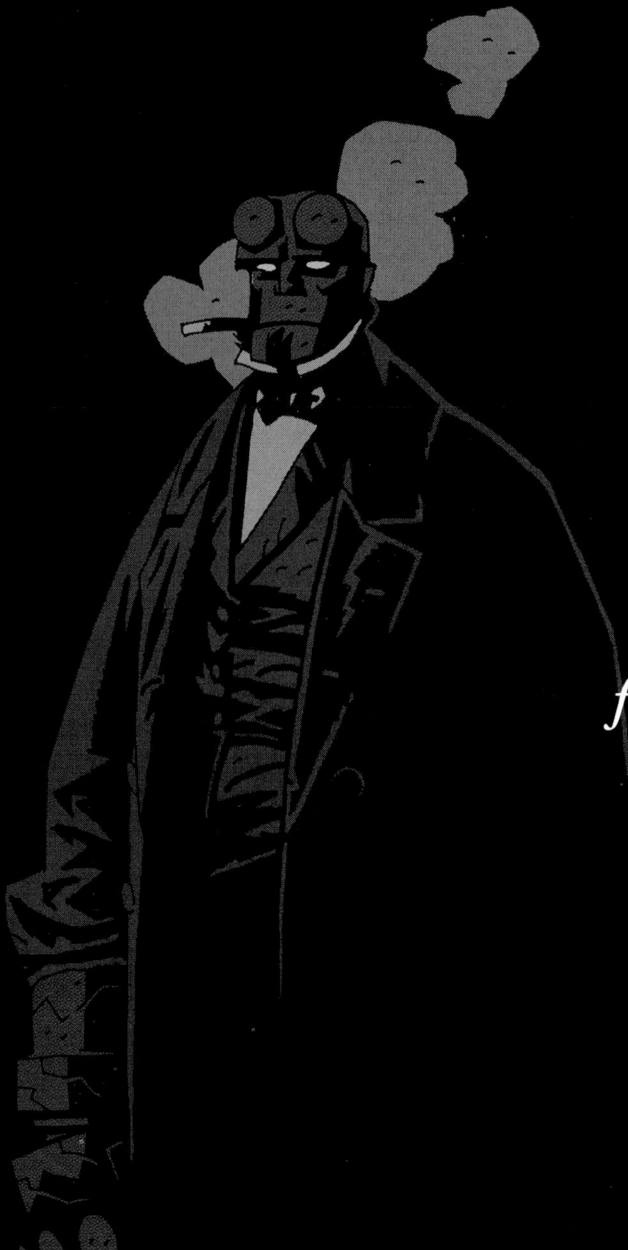

featuring

SIMON BISLEY
colored by Matthew Hollingsworth

MIKE ALLRED

ART ADAMS
colored by Matthew Hollingsworth

FRANK MILLER

FRED BLANCHARD

and

GARY GIANNI

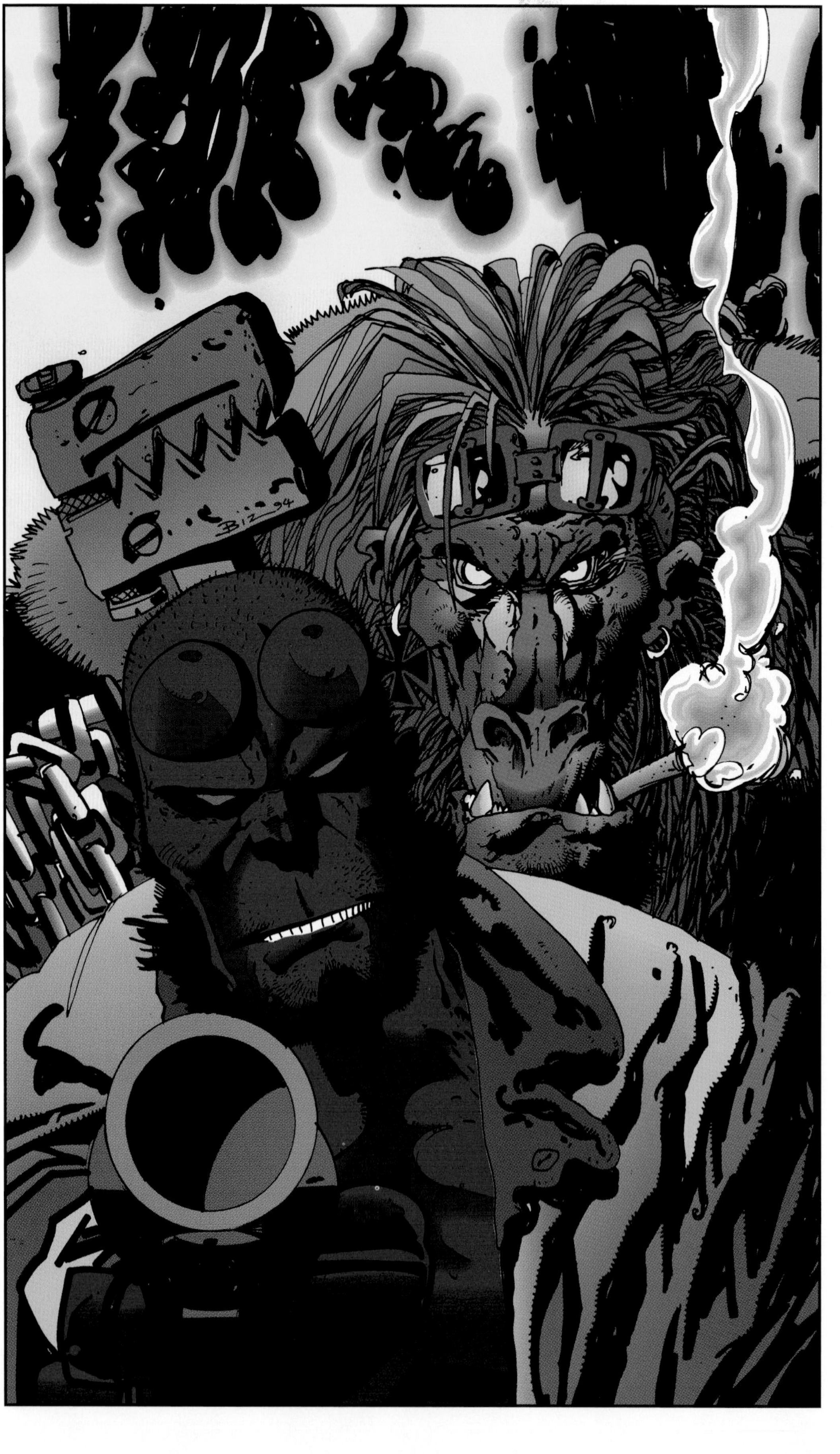

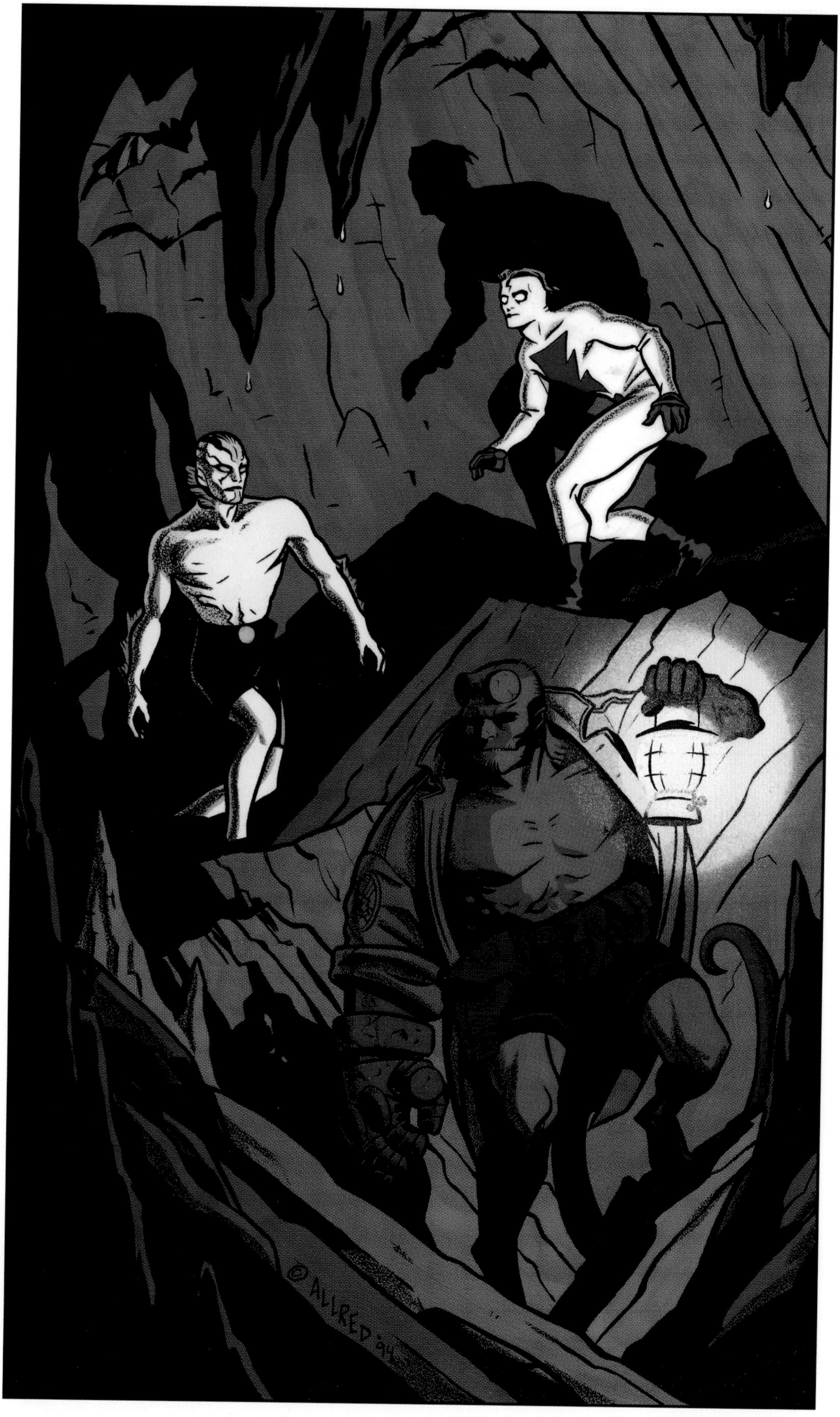
© ALLRED '04

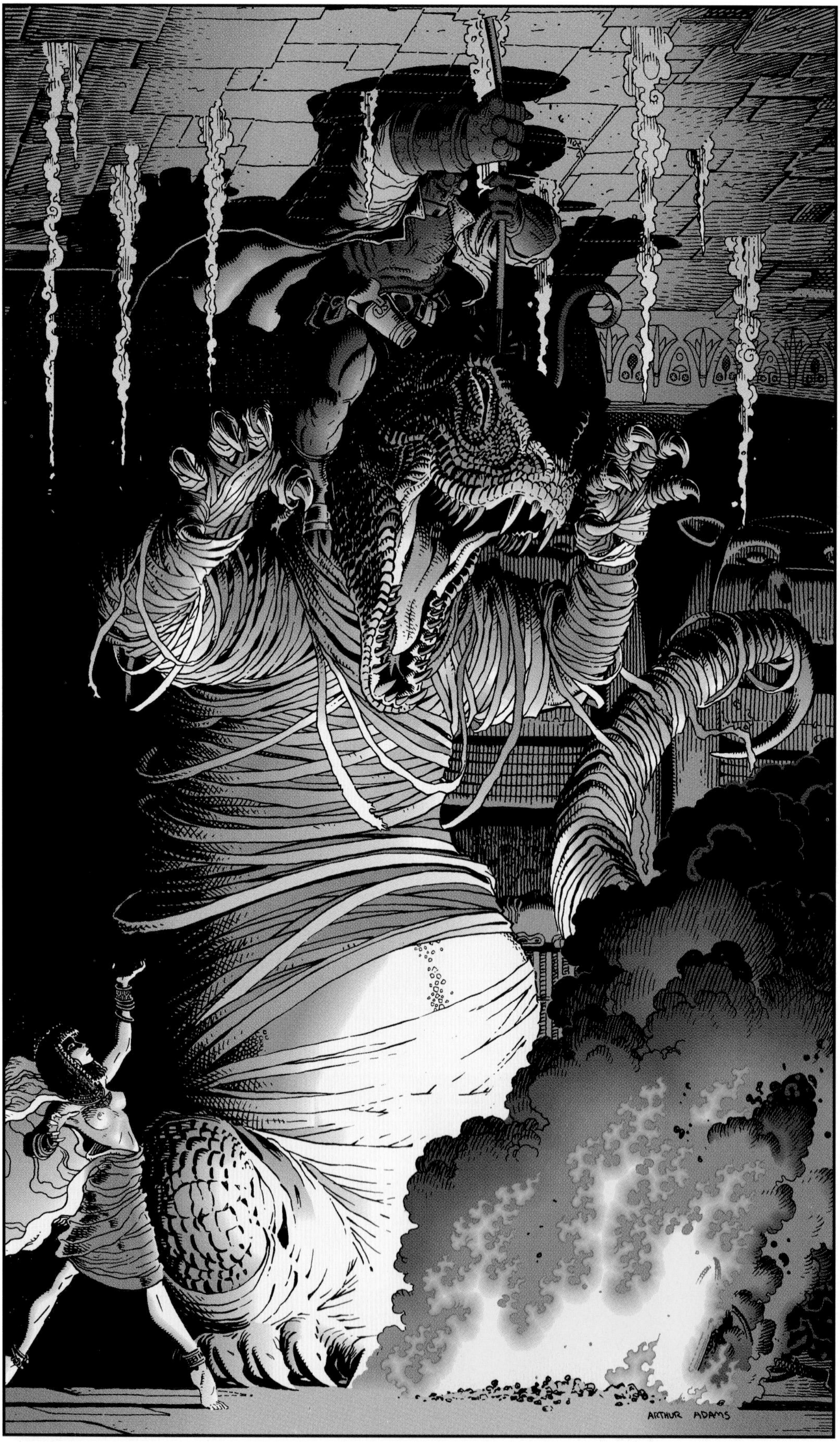
ARTHUR ADAMS

FM

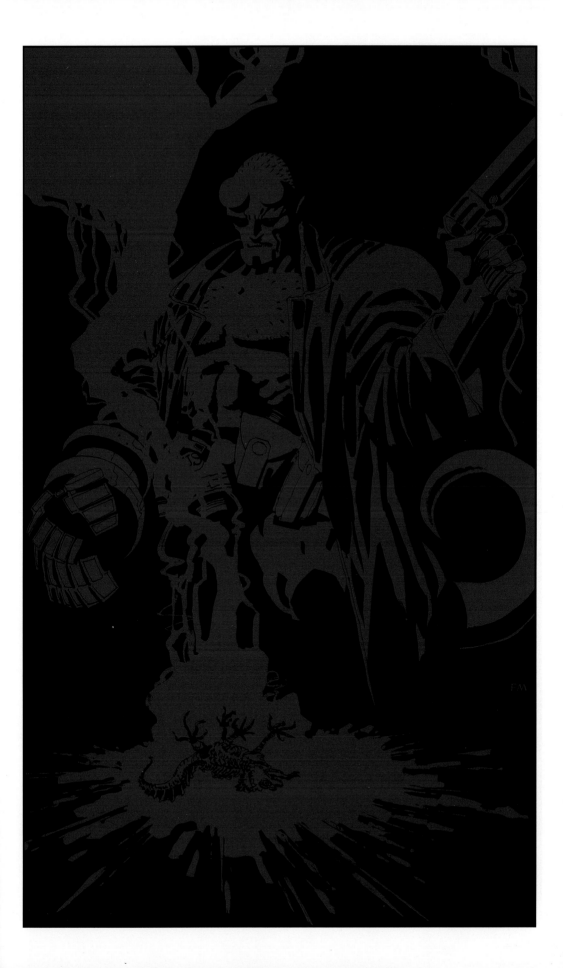

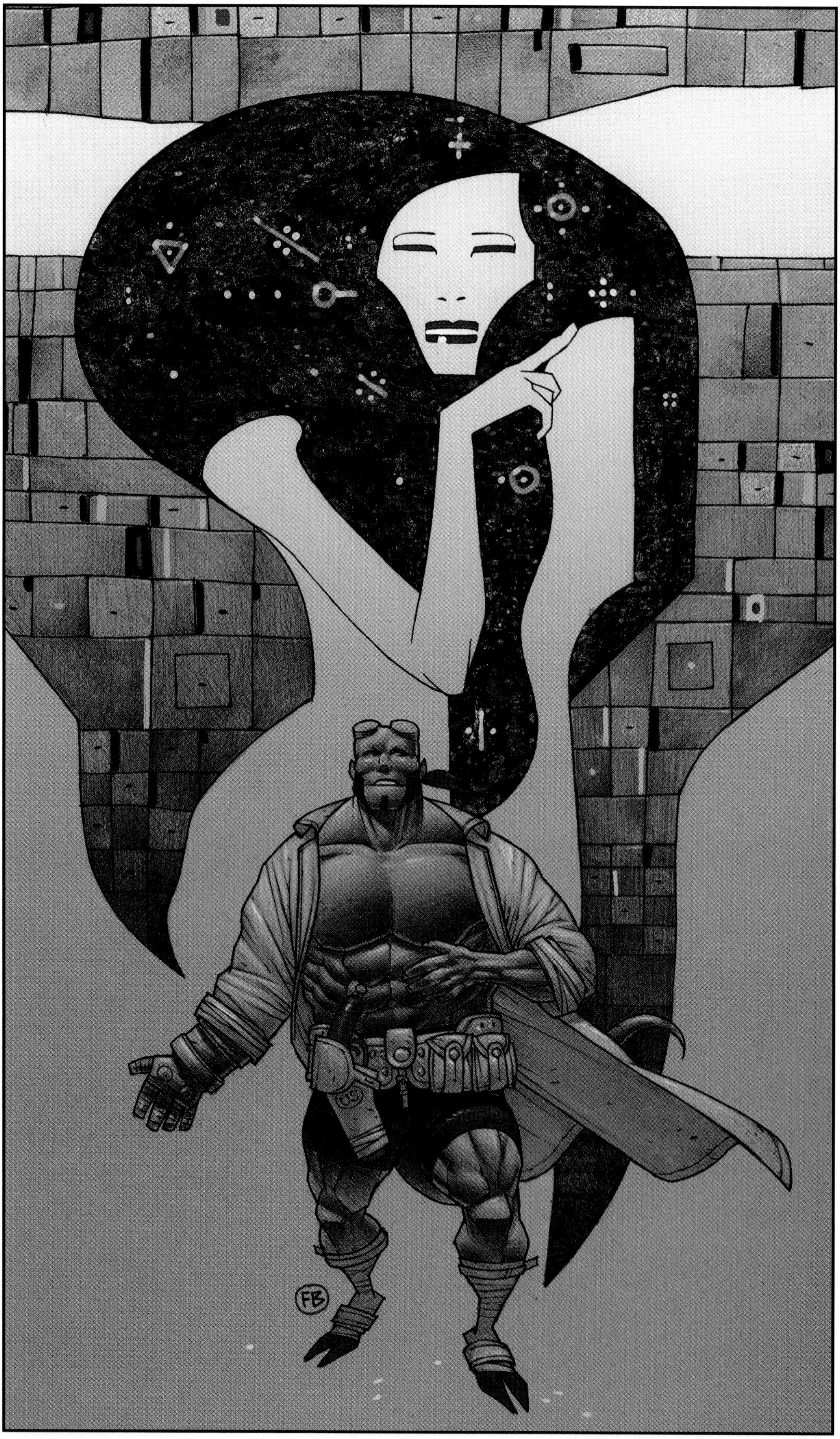

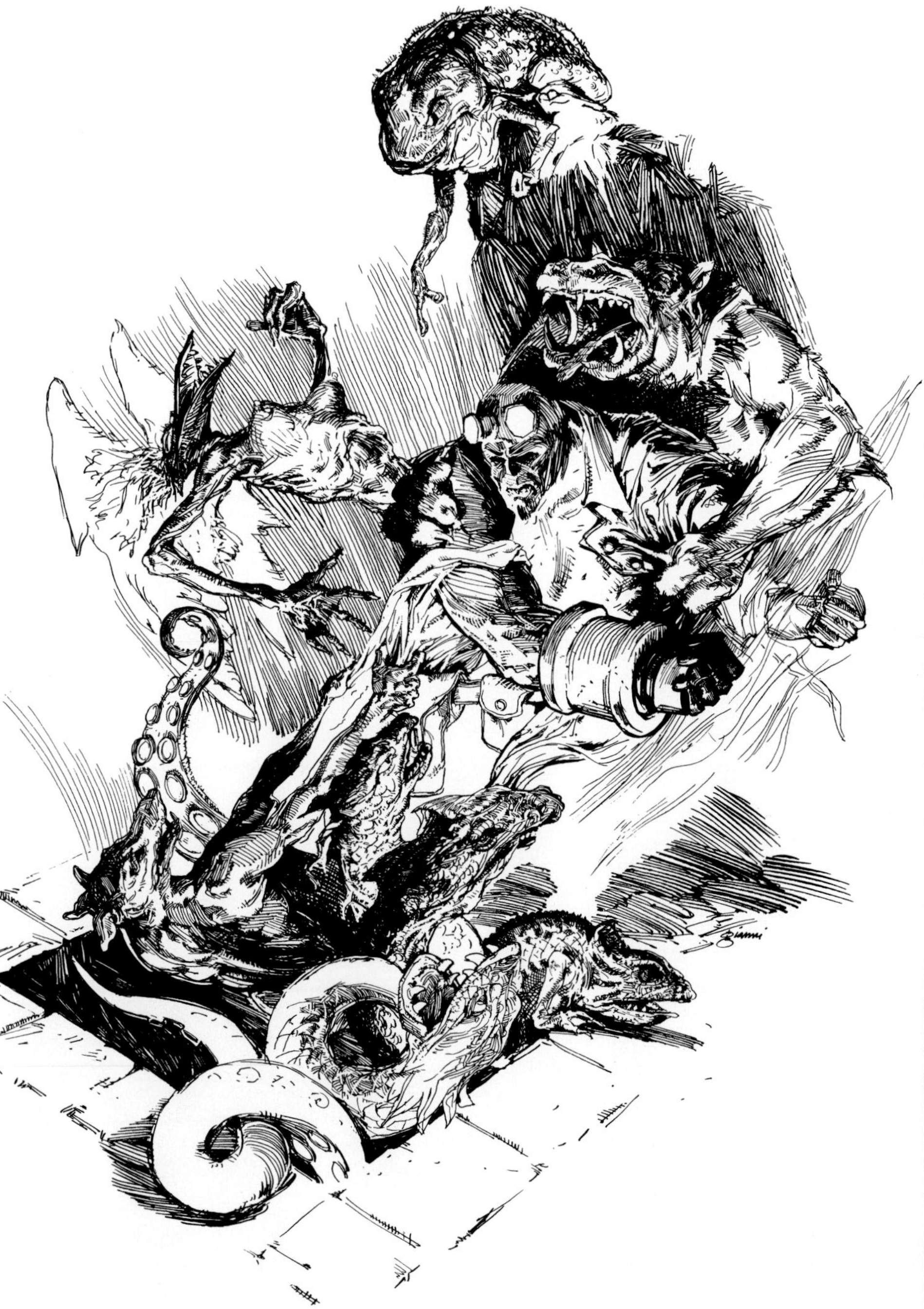

HELLBOY

by MIKE MIGNOLA

DARK HORSE MAVERICK